FRUIT AND VEGGIES 101 VEGETABLE COMPANION PLANTING

COMPANION GUIDE ON HOW TO GROW VEGETABLES USING ESSENTIAL, ORGANIC & SUSTAINABLE GARDENING STRATEGIES (PERFECT FOR BEGINNERS)

GREEN ROOTS

Fruit and Veggies 101

VEGETABLE COMPANION PLANTING

Companion Guide On How To Grow Vegetables Using Essential Organic & Sustainable Gardening Strategies

(Perfect For Beginners)

GREEN ROOTS

CONTENTS

A Special Gift To Our Readers	xi
Introduction	xiii

1. THE ART OF VEGETABLE COMPANION PLANTING - TECHNIQUES — 1
   - The Role Of Companion Planting In Organic & Sustainable Gardening Practices — 2
   - Advantages & Disadvantages Of Using Companion Planting In A Vegetable Garden — 4
   - Types Of Sustainable Companion Gardening Strategies — 6
   - Selecting Where Your Garden Will Grow — 20
   - Types Of Vegetable Companion Gardens — 23

2. THE ART OF VEGETABLE COMPANION PLANTING - PREPARATION — 33
   - Essential Tools For Vegetable Companion Gardening — 34
   - The Basics Of Garden Soil Preparation — 41
   - Seven Types Of Soils — 42
   - Signs Of Fertile & High-Quality Soil — 53
   - How To Create The Perfect Soil Condition — 55
   - Store Bought Vs. Homemade Soil Treatment — 59

3. BRASSICA "CABBAGE" FAMILY COMPANION PLANTING — 64
   - Brassica Family Vegetable Plants — 65
   - Brassica Family Companion Vegetables — 68
   - Brassica Family Non-Companion Plants — 70
   - The Right Soil For Brassica Family Vegetables — 72
   - Sowing Brassica Family Vegetables — 75
   - Correct Season To Sow Brassica Vegetable Plants — 75
   - Planting Needs & Requirements — 78
   - Spacing & Measurements — 80

Maintaining Brassica Vegetable Plants	82
Pruning and Thinning Brassica Vegetable Plants	83
Watering Brassica Vegetable Plants	85
Organic Fertilisation For Brassica Vegetable Plants	88
Protecting Brassica Vegetable Plants	91
Protecting Brassica Vegetables From Pest	93
Protecting Brassica Vegetables From Diseases	95
Harvesting Brassica Vegetable Plants	97
Crop Rotation for Brassica Vegetable Plants	99
4. ALLIUM "ONION" FAMILY COMPANION PLANTING	**103**
Allium Family Vegetable Plants	104
Allium Family Companion Vegetables	106
Allium Family Non-Companion Plants	109
The Right Soil For Allium Family Vegetables	110
Sowing Allium Family Vegetables	113
Correct Season To Sow Allium Vegetable Plants	113
Planting Needs & Requirements	115
Spacing & Measurements	117
Maintaining Allium Vegetable Plants	119
Pruning and Thinning Allium Vegetable Plants	120
Watering Allium Vegetable Plants	123
Organic Fertilisation For Allium Vegetable Plants	125
Protecting Allium Vegetable Plants	127
Extreme Temperatures	127
Protecting Allium Vegetables From Pest	129
Protecting Allium Vegetables From Diseases	131
Harvesting Allium Vegetable Plants	133
Crop Rotation for Allium Vegetable Plants	135
5. CUCURBITACEAE "SQUASH" FAMILY COMPANION PLANTING	**137**
Cucurbitaceae Family Vegetable Plants	138
Cucurbitaceae Family Companion Vegetables	140
Cucurbitaceae Family Non-Companion Plants	142
The Right Soil For Cucurbitaceae Family Vegetables	144

Sowing Cucurbitaceae Family Vegetables	146
Correct Season To Sow Cucurbitaceae Vegetable Plants	146
Planting Needs & Requirements	149
Spacing & Measurements	152
Maintaining Cucurbitaceae Vegetable Plants	154
Pruning and Thinning Cucurbitaceae Vegetable Plants	155
Watering Cucurbitaceae Vegetable Plants	158
Organic Fertilisation For Cucurbitaceae Vegetable Plants	160
Protecting Cucurbitaceae Vegetable Plants	163
Extreme Temperatures	163
Protecting Cucurbitaceae Vegetables From Pest	165
Protecting Cucurbitaceae Vegetables From Diseases	168
Harvesting Cucurbitaceae Vegetable Plants	170
Crop Rotation for Cucurbitaceae Vegetable Plants	172

6. **LEGUMINOSAE "PEA" FAMILY COMPANION PLANTING** — 175

Leguminosae Family Vegetable Plants	176
Leguminosae Family Companion Vegetables	179
Leguminosae Family Non-Companion Plants	181
The Right Soil For Leguminosae Family Vegetables	182
Sowing Leguminosae Family Vegetables	183
Correct Season To Sow Leguminosae Vegetable Plants	183
Planting Needs & Requirements	185
Spacing & Measurements	188
Maintaining Leguminosae Vegetable Plants	190
Pruning and Thinning Leguminosae Vegetable Plants	190
Watering Leguminosae Vegetable Plants	193
Organic Fertilisation For Leguminosae Vegetable Plants	194
Protecting Leguminosae Vegetable Plants	197
Extreme Temperatures	197

Protecting Leguminosae Vegetables From Pest	198
Protecting Leguminosae Vegetables From Diseases	200
Harvesting Leguminosae Vegetable Plants	202
Crop Rotation for Leguminosae Vegetable Plants	204

7. SOLANACEAE "NIGHTSHADE" FAMILY COMPANION PLANTING — 206

Solanaceae Family Vegetable Plants	208
Solanaceae Family Companion Vegetables	209
Solanaceae Family Non-Companion Plants	211
The Right Soil For Solanaceae Family Vegetables	212
Sowing Solanaceae Family Vegetables	213
Correct Season To Sow Solanaceae Vegetable Plants	213
Planting Needs & Requirements	215
Spacing & Measurements	217
Maintaining Solanaceae Vegetable Plants	219
Pruning and Thinning Solanaceae Vegetable Plants	220
Watering Solanaceae Vegetable Plants	222
Protecting Solanaceae Vegetable Plants	226
Extreme Temperatures	226
Protecting Solanaceae Vegetables From Pest	227
Protecting Solanaceae Vegetables From Diseases	229
Harvesting Solanaceae Vegetable Plants	231
Crop Rotation for Solanaceae Vegetable Plants	233

8. APIACEAE "CARROT" FAMILY COMPANION PLANTING — 235

Apiaceae Family Vegetable Plants	236
Apiaceae Family Companion Vegetables	238
Apiaceae Family Non-Companion Plants	239
The Right Soil For Apiaceae Family Vegetables	241
Sowing Apiaceae Family Vegetables	242
Correct Season To Sow Apiaceae Vegetable Plants	242
Planting Needs & Requirements	244
Spacing & Measurements	247

Maintaining Apiaceae Vegetable Plants	248
Pruning and Thinning Apiaceae Vegetable Plants	249
Watering Apiaceae Vegetable Plants	251
Organic Fertilisation For Apiaceae Vegetable Plants	253
Protecting Apiaceae Vegetable Plants	255
Extreme Temperatures	255
Protecting Apiaceae Vegetables From Pest	256
Protecting Apiaceae Vegetables From Diseases	258
Harvesting Apiaceae Vegetable Plants	260
Crop Rotation for Apiaceae Vegetable Plants	262
9. CROP ROTATION GUIDE	264
Six-Year Rotation Plan	265
10. ACKNOWLEDGEMENTS	267
Afterword	269
Also by Green Roots	273
11. GLOSSARY	276
Bibliography	287

© **Copyright 2023 - All rights reserved.**

The content contained within this book may not be reproduced, duplicated, or transmitted without direct written permission from the author or the publisher.

Under no circumstances will any blame or legal responsibility be held against the publisher, or author, for any damages, reparation, or monetary loss due to the information contained within this book, either directly or indirectly.

Legal Notice:

This book is copyright protected. It is only for personal use. You cannot amend, distribute, sell, use, quote, or paraphrase any part, or the content within this book, without the consent of the author or publisher.

Disclaimer Notice:

Please note the information contained within this document is for educational and entertainment purposes only. All effort has been executed to present accurate, up-to-date, reliable, and complete information. No warranties of any kind are declared or implied. Readers acknowledge that the author is not engaged in the rendering of legal, financial, medical, or professional advice. The content within this book has been derived from various sources. Please consult a licensed professional before attempting any techniques outlined in this book.

By reading this document, the reader agrees that under no circumstances is the author responsible for any losses, direct or indirect, that are incurred as a result of the use of the information contained within this document, including, but not limited to, errors, omissions, or inaccuracies.

A SPECIAL GIFT TO OUR READERS

Included with your purchase of this book is our list of "27 horticulture Myths Debunked"
This list will provide and aid you as a new (or soon-to-be) gardener by actively informing you of the myths and irrelevant practices to avoid during your gardening journey.

Visit the link below to let us know which email address to deliver to

www.gardengreenroots.com

INTRODUCTION

AN INTRODUCTION TO VEGETABLE COMPANION GARDENING

Welcome to the world of vegetable companion gardening, where the power of nature's relationships is harnessed to create a more productive, sustainable, and beautiful garden. This time-tested method not only maximizes the potential of your garden but also enhances its overall health and vitality. By understanding the principles of companion planting, you will unlock the secrets to a thriving garden ecosystem that benefits both you and the environment.

The concept of companion gardening is rooted in the understanding that certain plants grow better together than they do alone. Just as people form relationships that help them thrive, so too do plants. By strategically placing plants in close proximity, they can benefit from each other's strengths, providing support, deterring pests, and even improving soil fertility.

In this guide, we will explore the various aspects of vegetable companion gardening, from its history and underlying principles to practical tips and techniques that can be easily imple-

INTRODUCTION

mented in any garden. Whether you're an experienced gardener looking to elevate your garden's success or a beginner eager to learn the ropes, this guide is designed to provide you with all the necessary tools and knowledge to make companion gardening work for you.

Throughout the chapters, you will discover:

- The history and origins of companion gardening and why it remains relevant today
- The science behind companion planting, including the roles of allelopathy, nutrient sharing, and pest control
- A comprehensive list of compatible plant pairings in each vegetable family, as well as those to avoid
- How to plan, design, and maintain a successful vegetable companion garden
- Tips for maximizing space and yield in small gardens and urban settings
- The role of companion planting in organic and sustainable gardening practices
- Ways to attract beneficial insects and promote biodiversity in your garden

By the end of this journey, you will have a deeper understanding of the intricate relationships between vegetable plants and how they can be used to your gardens advantage. More importantly, you will be equipped with practical knowledge and strategies to create a thriving vegetable companion garden of your own.

So let's embark on this exciting adventure together and experience the transformative power of companion gardening as we unlock the full potential of our gardens and contribute to a healthier, more sustainable world.

INTRODUCTION

What Is Vegetable Companion Planting?

Vegetable companion gardening is a strategic method of cultivating plants in close proximity to one another, capitalizing on their natural synergies and interactions to create a more productive, healthy, and sustainable garden ecosystem.

This age-old practice acknowledges the fact that certain plant species, when grown together, can mutually benefit from each other's presence, providing support, enhancing soil fertility, and deterring pests. By understanding the specific needs and characteristics of various vegetables, as well as their compatibility with other plants, you can harness the power of these relationships to optimize your garden's yield, reducing the need for chemical interventions, can promote biodiversity, support pollinators, conserve water, and maintain healthy soil.

Understanding the concept of vegetable companion planting is crucial for any gardener seeking to optimize their garden's productivity, health, and sustainability. As a result, vegetable companion gardening not only contributes to a thriving and bountiful garden but also fosters a more harmonious relationship with nature.

The history and origins of companion gardening can be traced back thousands of years to various ancient civilizations, including the Romans, Greeks, and Native Americans, who recognized the benefits of growing certain plants together. One of the most famous examples is the "Three Sisters" planting method, utilized by the indigenous peoples of North America, which involves growing corn, beans, and squash together in a mutually beneficial arrangement.

Over time, these traditional practices have been passed down through generations, and their principles have been refined and expanded upon as our understanding of plant interactions has grown. Today, companion gardening remains relevant due to its ability to address modern agricultural challenges, such as the overuse of chemical fertilizers and pesticides, soil degradation, and loss of biodiversity. By embracing the wisdom of the past and applying it to contemporary gardening practices, we can create more sustainable, productive, and environmentally friendly gardens that contribute to a healthier planet for future generations.

The Science Behind Why Vegetable Companion Planting Works.

Vegetable companion planting works due to a combination of scientific principles and natural interactions between plants. By understanding these underlying mechanisms, gardeners can harness the power of these relationships to create thriving, sustainable gardens. Some key aspects of the science behind companion planting include allelopathy, nutrient sharing, and pest control.

Allelopathy

At the core of vegetable companion planting is the concept of allelopathy, which refers to the biochemical interactions between plants as they release various compounds into their surrounding environment.

These compounds, known as allelochemicals, can have either positive or negative effects on neighboring plants. For example, some allelochemicals may inhibit the growth of competing plants, while others may stimulate growth or even protect against pests and diseases. By strategically pairing plants with complementary allelopathic properties, gardeners can foster mutually beneficial relationships that promote overall plant health and productivity.

INTRODUCTION

Nutrient Sharing

Another critical aspect of vegetable companion planting is nutrient sharing, where certain plants help improve soil fertility and nutrient availability for their neighbors. Legumes, such as beans and peas, are well-known for their ability to fix nitrogen from the atmosphere and convert it into a form that can be readily absorbed by other plants.

This process, carried out by symbiotic bacteria living in the plants' root nodules, can significantly enhance soil nitrogen levels, providing essential nutrients for nitrogen-demanding vegetables like corn and leafy greens. Additionally, some plants are efficient at mining nutrients from deep within the soil and bringing them to the surface, making them more accessible to shallow-rooted plants.

Pest Control

Vegetable companion planting also plays a crucial role in natural pest control, reducing the need for chemical pesticides. Some plants produce compounds that repel or confuse common pests, protecting their more vulnerable neighbors. For example, marigolds emit a strong scent that deters nematodes and other soil-dwelling pests, while garlic and onions can help repel aphids and other insect pests.

Furthermore, companion planting can attract beneficial insects, such as ladybugs and lacewings, which prey on harmful pests. By providing a diverse habitat that supports a healthy population of natural predators, gardeners can maintain a balanced ecosystem that keeps pest populations in check.

In summary, the science behind vegetable companion planting is rooted in the complex and fascinating interactions between plants and their environment. By understanding these principles and applying them strategically, gardeners can create a harmonious and productive garden ecosystem that thrives with minimal intervention.

This natural approach not only leads to healthier, more resilient gardens but also contributes to a more sustainable and environmentally friendly approach to gardening.

The Importance of Balance & Diversity in A Sustainable Vegetable Garden

Achieving balance and diversity in a sustainable vegetable garden plan is essential to ensure long-term productivity, resilience, and environmental harmony. By carefully considering the composition and arrangement of plants within the garden, gardeners can create a self-sustaining ecosystem that thrives with minimal intervention. The importance of balance and diversity in a sustainable vegetable garden can be explored through several key aspects, including plant health, soil fertility, pest management, and ecological impact.

Plant Health

A diverse and balanced garden promotes overall plant health by reducing the risk of disease outbreaks and minimizing competition for resources. When various plant species are grown together, pathogens have a harder time spreading from one plant to another, lowering the chances of widespread infections. Moreover, a well-planned garden ensures that each plant has adequate access to sunlight, water, and nutrients, reducing stress and optimizing growth.

Soil Fertility

Maintaining soil fertility is crucial for a sustainable vegetable garden, and incorporating a diverse array of plants can help achieve this goal. Different plants have varying nutrient requirements and root structures, which can lead to more efficient nutrient cycling and reduced soil depletion. For example, deep-rooted plants can mine nutrients from lower soil layers, making them available to shallow-rooted plants. Additionally, incorporating nitrogen-fixing legumes and nutrient-accumulating plants, such as comfrey, can further enhance soil fertility and reduce the need for chemical fertilizers.

Pest Management

A balanced and diverse garden can contribute to effective pest management by creating an environment that supports a healthy population of natural predators. By providing a habitat for beneficial insects, such as ladybugs, lacewings, and parasitic wasps, gardeners can keep pest populations in check without relying on chemical pesticides. Moreover, a diverse garden makes it more difficult for pests to locate their preferred host plants, reducing the likelihood of infestations.

Ecological Impact

Promoting balance and diversity in a vegetable garden contributes to broader ecological sustainability. A diverse garden attracts a wider range of pollinators, which are essential for many flowering plants' reproductive success. Furthermore, sustainable garden practices, such as composting, mulching, and water conservation, can help minimize the garden's environmental footprint and promote a healthier, more resilient ecosystem.

Cultivating balance and diversity in a sustainable vegetable garden plan is vital for ensuring the long-term health, productivity, and ecological harmony of the garden. By thoughtfully selecting plant species and implementing environmentally friendly practices, gardeners can create a

INTRODUCTION

thriving garden that not only nourishes their families but also contributes to the well-being of the planet.

The time-honored practice of vegetable companion gardening is an environmentally responsible way to grow a flourishing and abundant vegetable garden. Gardeners can strengthen their plots by understanding the co-dependency of different plants and creating a new, diverse ecosystem.

These simple techniques offer great benefits, like staving off disease and boosting production, while pushing back against humanity's contemporary issues concerning human dependencies with chemicals and potential losses in biodiversity due to climate change. A commitment to mastering the principles of companion gardening will prove essential if we hope to balance sustainability and productivity.

By internalizing this tradition that weaves together an understanding of both science and history, gardeners can become a part of a bigger picture in protecting not only the health status of their gardens but also larger green initiatives that create a more blossoming future for our planet.

CHAPTER 1
THE ART OF VEGETABLE COMPANION PLANTING - TECHNIQUES

Sustainable gardening is not just a passing trend; it is an important process that aims to conserve the environment and maintain a healthy ecosystem. The use of sustainable gardening strategies has become increasingly popular in recent years and for all the right reasons. As the importance of sustainability and ecological stewardship comes to the forefront, gardeners are increasingly seeking ways to minimize their environmental impact while still cultivating productive and healthy landscapes.

In this chapter, we will explore the roles which companion planting plays in an organic and sustainable garden as well as a range of companion gardening strategies where each strategy offers unique benefits and challenges, allowing you to tailor your approach to your specific needs and goals. Join us as we delve into these gardening strategies, uncovering valuable insights and practical tips to help you create a flourishing vegetable garden that not only nourishes yourself but also contributes to the well-being of our planet.

THE ROLE OF COMPANION PLANTING IN ORGANIC & SUSTAINABLE GARDENING PRACTICES

Companion planting is a gardening technique that involves strategically placing different plant species near one another to create mutually beneficial relationships. This method has long been used in organic and sustainable gardening practices, as it can help improve soil fertility, manage pests and diseases, optimize space and resources, and enhance overall garden health and productivity. The role of companion planting in organic and sustainable gardening practices can be understood through several vital aspects.

Improved Soil Fertility

Companion planting can contribute to better soil fertility by promoting nutrient cycling and efficient resource use. For example, legumes, such as beans and peas, have the ability to fix atmospheric nitrogen and convert it into a form that plants can utilize. By planting nitrogen-fixing legumes alongside heavy nitrogen feeders like corn or tomatoes, gardeners can ensure a consistent supply of this essential nutrient without relying on synthetic fertilizers.

Pest And Disease Management

One of the primary roles of companion planting in organic and sustainable gardening is its contribution to natural pest and disease management. Certain plant combinations can deter pests, attract beneficial insects, or act as sacrificial plants that draw pests away from more valuable crops. For instance, planting marigolds near tomatoes can repel harmful nematodes, while planting basil alongside tomatoes can help deter aphids and other pests. These relationships reduce the need

CHAPTER 1

for chemical pesticides, promoting a healthier and more balanced garden ecosystem.

Efficient Use Of Space And Resources

Companion planting can optimize space and resource use in the garden by taking advantage of the different growth habits and resource requirements of various plant species. For example, growing shade-tolerant lettuce or spinach under taller, sun-loving tomato plants can maximize vertical space and ensure that both plants receive the appropriate amount of sunlight. This efficient use of space and resources is particularly valuable in small-scale or urban gardens with little room for expansion.

Increased Biodiversity And Ecosystem Services

Implementing companion planting encourages biodiversity within the garden, which can contribute to its overall health and resilience. A diverse array of plants can provide various ecosystem services, such as nutrient cycling, erosion control, habitat for beneficial organisms, and pollination. By creating a more robust and balanced garden ecosystem, companion planting supports the long-term sustainability and productivity of the garden.

Enhanced Aesthetics And Sensory Experiences

Companion planting can also play a role in creating visually appealing and sensory-rich garden spaces. By combining different colors, textures, and scents, gardeners can create vibrant and stimulating environments that are not only productive but also enjoyable to experience. This aspect of companion planting can contribute to the overall well-being and satisfaction of the gardener, promoting a deeper connection with nature and sustainable living practices.

Companion planting plays a significant role in organic and sustainable gardening practices by improving soil fertility, managing pests and diseases, optimizing space and resources, increasing biodiversity, and enhancing aesthetics and sensory experiences. By understanding the relationships between different plant species and harnessing their complementary qualities, gardeners can create thriving, productive, and sustainable gardens that support both human and environmental well-being.

ADVANTAGES & DISADVANTAGES OF USING COMPANION PLANTING IN A VEGETABLE GARDEN

Companion planting in a vegetable garden offers a multitude of benefits, as well as some potential disadvantages, which should be considered when deciding whether to adopt this approach. By weighing the pros and cons, gardeners can make informed decisions about the best practices for their specific circumstances.

Benefits Of Companion Planting

Increased Productivity: One of the primary advantages of companion planting is the potential for increased productivity. When plants with complementary growth habits and needs are paired together, they can support each other's growth, leading to higher yields. For example, tall plants like corn can provide shade for heat-sensitive plants, while low-growing plants can help suppress weeds and maintain soil moisture.

Improved Soil Fertility: Companion planting can also contribute to better soil health and fertility. As mentioned earlier, legumes can fix nitrogen from the atmosphere, making it available to neighboring plants. Additionally, some plants can help break up compacted soil, allowing for better root penetration and nutrient absorption.

Natural Pest Control: By strategically pairing plants that deter pests or attract beneficial insects, companion planting can reduce the need for chemical pesticides. This not only lowers the environmental impact of gardening but also promotes a healthier garden ecosystem.

Biodiversity: Incorporating a diverse array of plant species in your vegetable garden can lead to a more resilient and balanced ecosystem. Biodiversity helps to create a stable environment that can better withstand disease outbreaks, pest infestations, and fluctuations in weather conditions.

Disadvantages Of Companion Planting

Complexity: One potential drawback of companion planting is the complexity involved in planning and executing an effective layout. Gardeners must research plant pairings and consider factors such as growth habits, nutrient requirements, and pest resistance. This can be time-consuming and may require a steeper learning curve than traditional monoculture gardening.

Competition: While some plant pairings can be mutually beneficial, others may compete for resources such as light, water, and nutrients. If not planned carefully, companion planting can inadvertently lead to reduced productivity and plant stress.

Limited Space: In small gardens or urban settings, it can be challenging to implement companion planting effectively due to space constraints. Gardeners may need to be more creative in their plant pairings and garden design to maximize the benefits of companion planting in limited areas.

The practice of companion planting brings multiple benefits to vegetable gardens, such as boosting productivity, enriching soil fertility, providing organic pest management, and promoting biodiversity. Yet, it does come with a set of hurdles, including its intricate nature, potential competition, and the constraints of space. By thoughtfully addressing these elements and crafting a well-studied companion planting scheme, garden enthusiasts can leverage this age-old technique to cultivate flourishing, eco-friendly gardens.

TYPES OF SUSTAINABLE COMPANION GARDENING STRATEGIES

Mono-Cropping

Mono-cropping, also known as monoculture, is an agricultural practice in which a single crop species is grown over a large area, often for several consecutive seasons. This method has been widely adopted in modern industrial agriculture due to its perceived efficiency and potential for increased short-term yields. However, when implemented in a vegetable garden, mono-cropping presents various benefits and disadvantages that need to be carefully considered.

CHAPTER 1

Benefits Of Mono-Copping In A Vegetable Garden

Simplified Planting And Harvesting: One of the main advantages of mono-cropping is the ease of planting and harvesting. When only one type of plant is grown, gardeners can streamline their processes, making it easier to manage tasks such as seeding, transplanting, and harvesting. This can save time and labor, particularly for larger-scale gardens or commercial operations.

Potential For Increased Short-Term Yields: Mono-cropping can lead to higher short-term yields, as the focus on a single crop allows gardeners to optimize growing conditions and inputs specifically tailored to that plant's needs. This targeted approach can result in more substantial harvests within a single growing season.

Disadvantages Of Mono-Cropping In A Vegetable Garden

Increased Vulnerability To Pests And Diseases: One of the most significant drawbacks of mono-cropping is its susceptibility to pest and disease outbreaks. A uniform crop provides an ideal environment for pests and pathogens to thrive, leading to more frequent and severe infestations. Additionally, the lack of diversity in a monoculture system eliminates natural predators that would otherwise keep pest populations in check.

Soil Nutrient Depletion: Growing the same crop repeatedly can lead to soil nutrient depletion, as each plant species has specific nutrient requirements. Over time, this can reduce soil fertility, necessitating the use of chemical fertilizers to maintain productivity. This not only increases the environmental impact of gardening but also contributes to soil degradation and erosion.

Reduced Biodiversity: Mono-cropping reduces biodiversity within the garden ecosystem, making it less resilient to environmental stressors such as climate fluctuations, invasive species, and natural disasters. A diverse garden is more likely to withstand these challenges, as different plant species can provide various ecosystem services, such as pest control, pollination, and soil fertility maintenance.

Long-term Yield Instability: While mono-cropping may result in increased short-term yields, it can also lead to long-term yield instability due to its vulnerability to pests, diseases, and soil degradation. Over time, these factors can result in declining productivity and increased reliance on chemical inputs, undermining the sustainability of the garden.

Although mono-cropping provides certain advantages like streamlined planting and harvesting procedures and the possibility of enhanced immediate yields, it comes with notable drawbacks when implemented in a vegetable garden.

These include heightened susceptibility to pests and diseases, soil nutrient exhaustion, diminished biodiversity, and instability of long-term yields, which collectively render mono-cropping a less sustainable choice for vegetable gardening. By incorporating different strategies that foster variety and ecological equilibrium, gardeners can establish sturdier and more fruitful gardens while reducing their environmental footprint.

CHAPTER 1

Crop Rotation

Crop rotation is the practice of growing different types of crops in a specific sequence in the same area over multiple seasons. This method has been used for centuries by farmers and gardeners to improve soil fertility, manage pests and diseases, and optimize crop yields. When applied in a vegetable garden, crop rotation offers several benefits and some potential disadvantages that need to be carefully weighed.

Benefits Of Crop Rotation In A Vegetable Garden

Improved Soil Fertility: One of the primary benefits of crop rotation is its ability to enhance soil fertility. Different plants have varying nutrient requirements and can contribute to or draw from the soil's nutrient reserves in unique ways. By rotating crops, gardeners can prevent the depletion of specific nutrients and promote more efficient nutrient cycling. For example, planting nitrogen-fixing legumes after a heavy nitrogen-feeding crop can help replenish the soil's nitrogen levels.

Pest And Disease Management: Crop rotation can help reduce the prevalence of pests and diseases in a vegetable garden. Many pests and pathogens are host-specific, meaning they target particular plant species or families. By changing the crops grown in a given area each season, gardeners can disrupt the life cycles of these pests and pathogens, reducing their populations and minimizing the need for chemical interventions.

Increased Biodiversity: Implementing crop rotation encourages biodiversity within the garden ecosystem, which can contribute to its overall health and resilience. A diverse array of plants can attract beneficial insects, such as pollinators and natural predators, and support a more balanced and robust ecosystem.

Higher Crop Yields: Practicing crop rotation can lead to higher crop yields over time by maintaining soil fertility, reducing pest and disease pressures, and promoting a healthier garden ecosystem. This sustainable approach allows for more productive and environmentally friendly gardening.

Disadvantages Of Crop Rotation In A Vegetable Garden

Complex Planning: One of the main challenges of implementing crop rotation in a vegetable garden is the need for careful planning. Gardeners must consider each crop's specific nutrient requirements, growth habits, and potential pest and disease issues when designing a rotation plan. This can be time-consuming and require a deeper understanding of plant biology and ecology.

Limited Space: For small-scale vegetable gardens or urban settings with limited space, implementing a proper crop rotation plan can be difficult. Limited space may restrict the variety of crops that can be grown or the ability to rotate them effectively. In such cases, gardeners may need to explore alternative strategies, such as intercropping or container gardening, to achieve some of the benefits of crop rotation.

Crop rotation is a beneficial and eco-friendly gardening technique that brings multiple advantages such as enhanced soil fertility, efficient pest and disease control, augmented biodiversity, and superior crop yields.

Despite some challenges it may pose, like intricate planning and limited space, the enduring benefits of introducing crop rotation in a vegetable garden significantly outweigh these minor inconveniences. By gaining knowledge about various crops and their interplay, garden enthusiasts can utilize the potency of crop rotation to cultivate a flourishing, bountiful, and green-conscious garden.

Cover Crops

Cover crops, also known as green manure, are plants grown primarily for their ability to improve soil health, suppress weeds, and manage pests and diseases. They are typically planted during fallow periods or between rows of cash crops and are later incorporated into the soil or left on the surface as mulch. When used in a vegetable garden, cover crops offer several benefits, but there are also some potential disadvantages to consider.

Benefits Of Cover Crops In A Vegetable Garden

Improved Soil Fertility: One of the most significant advantages of using cover crops is their ability to enhance soil fertility. Certain cover crops, such as legumes, have nitrogen-fixing properties, which means they can convert atmospheric nitrogen into a form that plants can use. When these cover crops are incorporated into the soil or left as mulch, they can provide valuable nutrients for subsequent vegetable crops.

Soil Structure And Erosion Control: Cover crops can help improve soil structure by adding organic matter and promoting the growth of beneficial microorganisms. Their root systems help bind soil particles together, reducing erosion and runoff. This can be particularly beneficial in areas prone to heavy rainfall or on sloped garden sites.

Weed Suppression: As they grow, cover crops can outcompete weeds for resources such as light, water, and nutrients. This can result in reduced weed pressure, making it easier to maintain a clean and productive vegetable garden.

Pest And Disease Management: Some cover crops can help manage pests and diseases by acting as trap crops or by releasing compounds that deter harmful insects. For example, certain brassicas release chemicals that can suppress soil-borne diseases like nematodes, while buckwheat attracts beneficial insects that prey on common garden pests.

Disadvantages Of Cover Crops In a Vegetable Garden

Additional Labor And Planning: Planting, maintaining, and incorporating cover crops can require additional labor and planning, particularly for small-scale or urban gardeners with

CHAPTER 1

limited time and resources. Gardeners must also carefully select cover crop species that are compatible with their vegetable crops and local climate conditions.

Potential Competition With Cash Crops: If not managed properly, cover crops can compete with vegetable crops for resources like water, nutrients, and sunlight. This can be especially problematic in smaller gardens or during periods of limited resource availability, such as droughts.

Pest and Disease Harboring: While some cover crops can help manage pests and diseases, others may inadvertently provide a habitat for harmful insects or pathogens. It is essential to select cover crop species that are not hosts for pests or diseases that affect the primary vegetable crops being grown.

To sum up, cover crops can provide a host of advantages to a vegetable garden, including enhanced soil fertility, better soil structure, control of erosion, suppression of weeds, and management of pests and diseases. Yet, it's important to note potential downsides too, such as increased labor and planning needs, competition with primary crops, and the possibility of fostering pests and diseases. By judiciously choosing and handling cover crops, you can amplify the benefits while curtailing potential negatives, thereby fostering a more fruitful and ecologically sustainable vegetable garden.

Intercropping

Intercropping, also known as interplanting, is the practice of growing two or more different crops together in the same area, often with complementary growth habits or resource requirements. This method promotes efficient use of space and resources and can provide a range of benefits for a vegetable garden. However, there are also some potential disadvantages to consider when implementing intercropping.

Benefits Of Intercropping In A Vegetable Garden

Efficient Use Of Space: One of the primary advantages of intercropping is its ability to maximize space utilization in a vegetable garden. By growing multiple crops together, gardeners can make better use of available space, particularly in small or urban gardens with little room for expansion.

Resource Sharing: Intercropping can promote more efficient resource sharing between plants, as different crops may have varying nutrient, water, and light requirements. For example, shallow-rooted crops can be grown alongside deep-rooted crops, allowing both to access nutrients and water at different soil depths without competing for resources.

CHAPTER 1

Improved Pest And Disease Management: Growing multiple crop species together can help disrupt the life cycles of pests and diseases, reducing the likelihood of severe infestations. Diverse plantings can also attract beneficial insects, such as pollinators and natural predators, which can help control pest populations and maintain a balanced garden ecosystem.

Increased Biodiversity: Intercropping encourages biodiversity within the garden, which can contribute to its overall health and resilience. A diverse array of plants can provide various ecosystem services, such as nutrient cycling, erosion control, and habitat for beneficial organisms.

Higher Overall Yields: By planting complementary crops together, gardeners can potentially achieve higher overall yields compared to growing each crop individually. The efficient use of space and resources, combined with improved pest and disease management, can result in increased productivity for the garden as a whole.

Disadvantages Of Intercropping In A Vegetable Garden

Complex Planning and Management: Implementing successful intercropping requires careful planning and management. Gardeners must consider factors such as growth habits, resource requirements, and compatibility between different crops when designing an intercropping plan. This can be time-consuming and may require a deeper understanding of plant biology and ecology.

Potential Competition Between Crops: If not planned correctly, intercropping can lead to competition between crops for resources like light, water, and nutrients. This can result in reduced growth and productivity for one or both crops, negating the potential benefits of intercropping.

Harvesting Challenges: Intercropping can make harvesting more difficult, as different crops may have varying maturity times and growth habits. Gardeners may need to carefully navigate through mixed plantings to harvest their crops without damaging neighboring plants.

Intercropping is a valuable gardening practice that offers several benefits, including efficient use of space, resource sharing, improved pest and disease management, increased biodiversity, and potentially higher overall yields. However, it also presents some challenges, such as complex planning and management, potential competition between crops, and harvesting difficulties. By thoughtfully selecting compatible crops and carefully managing their growth, gardeners can harness the power of intercropping to create a thriving, productive, and sustainable vegetable garden.

The Three Sisters

The Three Sisters is a traditional Native American companion planting technique that involves growing corn, beans, and squash together in the same area. This ancient agricultural method creates a mutually beneficial relationship between the three crops, promoting their growth and health while maximizing space and resources. Although the Three Sisters method offers several advantages for a vegetable garden, there are also some potential disadvantages to consider.

Benefits Of The Three Sisters In A Vegetable Garden

Mutual Support: The Three Sisters planting technique provides each crop with unique support. The cornstalks act as natural trellises for the beans to climb, eliminating the need for additional support. Meanwhile, the beans help stabilize the corn plants, making them less susceptible to wind damage. The large leaves of the squash plants shade the soil, helping to conserve moisture and suppress weed growth.

Improved Nutrient Cycling: Each of the Three Sisters contributes to the garden's nutrient cycling. Beans, being legumes, have nitrogen-fixing properties, converting atmospheric nitrogen into a form that plants can use. Corn, a heavy nitrogen feeder, benefits from this nitrogen supply, while the squash plants provide ground cover that helps retain soil moisture and nutrients.

Pest And Disease Management: Growing the Three Sisters together can help deter pests and diseases by creating a diverse planting environment. The intermingling of different plant species makes it more difficult for pests to locate their preferred host plants, reducing the likelihood of severe infestations. Additionally, the large squash leaves can deter some pests, such as raccoons, from accessing the corn and beans.

Efficient Use Of Space: The Three Sisters method allows gardeners to grow three crops together in a relatively small area, making efficient use of available garden space. This can be particularly advantageous for small-scale or urban gardeners with limited room for expansion.

Disadvantages Of The Three Sisters In a Vegetable Garden

Complex Planning And Management: Implementing the Three Sisters method requires careful planning and management to ensure that each crop receives the appropriate sunlight, water, and nutrients. Gardeners need to consider factors such as planting times, spacing, and crop compatibility when designing their Three Sisters garden.

Potential Competition Between Crops: If not managed correctly, the Three Sisters can compete with one another for resources like light, water, and nutrients. For example, if the corn grows too quickly, it may shade out the beans and squash, reducing their growth and productivity.

Harvesting Challenges: The intermingling of the Three Sisters can make harvesting more difficult, as each crop may have different maturity times and growth habits. Gardeners may need to carefully navigate through the mixed plantings to harvest their crops without damaging neighboring plants.

The Three Sisters planting technique offers numerous benefits for a vegetable garden, including mutual support, improved nutrient cycling, effective pest and disease management, and efficient use of space.

However, it also presents some challenges, such as complex planning and management, potential competition between crops, and harvesting difficulties. By carefully planning and managing their Three Sisters garden, gardeners can create a thriving, productive, and sustainable growing environment that honors an ancient agricultural tradition.

The Guild System

The Guild System, often associated with permaculture and forest gardening, is a method of grouping plants together based on their complementary relationships and ecological functions. The primary goal of this approach is to create a diverse, self-sustaining, and resilient garden ecosystem that mimics natural systems. In a vegetable garden, the Guild System can offer several benefits, but there are also potential disadvantages to consider.

Benefits Of The Guild System In A Vegetable Garden

Increased Biodiversity: The Guild System fosters biodiversity by encouraging the planting of a wide variety of plant species. This increased diversity can result in a healthier and more resilient garden ecosystem, better able to withstand environmental stressors such as climate fluctuations, pests, and diseases.

Improved Resource Use Efficiency: By grouping plants with complementary resource requirements, the Guild System promotes more efficient use of water, nutrients, and sunlight. For example, planting deep-rooted vegetables alongside shallow-rooted ones can help ensure that both access resources at different soil depths without competing with each other.

Natural Pest And Disease Management: Planting diverse guilds can help reduce the prevalence of pests and diseases by disrupting their life cycles and attracting beneficial insects that prey on common garden pests. This can reduce the need for chemical interventions and promote a more balanced garden ecosystem.

Enhanced Pollination: The Guild System encourages the inclusion of flowering plants that attract pollinators, which can improve the pollination of vegetable crops and increase overall productivity. A diverse array of flowers can also provide habitat and food sources for beneficial insects, further supporting garden health.

Reduced Maintenance: By creating a self-sustaining garden ecosystem, the Guild System can reduce the need for external inputs such as fertilizers and pesticides. This can save time, money, and effort while minimizing the garden's environmental impact.

Disadvantages Of The Guild System In A Vegetable Garden

Complex Planning and Design: The Guild System requires a deep understanding of plant relationships and ecological functions, which can make planning and designing a guild-based vegetable garden more complex and time-consuming than traditional gardening methods.

Potential Competition Between Plants: If not designed correctly, the Guild System can result in competition between plants for resources like light, water, and nutrients. This can lead to reduced growth and productivity for some plants within the guild.

Initial Establishment Challenges: Establishing a guild-based garden can require significant upfront effort and resources, particularly if starting from scratch or converting an existing garden. It may take several years for the guilds to become fully established and reach their full potential in terms of productivity and resilience.

Embracing the Guild System can dramatically transform your vegetable garden, bringing about a surge in biodiversity, boosting resource utilization efficiency, offering natural solutions for pest and disease control, enhancing pollination, and even cutting down on maintenance.

Of course, it's not without its challenges: intricate planning and design, possible plant rivalry, and hurdles during initial set up are all part of the package. Yet, with thoughtful consideration of plant associations and ecological roles, gardeners can masterfully apply the Guild System, paving the way for a bountiful, dynamic, and eco-friendly vegetable garden.

SELECTING WHERE YOUR GARDEN WILL GROW

Selecting the right location when growing vegetables using companion planting is crucial for the success of this gardening technique. A well-chosen location ensures that each plant receives the appropriate amount of sunlight, water, and nutrients, creating an environment in which plants can thrive and support one another. Additionally, by considering factors such as microclimates, soil type, and drainage, gardeners can optimize the growing conditions for their chosen plant combinations, allowing them to fully benefit from the symbiotic relationships that companion planting provides.

Furthermore, a strategically planned location can help reduce the risk of pest and disease infestations by disrupting their life cycles and making it more difficult for them to locate their preferred host plants. In summary, selecting the right location for a companion-planted vegetable garden is essential to maximize plant health, productivity, and overall garden sustainability, ultimately contributing to a more successful and rewarding gardening experience.

Sunlight Exposure

One of the most critical factors to consider when selecting a garden location is sunlight exposure. Most vegetables require at least six to eight hours of direct sunlight per day to grow and produce optimally. Gardeners should observe the sun patterns in their garden and choose a spot where their plants will receive sufficient light. When planning companion planting, it's essential to consider the light requirements of each plant species and arrange them accordingly, ensuring that taller plants do not shade out smaller or more shade-sensitive companions.

Soil Quality

Healthy soil is the foundation of a successful vegetable garden. Gardeners should assess the soil quality in their chosen location, considering factors such as texture, structure, pH, and nutrient content. Ideally, the soil should be well-draining, rich in organic matter, and have a neutral to slightly acidic pH. It may be necessary to amend the soil with compost, manure, or other organic materials to improve its fertility and structure. Additionally, gardeners should be aware of the specific nutrient requirements of their companion-planted vegetables and plan accordingly to avoid competition for resources.

Water Availability

Consistent and adequate water availability is crucial for healthy vegetable growth. When choosing a garden location, gardeners should ensure that they have easy access to a water source, such as a hose or irrigation system. The site should also have proper drainage to prevent waterlogged soil, which can lead to root rot and other issues. In a companion planting scenario, it's essential to group plants with similar water requirements together to avoid over- or under-watering and ensure that each plant receives the appropriate amount of moisture.

Existing Microclimates

Microclimates are small areas within a garden that have unique environmental conditions, such as temperature, humidity, and wind exposure. When planning a companion-planted vegetable garden, gardeners should be aware of any existing microclimates in their chosen location and use them to their advantage.

For example, heat-loving plants like tomatoes and peppers can be planted in a sunny, south-facing spot, while cool-season vegetables like lettuce and spinach may benefit from the shade provided by a fence or taller plants. By understanding and leveraging these microclimates, gardeners can

CHAPTER 1

create customized growing conditions for their companion plants, promoting optimal growth and productivity.

Pinpointing the perfect spot for a companion-planted vegetable garden isn't an off-the-cuff decision. It requires meticulous pondering over elements like how much sunlight the area gets, the quality of soil present, water accessibility, and the unique microclimates within. By diligently assessing these facets and customizing their garden blueprints to suit, garden enthusiasts can cultivate a vibrant, fruitful, and eco-friendly garden that truly capitalizes on the magic of companion planting.

TYPES OF VEGETABLE COMPANION GARDENS

Vegetable companion gardens can be effectively established in various settings, including raised beds, container gardens, and in-ground gardens, each offering unique advantages for implementing companion planting techniques. Raised bed gardens provide excellent drainage, precise control over soil quality, and the ability to create clearly defined planting zones, making it easier to plan and manage companion plant relationships.

Container gardens offer flexibility and mobility, allowing gardeners to experiment with different plant combinations and move containers as needed to optimize growing conditions, such as sunlight exposure. In-ground gardens provide the most traditional and expansive setting for companion planting, offering ample space for creating diverse and intricate planting schemes that maximize the benefits of plant relationships.

By understanding the unique characteristics and requirements of each garden style, gardeners can effectively incorporate companion planting principles, fostering healthier, more productive, and sustainable vegetable gardens.

Container Gardens

Container gardening has become increasingly popular for growing vegetables, especially in urban environments or areas with limited space. When combined with companion planting techniques, container gardens can offer several benefits, but there are also potential disadvantages to consider.

Benefits Of Container Gardening For Vegetable Companion Planting

Flexibility and Mobility: One of the primary benefits of container gardening is the flexibility it provides. Gardeners can easily rearrange containers to experiment with different plant combinations or move them to optimize growing conditions, such as sunlight exposure or temperature. This adaptability can help maximize the benefits of companion planting and create a more successful garden.

Control Over Soil Quality: In container gardens, gardeners have complete control over the soil used for their plants. This allows them to tailor the soil mix to suit the specific needs of their companion-planted vegetables, ensuring optimal nutrient availability and soil structure. This level of control can be particularly beneficial for gardeners dealing with poor native soil or contaminated sites.

Reduced Weed Pressure: Container gardening can significantly reduce weed pressure compared to in-ground gardens. By using high-quality, weed-free potting mixes and closely monitoring the containers, gardeners can minimize weed competition and devote more time and energy to nurturing their companion-planted vegetables.

Accessibility: Container gardens are often more accessible than in-ground gardens, making them an attractive option for individuals with limited mobility or those looking to minimize physical strain. Raised containers can be brought to a comfortable working height, allowing gardeners to tend to their companion plants more easily and efficiently.

Disadvantages Of Container Gardening For Vegetable Companion Planting

Limited Space: The most significant disadvantage of container gardening is the limited space available for plant growth. This constraint can make it difficult to accommodate larger companion planting schemes or grow a wide variety of vegetables. Gardeners may need to prioritize specific plant combinations or choose smaller, dwarf varieties to make the most of their available space.

Increased Water And Nutrient Requirements: Container-grown plants typically require more frequent watering and fertilization than in-ground plants due to the restricted root space and faster evaporation rates. This can be both time-consuming and resource-intensive for gardeners, particularly during hot or dry periods.

Temperature Fluctuations: Containers can be more susceptible to temperature fluctuations than in-ground gardens, as the soil in containers can heat up or cool down more quickly. These fluctuations can create stress for plants and may require additional monitoring and management to ensure optimal growing conditions for companion-planted vegetables.

Cost: Container gardening can be more expensive than in-ground gardening, particularly when it comes to purchasing high-quality containers, potting mixes, and irrigation systems. Gardeners must weigh these costs against the benefits of container gardening to determine if it is the best option for their situation.

Venturing into container gardening for vegetable companion planting can be a game-changer, offering you the perks of adaptability, control over soil health, diminished weed trouble, and easy reach.

Yet, it's not without its fair share of hurdles: space constraints, amplified water and nutrient needs, temperature swings, and possible escalated expenses. By thoughtfully weighing these elements, green thumbs can decide if container gardening is the perfect fit for their companion-planted vegetable garden, and unlock its full potential to bloom.

CHAPTER 1

Raised Bed Gardens

Raised bed gardening has become a popular choice for many gardeners who seek an effective way to grow vegetables using companion planting techniques. This method offers various benefits, but there are also potential disadvantages that should be taken into account.

Benefits Of Raised Bed Gardening For Vegetable Companion Planting

Improved Drainage and Soil Quality: Raised beds provide better drainage than traditional in-ground gardens, reducing the risk of waterlogged soil and root rot. They also allow gardeners to have complete control over the soil composition, making it easier to provide the ideal growing conditions for their chosen companion plants. Improved soil quality can lead to healthier plants and increased productivity.

Defined Planting Zones: Raised beds create clearly defined planting zones, simplifying the planning and management of companion planting schemes. Gardeners can easily organize their beds according to plant families or specific companion relationships, making it easier to rotate crops and maintain soil fertility.

Reduced Weed Pressure and Pest Issues: Raised beds can help decrease weed pressure by providing a physical barrier between the garden soil and the surrounding environment. Additionally, some pests may find it more difficult to access plants in raised beds, reducing the need for chemical pesticides and promoting a healthier garden ecosystem.

Accessibility and Ergonomic Benefits: Raised beds offer improved accessibility for individuals with limited mobility or those looking to minimize physical strain. By elevating the garden bed, gardeners can tend to their companion plants more comfortably, reducing the need for bending and kneeling.

Disadvantages Of Raised Bed Gardening For Vegetable Companion Planting

Initial Cost and Setup: One of the primary disadvantages of raised bed gardening is the initial cost and setup required. Constructing raised beds can be labor-intensive and expensive, particularly if high-quality materials are used. However, these costs can be offset over time by the long-term benefits of improved soil quality and reduced maintenance.

Water Requirements: Raised beds tend to dry out more quickly than in-ground gardens due to their improved drainage and elevated position. This can lead to increased water requirements, especially during hot or dry periods. Gardeners should plan for consistent watering and consider implementing an efficient irrigation system to ensure their companion plants receive adequate moisture.

Potential Limitations on Plant Selection: In some cases, raised beds may not be suitable for all types of vegetables or companion planting arrangements. Some plants with deep root systems may struggle in the confined space of a raised bed, and gardeners may need to choose specific plant varieties or combinations that are well-suited to this growing environment.

Temperature Fluctuations: Similar to container gardens, raised beds can be more susceptible to temperature fluctuations due to their elevated position and smaller soil volume. Gardeners will need to monitor soil temperatures closely and may need to provide additional insulation or protection for their companion plants during extreme weather conditions.

Venturing into raised bed gardening for vegetable companion planting can be a thrilling journey, offering the perks of superior drainage, enhanced soil quality, clear-cut planting zones, and diminished weed woes. Yet, it's not without its own set of challenges: initial setup costs, heightened water needs, restrictions on plant choice, and temperature variances. By thoughtfully weighing these elements, green thumbs can decide if raised bed gardening is their perfect match for a companion-planted vegetable garden, and unlock its full potential to flourish.

In-Ground Gardens

In-ground gardening is the most traditional method for growing vegetables and can be an effective approach for implementing companion planting techniques. Just like the previously mentioned garden types, there are both benefits and disadvantages to consider when using in-ground gardens for vegetable companion planting.

Benefits of In-Ground Gardening For Vegetable Companion Planting

Natural Soil Ecosystem: In-ground gardens benefit from the existing soil ecosystem, which includes beneficial microorganisms, insects, and earthworms that contribute to soil fertility and plant health. This natural environment can support complex companion planting schemes and help create a balanced and sustainable garden ecosystem.

Larger Planting Area: In-ground gardens typically offer more space for planting compared to raised beds or container gardens. This allows gardeners to grow a wider variety of vegetables and experiment with more extensive companion planting arrangements, ultimately increasing the potential for a diverse and productive garden.

Lower Initial Costs: In-ground gardens generally have lower initial costs compared to raised beds or container gardens. There is no need for constructing garden beds or purchasing containers and potting soil, making in-ground gardening more accessible and cost-effective for many gardeners.

Improved Moisture Retention: In-ground gardens tend to retain moisture better than raised beds or container gardens due to their larger soil volume and direct contact with the ground. This can result in less frequent watering requirements, conserving water resources, and reducing maintenance efforts.

Disadvantages Of In-Ground Gardening For Vegetable Companion Planting

Soil Quality and Drainage Issues: One of the main challenges of in-ground gardening is dealing with the native soil quality, which may not be ideal for growing vegetables. Gardeners may need to amend the soil with organic matter, nutrients, or other materials to improve its fertility and structure. Additionally, poorly draining soil can lead to waterlogged conditions and root rot, requiring further interventions such as installing drainage systems or choosing plants that tolerate wet conditions.

Increased Weed Pressure and Pest Issues: In-ground gardens are more susceptible to weed pressure and pest issues compared to raised beds or container gardens. Gardeners may need to spend more time on weed control and pest management, which could involve the use of chemical pesticides or other interventions that may not align with sustainable gardening practices.

Less Accessibility and Ergonomic Challenges: In-ground gardens can be more physically demanding than raised beds or container gardens, requiring gardeners to bend, kneel, or squat while tending to their companion plants. This can be challenging for individuals with limited mobility or those looking to minimize physical strain.

Difficulty In Defining Planting Zones: In-ground gardens may not have clearly defined planting zones compared to raised beds, making it more challenging to plan and manage companion planting schemes. Gardeners will need to be diligent in organizing their planting areas and maintaining accurate records to ensure proper crop rotation and soil fertility management.

Wrapping up, delving into in-ground gardening for vegetable companion planting can be an exciting endeavor, offering the advantages of a natural soil habitat, expansive planting space, lower startup costs, and superior moisture retention.

Yet, it's not without its challenges: possible issues with soil quality and drainage, heightened weed problems, lesser accessibility, and complications in demarcating planting zones. By thoughtfully weighing these aspects, garden enthusiasts can decide if in-ground gardening hits the sweet spot for their companion-planted vegetable garden, thereby unlocking its full potential to thrive.

CHAPTER 2
THE ART OF VEGETABLE COMPANION PLANTING - PREPARATION

P reparation is a crucial aspect of vegetable companion gardening, as it sets the foundation for a successful and sustainable garden ecosystem. Proper planning and preparation ensure that compatible plant species are intentionally placed together to maximize the benefits of their relationships, such as pest control, pollination, nutrient uptake, and overall plant health.

By carefully selecting plant combinations that complement each other, gardeners can create a harmonious environment where plants thrive and support one another's growth. Additionally, preparing the garden site by amending the soil, installing appropriate irrigation systems, and considering factors such as sunlight exposure and drainage helps establish optimal growing conditions for the chosen companion plants. In essence, thorough preparation not only enhances the productivity and resilience of a vegetable companion garden but also promotes a more enjoyable and rewarding gardening experience.

ESSENTIAL TOOLS FOR VEGETABLE COMPANION GARDENING

Utilizing the right tools for vegetable companion gardening is essential in ensuring the success and efficiency of your gardening efforts. By selecting appropriate tools tailored to the specific needs of your garden, you can minimize physical strain, save time, and achieve more accurate and precise results when planting, maintaining, and harvesting your vegetables.

High-quality tools can also contribute to the longevity and overall health of your plants by promoting proper care and reducing the risk of damage or stress. Furthermore, understanding how and when to use these tools enhances your gardening skills and knowledge, empowering you to make informed decisions and adapt your techniques as needed. In summary, investing in the right tools and mastering their use is a critical aspect of vegetable companion gardening that supports a thriving, productive, and sustainable garden ecosystem. So here is a list of essential tools for vegetable companion gardening.

Garden Trowel

A garden trowel is an indispensable tool for vegetable companion gardening, as its compact and ergonomic design makes it perfect for working in close quarters among various plant species. The trowel's versatility allows gardeners to dig small holes, transplant seedlings, and add soil amendments with precision, ensuring minimal disturbance to neighboring plants and their delicate root systems.

Additionally, the garden trowel enables gardeners to efficiently weed around companion plants without causing damage or uprooting the desired vegetation. Overall, a garden trowel is essential for maintaining the delicate balance within a vegetable companion garden, contributing to a thriving ecosystem where plants can grow harmoniously and support one another.

Garden Fork

A garden fork is a vital tool for vegetable companion gardening, as it allows gardeners to effectively cultivate and aerate the soil without damaging the intricate root systems of companion plants. The sturdy, pronged design of a garden fork facilitates the loosening of compacted soil, enabling better drainage, improved root penetration, and enhanced nutrient uptake for all plants within the garden ecosystem.

Additionally, garden forks are highly effective in turning compost and incorporating organic matter into the soil, which is essential for maintaining soil fertility and providing essential nutrients for companion plants. In essence, a garden fork plays a significant role in creating and maintaining optimal growing conditions for companion plants, contributing to a thriving and productive garden.

Hand Cultivator

A hand cultivator is an essential tool for vegetable companion gardening, as its compact design and pronged head make it ideal for working in tight spaces between various plant species. This versatile tool allows gardeners to gently break up the soil, mix in amendments, and remove weeds with precision, ensuring minimal disturbance to neighboring plants and their delicate root systems. By maintaining well-aerated and weed-free soil, a hand cultivator helps promote healthy root growth, improved nutrient uptake, and better water infiltration for all plants within the companion garden.

Moreover, using a hand cultivator can assist in the even distribution of organic matter, such as compost or mulch, which further contributes to a fertile and balanced garden ecosystem. In summary, a hand cultivator is a valuable tool for fostering optimal growing conditions in a vegetable companion garden, leading to a more productive and harmonious environment for plants to thrive.

Pruning Shears

Pruning shears are a critical tool for vegetable companion gardening, as they facilitate the selective removal of plant material to promote healthy growth, prevent disease, and encourage higher yields. By enabling precise cuts that minimize damage to the plant, pruning shears ensure that gardeners can effectively trim away dead, diseased, or overcrowded branches and leaves without harming nearby companion plants.

Regular pruning with shears also helps maintain the desired shape and size of plants, which is crucial in companion gardening, where space is often shared among various species. Furthermore, pruning shears are instrumental in harvesting ripe produce without causing damage to the plant or surrounding vegetation. In essence, pruning shears play a pivotal role in managing the health and productivity of a vegetable companion garden, contributing to an organized and flourishing ecosystem where plants can thrive together.

Garden Gloves

Garden gloves are an essential accessory for vegetable companion gardening, as they provide much-needed protection and comfort while working in close proximity to various plant species. Gardening tasks often involve handling soil, compost, sharp tools, and prickly or abrasive plant materials, which can lead to cuts, scratches, or skin irritation. By wearing garden gloves, gardeners can safeguard their hands from potential injuries and maintain a clean and hygienic environment for their plants.

Additionally, gloves enhance grip and dexterity, allowing for more accurate and efficient completion of tasks such as planting, weeding, and pruning. In the context of companion gardening, where careful and precise handling is crucial to avoid disturbing neighboring plants and their delicate root systems, garden gloves play an important role in ensuring the overall health and success of the garden ecosystem.

Watering Can or Hose with a Nozzle

A watering can or hose with a nozzle is an indispensable tool for vegetable companion gardening, as it ensures proper and efficient hydration of the diverse plant species sharing the same garden space. Different plants have varying water requirements, and the adjustable nozzle allows gardeners to customize the water flow and pressure to suit the specific needs of each plant without causing damage or overwatering.

Additionally, a gentle shower setting helps to evenly distribute water and minimize soil erosion, which is particularly important in companion gardens where plants are closely spaced and rely on a delicate balance of nutrients. By providing precise control over water delivery, a watering can or hose with a nozzle enables gardeners to maintain optimal moisture levels within the companion garden, fostering a thriving and harmonious environment where plants can grow together successfully.

Garden Rake

A garden rake is a crucial tool for vegetable companion gardening, as its durable and wide-toothed design allows gardeners to effectively maintain the soil surface and keep the garden environment clean and organized. The rake's primary function is to level and smooth out the soil, ensuring an even distribution of nutrients and promoting proper drainage, both of which are essential for the healthy growth of companion plants.

Additionally, a garden rake can be used to remove debris, such as fallen leaves or weeds, which helps prevent the spread of diseases and pests that could harm the delicate balance within a companion garden. By facilitating proper soil management and garden maintenance, a garden rake contributes significantly to the overall health and productivity of a vegetable companion garden, creating an optimal environment where plants can flourish together.

Garden Hoe

A garden hoe is an important tool for vegetable companion gardening, as its versatile design enables gardeners to perform a variety of tasks that contribute to the overall health and success of the garden ecosystem. With its long handle and flat, sharp blade, a garden hoe allows for the efficient removal of weeds that compete with companion plants for nutrients, water, and sunlight. By eliminating weeds without disturbing the delicate root systems of neighboring plants, gardeners can maintain the balance and harmony within the companion garden.

Additionally, a garden hoe can be used to break up compacted soil, create furrows for planting seeds, and incorporate organic matter, such as compost or mulch, into the soil. These actions improve soil structure, promote proper drainage, and enhance nutrient availability for all companion plants. In essence, a garden hoe plays a vital role in fostering a thriving and productive vegetable companion

CHAPTER 2

garden by facilitating effective soil management and weed control.

Wheelbarrow or Garden Cart

A wheelbarrow or garden cart is an indispensable tool for vegetable companion gardening, as it greatly enhances efficiency and reduces physical strain when transporting materials throughout the garden.

These sturdy and mobile devices are designed to carry heavy loads, such as soil, compost, mulch, tools, and harvested produce, allowing gardeners to conveniently move large quantities of essential resources without causing fatigue or injury. In a companion garden, where different plant species coexist in close proximity, the efficient distribution of resources like soil amendments or mulch is crucial for maintaining a balanced and healthy ecosystem.

Moreover, a wheelbarrow or garden cart can also be utilized for collecting garden waste, such as weeds, pruned branches, and fallen leaves, ensuring a tidy and well-maintained garden environment that minimizes the risk of diseases and pests. In summary, a wheelbarrow or garden cart plays a significant role in optimizing productivity and organization within a vegetable companion garden, ultimately contributing to a flourishing and harmonious growing space.

Garden Spade or Shovel

A garden spade or shovel is a fundamental tool for vegetable companion gardening, as its robust and versatile design enables gardeners to perform essential tasks that contribute to the establishment and maintenance of a thriving garden ecosystem. With its sharp, flat blade and sturdy handle, a garden spade or shovel allows for efficient digging and lifting of soil, making it indispensable for tasks such as planting new seedlings, transplanting established plants, and incorporating amendments like compost or manure into the soil.

These actions help to create an optimal growing environment for companion plants by improving soil structure, drainage, and nutrient availability. Additionally, a garden spade or shovel can be used to edge garden beds, creating clean boundaries that enhance the overall aesthetics and organization of the companion garden.

By facilitating effective soil management and garden bed preparation, a garden spade or shovel plays a critical role in promoting the health and productivity of a vegetable companion garden, laying the foundation for a successful and harmonious growing space.

Garden Stakes or Plant Supports

Garden stakes or plant supports are essential tools for vegetable companion gardening, as they provide the necessary structure and stability for various plant species to grow and thrive together in a shared space. As plants mature, some may require additional support to prevent them from toppling over or encroaching on their neighbors, which could disrupt the delicate balance within the companion garden.

Stakes and supports help ensure that each plant receives adequate sunlight, air circulation, and access to nutrients, thereby promoting optimal growth and productivity. Furthermore, these tools can also be used to train climbing plants, such as beans or peas, to grow vertically, maximizing the use of available space and reducing competition among companion plants.

By offering targeted support and guidance, garden stakes and plant supports play a pivotal role in maintaining harmony and organization within a vegetable companion garden, ultimately contributing to a healthy, productive, and visually appealing growing environment.

Garden Twine or Plant Ties

Garden twine or plant ties are vital tools for vegetable companion gardening, as they provide a gentle yet effective means of securing and organizing plants within the shared garden space. Made from soft, flexible materials, these ties ensure that plants receive the support they need without causing damage to their delicate stems and branches.

In a companion garden, where diverse plant species coexist in close proximity, it's essential to maintain order and prevent overcrowding. Garden twine or plant ties can be used to train climbing plants to grow vertically on trellises or stakes, maximizing the use of available space and reducing competition for resources among neighboring plants. Additionally, these ties can help keep sprawling plants contained, preventing them from encroaching on other plants' growing areas and maintaining optimal air circulation, which is crucial for minimizing the risk of diseases and pests.

By offering a simple and effective solution for plant management, garden twine and plant ties play a key role in fostering a harmonious and well-organized vegetable companion garden, ultimately contributing to a thriving and productive growing environment.

THE BASICS OF GARDEN SOIL PREPARATION

Understanding your soil is of paramount importance for vegetable companion gardening, as it lays the foundation for a thriving and harmonious growing environment. Comprehensive knowledge of soil properties, such as texture, structure, pH level, and nutrient content, enables gardeners to make informed decisions about which plants will grow best together and how to optimize their garden's overall health and productivity.

By selecting compatible plant combinations that share similar soil requirements, gardeners can ensure that each species receives the necessary nutrients, water, and growing conditions to flourish. Moreover, understanding the soil allows for the targeted application of amendments, such as compost, manure, or lime, to improve soil fertility, structure, and pH balance, ultimately enhancing the vitality of the entire garden ecosystem.

Furthermore, healthy soil promotes beneficial microorganisms and suppresses harmful pests and diseases, contributing to the longevity and resilience of the companion garden. In essence, a deep understanding of one's soil is the key to unlocking the full potential of vegetable companion gardening, encouraging a vibrant and bountiful growing space where diverse plant species can coexist and support one another.

SEVEN TYPES OF SOILS

Understanding the seven types of soil is crucial for gardeners seeking to optimize their vegetable companion planting strategies. Each soil type presents unique characteristics, benefits, and challenges that can significantly influence plant growth, health, and productivity in a companion garden. Here we will provide an overview of the seven soil types – clay, silt, sand, peat, chalk, loam, and saline – and discuss how they impact vegetable companion planting. By gaining a deeper knowledge of these soil types and their properties, gardeners can make informed decisions about soil amendments and management practices, ultimately creating a thriving and well-balanced garden that leverages the full potential of companion planting.

Sandy Soil

Sandy soil is a type of garden soil characterized by its coarse texture and large mineral particles, primarily composed of sand. The high sand content in this soil type creates a light, well-draining structure that allows water and air to easily penetrate through the soil layers.

While sandy soil has certain unique properties that can provide both benefits and challenges for vegetable gardening, understanding these characteristics can help gardeners make informed decisions when working with this type of soil.

One of the primary benefits of sandy soil in a vegetable garden is its excellent drainage. Excess water quickly passes through the soil, preventing the roots from becoming waterlogged and reducing the risk of root rot. This characteristic makes sandy soil particularly well-suited for vegetables that require good drainage, such as root crops like carrots, radishes, and parsnips, which can grow long and straight without encountering obstacles or becoming deformed.

Additionally, sandy soil tends to warm up more quickly in the spring compared to other soil types, providing a head start for early-season planting and potentially extending the growing season.

However, there are also several disadvantages to using sandy soil in a vegetable garden. Due to its loose structure, sandy soil struggles to retain water and nutrients, which can result in plants becoming stressed or malnourished. This may necessitate more frequent watering and fertilization to ensure that plants receive the necessary resources to grow and thrive. Furthermore, sandy soil often lacks the beneficial microorganisms and organic matter found in richer soil types, which play a crucial role in promoting plant health and resilience.

To overcome these challenges, gardeners can take steps to improve the quality of sandy soil in their vegetable gardens. Incorporating organic matter, such as compost, aged manure, or well-rotted leaves, can help increase the soil's nutrient content, water retention, and overall fertility. Adding organic amendments will also encourage the growth of beneficial microorganisms and improve soil structure, making it more conducive to healthy plant growth. Cover crops and mulching can also be employed to protect the soil surface, reduce erosion, and conserve moisture.

Silty Soil

Silty soil is a type of garden soil that has a fine, smooth texture due to its composition of small mineral particles, predominantly silt. Silt particles are intermediate in size between sand and clay, giving silty soil properties that fall somewhere between these two soil types. While silty soil offers certain advantages for vegetable companion gardening, it also presents specific challenges that gardeners must address to create a thriving and productive growing environment.

One of the primary benefits of silty soil in a vegetable companion garden is its ability to retain moisture and nutrients. The smaller particle size allows silty soil to hold on to water more effectively than sandy soil, ensuring that plants have consistent access to the resources they need to grow. Additionally, silty soil often has a higher nutrient content compared to sandy soil, providing a fertile environment for a diverse range of vegetable plants. The smooth, workable texture of silty soil also makes it easy to cultivate, plant, and maintain garden beds.

However, there are also several disadvantages to using silty soil in a vegetable companion garden. Due to its fine texture and high water retention, silty soil can become easily compacted, which can lead to poor drainage and reduced aeration. This may result in waterlogged soil and increased risk of root rot, particularly during periods of heavy rainfall or overwatering. Furthermore, poorly drained silty soil can create anaerobic conditions that inhibit the growth of beneficial microorganisms and promote the proliferation of harmful pathogens.

To overcome these challenges, gardeners working with silty soil should implement appropriate management practices to improve soil structure and drainage. One effective strategy is to incorporate organic matter, such as compost, aged manure, or well-rotted leaves, into the soil. This will help to increase aeration, reduce compaction, and promote the growth of beneficial microorganisms that improve overall soil health. Additionally, gardeners can use raised beds or berms to elevate planting areas, further enhancing drainage and preventing waterlogging.

Clay Soil

Clay soil is a type of garden soil that is characterized by its dense, heavy texture and minute mineral particles, primarily composed of clay. The small particle size and high clay content in this soil type create a compact structure that can hold water and nutrients effectively. While clay soil has certain unique properties that can provide both benefits and challenges for vegetable companion gardening, understanding these characteristics can help gardeners make informed decisions when working with this type of soil.

One of the primary benefits of clay soil in a vegetable companion garden is its ability to retain moisture and nutrients. Due to its dense structure, clay soil can hold onto water and essential minerals more effectively than sandy or silty soils, ensuring that plants have consistent access to the resources they need to grow. Additionally, clay soil often has a rich nutrient content, providing a fertile environment for a diverse range of vegetable plants. This fertility can be particularly beneficial in a companion garden, where different plant species can help support one another's growth and health.

However, there are also several disadvantages to using clay soil in a vegetable companion garden. Due to its dense texture and high water retention, clay soil can become easily compacted, which can lead to poor drainage and reduced aeration. This may result in waterlogged soil and increased risk of root rot, particularly during periods of heavy rainfall or overwatering. Furthermore, poorly drained clay soil can create anaerobic conditions that inhibit the growth of beneficial microorganisms and promote the proliferation of harmful pathogens.

To overcome these challenges, gardeners working with clay soil should implement appropriate management practices to improve soil structure and drainage. One effective strategy is to incorporate organic matter, such as compost, aged manure, or well-rotted leaves, into the soil. This will help to increase aeration, reduce compaction, and promote the growth of beneficial microorganisms that improve overall soil health. Additionally, gardeners can use raised beds or berms to elevate planting areas, further enhancing drainage and preventing waterlogging.

Loamy Soil

Loamy soil is a type of garden soil that is characterized by its balanced composition of sand, silt, and clay particles. This well-proportioned mixture of particle sizes creates a fertile,

CHAPTER 2

well-draining structure that is highly desirable for gardening, particularly in vegetable companion gardens. While loamy soil is often considered the ideal soil type for many types of plants, it is essential to understand its characteristics and any potential challenges to ensure a thriving and productive growing environment.

One of the primary benefits of loamy soil in a vegetable companion garden is its excellent balance of water retention and drainage. The combination of sand, silt, and clay allows loamy soil to hold moisture and nutrients effectively while still providing sufficient drainage to prevent waterlogging. This characteristic ensures that plants have consistent access to the resources they need to grow without the risk of root rot or other moisture-related issues. Additionally, loamy soil often has a rich nutrient content and a high concentration of organic matter, which supports a diverse range of vegetable plants and promotes a healthy garden ecosystem.

Another advantage of loamy soil in a vegetable companion garden is its workability. The balanced texture of loamy soil makes it easy to cultivate, plant, and maintain garden beds, facilitating efficient gardening practices and reducing the labor required for garden maintenance. Furthermore, the well-aerated structure of loamy soil encourages the growth of beneficial microorganisms, which play a crucial role in promoting plant health and resilience.

Despite its many advantages, there can be some challenges when using loamy soil in a vegetable companion garden. One potential issue is that loamy soil can sometimes become compacted if not managed properly, leading to reduced aeration and drainage. To avoid this, gardeners should take care not to overwork the soil or walk on planting areas, which can contribute to soil compaction.

To maintain the quality of loamy soil in a vegetable companion garden, gardeners should implement proper management practices such as regular addition of organic matter, crop rotation, and mulching. Incorporating compost, aged manure, or well-rotted leaves can help to maintain the soil's nutrient content, structure, and overall fertility. Crop rotation can prevent nutrient depletion and reduce the buildup of pests and diseases, while mulching helps to conserve moisture, suppress weeds, and protect the soil surface.

Peaty Soil

Peaty soil is a type of garden soil that is characterized by its high organic matter content, primarily composed of decomposed plant material known as peat. This dark, nutrient-rich soil is often found in wetland areas and can form over thousands of years as plant material accumulates and decomposes slowly in waterlogged conditions. While peaty soil offers certain unique properties for vegetable companion gardening, it also presents specific challenges that gardeners must address to create a thriving and productive growing environment.

One of the primary benefits of peaty soil in a vegetable companion garden is its high nutrient content. The decomposed plant material in peaty soil provides a rich source of essential nutrients, such as nitrogen and phosphorus, which can support the growth of a diverse range of vegetable plants. Additionally, peaty soil has a high water-holding capacity, ensuring that plants have consistent access to moisture even during drier periods. This characteristic can be particularly beneficial for moisture-loving vegetable plants, such as lettuce, celery, and spinach.

CHAPTER 2

Another advantage of peaty soil is its naturally acidic pH, which can be well-suited for acid-loving vegetables and companion plants, such as blueberries, potatoes, and rhododendrons. Furthermore, the lightweight and fluffy texture of peaty soil makes it easy to cultivate and work with, reducing the labor required for garden maintenance and planting tasks.

However, there are also several disadvantages to using peaty soil in a vegetable companion garden. Due to its high water retention, peaty soil can become easily waterlogged, which can lead to poor drainage and reduced aeration. This may result in an increased risk of root rot and the development of anaerobic conditions that inhibit the growth of beneficial microorganisms and promote the proliferation of harmful pathogens.

Additionally, peaty soil can be prone to rapid drying and compaction when not managed properly. As peat dries out, it can become challenging to rehydrate, leading to issues with water penetration and moisture distribution within the soil. This can result in uneven watering and potential plant stress.

To overcome these challenges, gardeners working with peaty soil should implement appropriate management practices to improve soil structure and drainage. One effective strategy is to incorporate organic matter, such as compost, aged manure, or well-rotted leaves, into the soil. This will help to increase aeration, reduce compaction, and promote the growth of beneficial microorganisms that improve overall soil health. Additionally, gardeners can use raised beds or berms to elevate planting areas, further enhancing drainage and preventing waterlogging.

Chalky Soil

Chalky soil is a type of garden soil that is characterized by its high content of calcium carbonate, often in the form of chalk or limestone. This alkaline soil type can be found in regions with underlying chalk or limestone bedrock and is typically well-draining and stony. While chalky soil offers certain unique properties for vegetable companion gardening, it also presents specific challenges that gardeners must address to create a thriving and productive growing environment.

One of the primary benefits of chalky soil in a vegetable companion garden is its excellent drainage. The stony composition and large pore spaces in chalky soil allow water to pass through quickly, preventing the roots from becoming waterlogged and reducing the risk of root rot. This characteristic makes chalky soil particularly well-suited for vegetables that require good drainage, such as root crops like carrots, parsnips, and onions. Additionally, the alkaline nature of chalky soil can benefit certain vegetable plants and companion plants that prefer higher pH levels, such as cabbage, cauliflower, and beetroot.

However, there are also several disadvantages to using chalky soil in a vegetable companion garden. Due to its high calcium carbonate content, chalky soil can cause nutrient imbalances, leading to deficiencies in essential elements such as iron, magnesium, and manganese. These deficiencies can result in poor plant growth, yellowing leaves, and reduced crop yields. Furthermore, the stony composition of chalky soil can make it more challenging to cultivate and maintain garden beds, as well as potentially impede the growth of certain root vegetables.

To overcome these challenges, gardeners working with chalky soil should implement appropriate management practices to improve soil fertility and structure. One effective strategy is to incorporate organic matter, such as compost, aged manure, or well-rotted leaves, into the soil. This will help to increase nutrient availability, improve moisture retention, and promote the growth of beneficial microorganisms that improve overall soil health. Additionally, the use of soil amendments, such as elemental sulfur or acidifying fertilizers, can help to lower the pH of chalky soil and correct nutrient imbalances.

Saline Soil

Saline soil is a type of garden soil that is characterized by its high salt content, which can occur naturally or result from poor irrigation practices, seawater intrusion, or the use of salt-laden fertilizers. The presence of excess salts in the soil can have a significant impact on plant growth and health, as well as the overall productivity of a vegetable companion garden.

While saline soil presents specific challenges for gardeners, understanding these characteristics and employing proper management techniques can help mitigate the negative effects of salinity on plant growth.

One potential benefit of saline soil in a vegetable companion garden is that a certain level of salinity can help control the growth of weeds and pests, as many common weed species and pests are less tolerant of high salt concentrations than most vegetable plants.

This natural form of pest and weed control can reduce the need for chemical herbicides and pesticides, leading to a healthier and more sustainable garden ecosystem. However, it is important to note that the advantages of saline soil are significantly outweighed by the challenges it presents.

The primary disadvantage of using saline soil in a vegetable companion garden is the negative impact of high salt levels on plant growth and health. Excess salts can cause osmotic stress, making it difficult for plants to take up water and essential nutrients, leading to reduced growth, wilting, and even plant death. Furthermore, high salinity can exacerbate nutrient imbalances, potentially causing deficiencies or toxicities that can further impair plant health and productivity.

To overcome these challenges, gardeners working with saline soil should implement appropriate management practices to reduce soil salinity and improve overall soil health. One effective strategy is to employ proper irrigation techniques, such as using low-salinity water sources and applying sufficient water to leach salts below the root zone.

Additionally, incorporating organic matter, such as compost, aged manure, or well-rotted leaves, into the soil can help improve soil structure, increase nutrient availability, and enhance the soil's ability to buffer against the negative effects of salinity.

Another approach to managing saline soil in a vegetable companion garden is to select salt-tolerant vegetable varieties and companion plants. Certain plant species, such as kale, spinach, and Swiss chard, are more resilient to high salt levels and can be grown successfully in moderately saline soils. By choosing appropriate plant species, gardeners can increase the likelihood of a successful harvest even in challenging soil conditions.

In conclusion, while saline soil presents significant challenges for vegetable companion gardening, understanding its unique properties and employing proper management techniques can help gardeners mitigate the negative effects of salinity on plant growth. By reducing soil salinity, improving soil health, and selecting salt-tolerant plant varieties, it is possible to create a productive vegetable companion garden despite the inherent challenges of saline soil.

SIGNS OF FERTILE & HIGH-QUALITY SOIL

Fertile and high-quality soil is the foundation of any successful vegetable companion garden, playing a crucial role in supporting plant growth, health, and productivity. A well-balanced and nutrient-rich soil provides the necessary conditions for plants to thrive while also advancing beneficial relationships between various plant species in a companion planting setup.

By recognizing and understanding the importance of optimal soil quality and implementing best practices in soil management, gardeners can create a flourishing and bountiful garden that maximizes the benefits of companion planting.

Key indicators of fertile and high-quality soil include:

Soil Structure: Fertile soil has a crumbly, well-aerated texture that allows for easy root penetration, water infiltration, and gas exchange. This type of soil structure promotes healthy root development and efficient nutrient uptake, which can result in stronger, more vigorous plants and higher crop yields in a vegetable companion garden.

Organic Matter Content: High-quality soil contains a significant amount of organic matter, such as decomposed plant material, compost, or aged manure. Organic matter contributes to soil fertility by providing essential nutrients, improving soil structure, and supporting the growth of beneficial microorganisms. In a vegetable companion garden, the presence of organic matter enhances overall garden health, leading to increased productivity and resilience against pests and diseases.

Nutrient Availability: Fertile soil contains an adequate supply of essential plant nutrients, such as nitrogen, phosphorus, and potassium, as well as micronutrients like iron, manganese, and zinc. A soil test can help determine the nutrient levels in the soil and guide any necessary amendments to improve fertility. In a vegetable companion garden, balanced nutrient availability supports the growth of diverse plant species, allowing them to thrive and support one another's health and development.

Soil pH: High-quality soil has a balanced pH level, which generally falls within the range of 6.0 to 7.0 for most vegetable crops and ornamental plants. A balanced pH ensures that nutrients are readily available to plants and supports the growth of beneficial microorganisms. In a vegetable companion garden, maintaining the appropriate pH level can help to create a thriving soil environment that promotes healthy plant growth and minimizes nutrient deficiencies or toxicities.

The benefits of using fertile and high-quality soil in a vegetable companion garden are numerous. By providing a rich, well-balanced growing environment, fertile soil supports the growth of diverse plant species, leading to increased productivity and resilience against pests and diseases. Additionally, high-quality soil promotes the establishment of beneficial microorganisms and insects, which play essential roles in nutrient cycling, pest control, and overall garden health.

In a nutshell, discerning the indicators of fertile, premium-grade soil is essential for the triumphant journey of a vegetable companion garden. By certifying their soil's alignment with these standards, garden lovers can cultivate a bustling, prolific garden ecosystem that harnesses the synergies between varied plant species, thereby enhancing overall garden vitality and sustainability.

HOW TO CREATE THE PERFECT SOIL CONDITION

Creating the perfect soil condition in a vegetable companion garden is essential for ensuring the health and productivity of your plants. By understanding the specific requirements of your chosen plant species and employing proper soil management techniques, you can create an optimal growing environment that promotes strong plant growth and promotes a thriving garden ecosystem.

Test Your Soil: Before making any changes to your garden soil, it's essential to assess its current state.

Testing your garden soil is essential for successful vegetable companion gardening, as it provides valuable information about the soil's nutrient levels, pH, and texture, which directly impact plant growth and health. By understanding your soil's unique characteristics, you can tailor your soil management practices to address deficiencies or imbalances and create an optimal growing environment for your plants.

To test your garden soil, you can use a home soil test kit or send a soil sample to a professional laboratory for analysis. Home soil test kits typically include instructions and all necessary materials to evaluate pH, nitrogen, phosphorus, and potassium levels. For a more comprehensive analysis, consider using a professional soil testing service, which can provide detailed information on micronutrient levels, soil texture, and organic matter content.

Based on the test results, you can make informed decisions about soil amendments, fertilization, and other practices to enhance your vegetable companion garden's productivity and overall health.

Clean Your Soil: Maintaining clean garden soil is crucial for successful vegetable companion gardening, as it helps prevent the spread of pests, diseases, and weeds that can negatively impact plant health and productivity. By keeping your soil clean, you create a healthier environment for your plants and minimize potential threats to their growth. To clean your garden soil, start by removing any plant debris, such as fallen leaves, branches, or spent crops, which can harbor pests and pathogens.

Regularly weed your garden to prevent invasive species from competing with your vegetables for nutrients and space. If you encounter any diseased plants, remove them promptly and dispose of them properly to avoid spreading the disease to other plants. Additionally, consider solarizing your soil by covering it with a clear plastic tarp during the hottest months of the year. This process uses the sun's heat to kill off pathogens, pests, and weed seeds in the soil, effectively sterilizing the area for future planting.

Remove Infestations: Removing infestations in garden soil is essential for successful vegetable companion gardening, as pests, pathogens, and invasive weeds can hinder plant growth, reduce productivity, and even cause plant death. By promptly addressing infestations, you protect your plants and maintain a healthy garden ecosystem. To remove infestations, first, identify the specific issue affecting your soil or plants.

If dealing with pests, consider using natural methods such as introducing beneficial insects, like ladybugs or lacewings, to control the pest population. For fungal or bacterial diseases, remove affected plant material and apply organic fungicides or bactericides as needed. In the case of invasive weeds, manually pull them out or use a hoe to cut them below the soil surface, taking care not to disturb your desired plants.

Implementing preventive measures, such as crop rotation, proper sanitation, and maintaining balanced soil conditions, can also help reduce the risk of future infestations. By actively removing infestations and practicing proactive garden management, you can promote a thriving and productive vegetable companion garden.

Treat Your Soil: One of the most effective ways to improve soil conditions is by incorporating organic matter, such as compost, aged manure, well-rotted leaves, or bone meal, to provide a slow-release source of nutrients that will benefit your vegetable companion plants throughout the growing season.

Organic matter not only provides essential nutrients for plant growth but also improves soil structure, water retention, and supports the growth of beneficial microorganisms. Regularly adding organic matter to your garden beds will help maintain a healthy soil environment for your vegetable companion plants, but be careful not to over-fertilize, as excessive nutrient levels can harm plants and disrupt the soil ecosystem.

Most vegetable plants prefer a slightly acidic to neutral pH range, typically between 6.0 and 7.0. Ensuring that your soil falls within this range will promote nutrient availability and support the growth of beneficial microorganisms. If your soil test reveals an overly acidic or alkaline pH, amend the soil with appropriate materials such as lime (to raise pH) or sulfur (to lower pH) to achieve the desired level.

Drainage and Aeration: A well-draining and aerated soil allows for healthy root growth and prevents issues related to waterlogging, such as root rot. To improve soil drainage and aeration, consider adding coarse materials like sand or perlite to heavy clay soils or building raised beds. Regularly loosening the soil surface with a garden fork or cultivating tool can also help maintain good aeration.

Crop Rotation and Cover Cropping: Rotating your vegetable crops and planting cover crops can help maintain soil fertility, prevent the buildup of pests and diseases, and improve soil structure. By changing the types of plants grown in a specific area each year and incorporating cover crops like legumes or grasses, you can reduce the depletion of essential nutrients and enhance the overall health of your garden soil.

Monitor and Adjust Soil Conditions Regularly: Creating the perfect soil condition is an ongoing process. Continuously monitor your garden's soil health by conducting periodic soil tests, observing plant growth and health, and adjusting your soil management practices as needed.

Creating the perfect soil condition in a vegetable companion garden requires understanding your soil's unique characteristics and employing effective soil management techniques. By amending and nurturing your garden soil, you can create a thriving environment that supports the growth of diverse vegetable plants and contributes to a healthy, productive, and sustainable garden ecosystem.

CHAPTER 2

STORE BOUGHT VS. HOMEMADE SOIL TREATMENT

When it comes to vegetable companion planting, gardeners often face the dilemma of choosing between store-bought and homemade soil treatments. Both options have their merits and drawbacks, and selecting the most suitable treatment depends on various factors such as individual gardening goals, budget constraints, and environmental considerations.

This comparison will delve into the benefits and limitations of store-bought versus homemade soil treatments, helping you make an informed decision that best supports the health and productivity of your vegetable companion garden. By understanding the unique characteristics of each option, you can optimize your soil management practices and create a thriving garden ecosystem tailored to your specific needs.

Store-Bought Soil Treatments

Store-bought soil treatments offer a convenient and readily available solution for addressing various soil issues in a vegetable companion garden. These treatments come in a wide range of formulations, from chemical fertilizers and pH adjusters to organic amendments and pest control products, allowing gardeners to select the best option for their specific needs.

Benefits of Store-Bought Soil Treatments:

Convenience: One of the primary advantages of store-bought soil treatments is their convenience. These products are easily accessible at garden centers or online retailers and come with clear instructions for use, making them a practical choice for busy gardeners.

Consistency: Store-bought soil treatments typically undergo rigorous quality control processes, ensuring that they consistently deliver the desired effect. This consistency can be particularly beneficial when addressing nutrient deficiencies or pH imbalances, as it allows for reliable and predictable results.

Variety: With a wide range of products available, store-bought soil treatments cater to diverse gardening needs, from boosting nutrient levels and improving soil structure to controlling pests and diseases. This variety makes it easier for gardeners to find a suitable product for their specific requirements.

Disadvantages Of Store-Bought Soil Treatments:

Cost: One of the main drawbacks of store-bought soil treatments is their cost. Depending on the product and brand, these treatments can be relatively expensive compared to homemade alternatives, potentially straining a gardener's budget.

Environmental impact: Some store-bought soil treatments, particularly chemical fertilizers and pesticides, can have adverse environmental effects. Overuse or improper application of these products may lead to water pollution, soil degradation, and harm to beneficial organisms, such as pollinators and soil microbes.

Potential health risks: Certain store-bought soil treatments, especially those containing synthetic chemicals, may pose potential health risks to both plants and humans. Prolonged exposure to these substances can negatively impact plant growth and, in some cases, result in the accumulation of harmful residues in the harvested produce. This is especially concerning for vegetable gardens, where the produce is directly consumed by humans.

Commercially available soil treatments offer a handy and varied array of solutions for catering to specific needs in a vegetable companion garden. However, they also carry potential downsides such as cost implications, environmental footprint, and health hazards. When choosing a store-bought soil treatment, it's critical to meticulously balance the advantages and drawbacks. This will aid in making a well-informed choice that not only bolsters your garden's health and yield but also resonates with your personal beliefs and priorities.

Homemade Soil Treatments

Homemade soil treatments present an alternative to store-bought options, allowing gardeners to create custom solutions for their vegetable companion garden using readily available materials. These treatments can include compost, homemade fertilizers, and natural pest control methods, which cater to a variety of gardening needs.

Benefits Of Homemade Soil Treatments:

Cost-Effectiveness: One of the most significant advantages of homemade soil treatments is their cost-effectiveness. By using readily available materials, such as kitchen scraps, yard waste, or locally sourced manure, gardeners can create nutrient-rich amendments at little to no expense.

Environmentally Friendly: Homemade soil treatments often have a lower environmental impact than their store-bought counterparts. By utilizing organic materials and avoiding synthetic chemicals, these treatments contribute to a more sustainable gardening approach that supports soil health, biodiversity, and ecosystem balance.

Customization: Homemade soil treatments allow gardeners to tailor their amendments to their garden's specific needs. By adjusting the ingredients and proportions in their homemade treatments, gardeners can create targeted solutions that address nutrient deficiencies, pH imbalances, or other soil-related issues.

Disadvantages Of Homemade Soil Treatments:

Time-consuming: One of the main drawbacks of homemade soil treatments is the time and effort required to create them. Composting, for instance, can take several months to produce nutrient-rich, finished compost. Additionally, sourcing and preparing materials for homemade treatments can be labor-intensive and time-consuming.

Inconsistency: Unlike store-bought soil treatments, homemade options may lack consistency in terms of nutrient content, pH, or effectiveness. This inconsistency can make it challenging to achieve predictable results, especially for gardeners with limited experience in creating and using homemade treatments.

Limited Options: While homemade soil treatments can address many common gardening issues, they may not provide a solution for every problem. In some cases, gardeners may still need to rely on store-bought treatments to tackle specific challenges, such as stubborn pests or diseases that require specialized interventions.

To sum up, home-crafted soil treatments extend a multitude of advantages for vegetable companion gardens, such as being cost-effective, environmentally sustainable, and adaptable to specific needs. However, they also bear certain downsides, like the required investment of time and effort,

CHAPTER 2

potential variability, and a limited spectrum of solutions for specific concerns. When contemplating homemade soil treatments, it's vital to strike a balance between the pros and cons, and discern if they resonate with your gardening objectives, resources at disposal, and personal tastes.

CHAPTER 3
BRASSICA "CABBAGE" FAMILY COMPANION PLANTING

The Brassica cabbage family, a diverse and nutrient-rich group of vegetables, plays a vital role in vegetable companion planting strategies. Comprising various species such as cabbage, broccoli, kale, cauliflower, and Brussels sprouts, these cruciferous vegetables offer numerous advantages when thoughtfully integrated into a companion planting scheme.

Planting companion plants within the Brassica family can be significantly beneficial to your garden, as these vegetables often share common growth requirements and pest deterrents, leading to improved overall garden health and productivity. Companion planting brassicas with complementary plant species can provide a range of advantages, such as enhanced soil fertility, efficient use of space and resources, and natural pest control through the presence of aromatic herbs that repel harmful insects while attracting beneficial ones.

Furthermore, incorporating a variety of brassicas in a companion planting scheme promotes biodiversity in the garden, which can lead to increased resilience against diseases and pests and a more balanced garden ecosystem. By understanding the unique characteristics and needs of each brassica vegetable, you can create thriving, symbiotic relationships between their plants, ultimately resulting in a more prosperous and sustainable garden.

In this chapter, we will delve into the unique characteristics, growth requirements, and beneficial relationships that the Brassica family shares with other plant species in a companion garden. By understanding the intricacies of the Brassica cabbage family and strategically incorporating them into your garden plan, you can improve overall plant health, enhance productivity, and create a more resilient and sustainable vegetable garden ecosystem.

BRASSICA FAMILY VEGETABLE PLANTS

The Brassica cabbage family, also known as cruciferous vegetables or brassicas, consists of a wide variety of nutrient-dense vegetables that provide numerous benefits in vegetable companion planting. By understanding the unique characteristics and growing needs of each brassica vegetable, gardeners can create thriving, symbiotic relationships between plants that promote overall garden health and productivity. In the following, we will explore several vegetables within the Brassica family and their roles in companion planting.

Cabbage (Brassica oleracea var. capitata): Cabbage is a cool-season crop that can benefit from companion planting with aromatic herbs such as dill, mint, and thyme, which help repel pests like cabbage worms and aphids. Additionally, interplanting cabbage with fast-growing leafy greens like lettuce or spinach can maximize garden space and provide shade to the soil, reducing weed growth and conserving moisture. However, cabbage should be kept away from tomatoes and strawberries, as these plants can inhibit its growth.

Broccoli (Brassica oleracea var. italica): Broccoli thrives in the company of other cool-season vegetables and herbs, such as onions, garlic, and rosemary, which can deter pests like cabbage loopers and flea beetles. Planting broccoli alongside nitrogen-fixing legumes like beans and peas can also improve soil fertility, benefiting both plants. It's important to avoid planting broccoli near tomatoes, peppers, or eggplants, as these plants can compete for nutrients and potentially increase the risk of disease.

Cauliflower (Brassica oleracea var. botrytis): Cauliflower can benefit from companion planting with various herbs, such as oregano, sage, and chamomile, which can help repel pests and attract beneficial insects. Intercropping cauliflower with fast-growing, shallow-rooted vegetables like radishes can also assist in suppressing weeds and maximizing garden space. Similar to other brassicas, cauliflower should be kept away from tomatoes and other nightshade family members.

Kale (Brassica oleracea var. acephala): Kale can form successful partnerships with several vegetables and herbs in a companion planting system. Aromatic herbs like basil, dill, and parsley can help deter pests while planting kale alongside root vegetables like beets or carrots can promote efficient use of space and resources. However, it is essential to avoid planting kale near beans, as they can compete for nutrients and attract similar pests.

Brussels sprouts (Brassica oleracea var. gemmifera): Brussels sprouts benefit from being planted near aromatic herbs such as mint, sage, and rosemary, which can repel pests and attract beneficial insects. Companion planting with legumes like peas can also improve soil fertility by fixing nitrogen while interplanting with lettuce or spinach can provide ground cover and suppress weeds. As with other brassicas, Brussels sprouts should not be planted close to tomatoes or other nightshades.

Collard greens (Brassica oleracea var. acephala): Collard greens can form beneficial relationships with various companion plants, including herbs like dill, mint, and thyme, which help repel pests and attract pollinators. Planting collard greens with root vegetables such as onions or turnips can maximize garden space and promote efficient resource use. However, collard greens should be kept away from beans and other legumes, as they can compete for nutrients and share common pests.

Kohlrabi (Brassica oleracea var. gongylodes): Kohlrabi can benefit from companion planting with aromatic herbs like sage, oregano, and marjoram, which can help deter pests and attract beneficial insects. Interplanting kohlrabi with fast-growing vegetables like lettuce or radishes can also maximize garden space and suppress weeds. As with other brassicas, it is essential to avoid planting kohlrabi near tomatoes, peppers, or eggplants.

The Brassica cabbage family offers a diverse range of vegetables that can contribute to successful vegetable companion planting strategies. By understanding the unique characteristics and requirements of each brassica vegetable, gardeners can create symbiotic relationships between plants that foster a healthy, productive, and resilient garden ecosystem.

BRASSICA FAMILY COMPANION VEGETABLES

Companion planting is a gardening technique that involves tactically pairing different vegetable plants to benefit each other's growth, health, and productivity. When companion planting with Brassica "Cabbage" Family vegetables, selecting the right partners can significantly enhance your garden's overall success. In the following paragraphs, we will explore various types of vegetable plants that make excellent companions for brassicas and offer tips on how to choose the best companion plants for this diverse family of vegetables.

Legumes (Beans and Peas): Legumes, such as beans and peas, are excellent companion plants for many brassicas due to their ability to fix nitrogen in the soil. Nitrogen is an essential nutrient for healthy plant growth, and brassicas are known to be heavy feeders. By planting legumes near brassicas, you can improve soil fertility and promote vigorous growth for both types of plants. However, it is essential to avoid planting kale or collard greens near beans, as they can compete for nutrients and attract similar pests.

Alliums (Onions, Garlic, and Leeks): Alliums are another group of vegetables that can benefit brassicas when planted together. These plants release sulfur compounds into the soil, which can help deter common brassica pests like cabbage worms, aphids, and root maggots. Additionally, the pungent aroma of alliums can mask the scent of brassicas, making it more difficult for pests to locate their host plants. When selecting alliums as companion plants for brassicas, consider planting them between rows or interspersed throughout your brassica patch.

Leafy Greens (Lettuce, Spinach, and Swiss Chard): Fast-growing leafy greens like lettuce, spinach, and Swiss chard make excellent companion plants for brassicas. These plants can be intercropped with brassicas, providing ground cover and suppressing weed growth while helping to conserve soil moisture. Additionally, leafy greens can act as a "living mulch," moderating soil temperature and preventing erosion. When choosing leafy greens to plant with brassicas, consider selecting varieties with different maturation times to maximize garden space and harvest windows.

Root Vegetables (Carrots, Beets, and Radishes): Root vegetables can be beneficial companion plants for brassicas, as they occupy different layers of the soil and don't compete for nutrients. Intercropping brassicas with root vegetables like carrots, beets, or radishes can help maximize garden space and promote efficient resource use. Moreover, some root vegetables, such as radishes, can deter pests like flea beetles, which are known to attack brassicas. When selecting root vegetables to plant with brassicas, consider their growth habits and maturity times to ensure harmonious coexistence.

Aromatic Herbs (Basil, Dill, and Mint): Aromatic herbs can play a crucial role in companion planting with brassicas, as their strong scents can repel pests and attract beneficial insects. Herbs like basil, dill, and mint can help deter common brassica pests like cabbage worms, aphids, and whiteflies.

Additionally, these herbs can attract pollinators and predator insects, such as ladybugs and lacewings, which prey on harmful pests. When choosing aromatic herbs to plant with brassicas, consider their growth habits, water requirements, and compatibility with your specific brassica varieties.

Selecting the right companion plants for Brassica "Cabbage" Family vegetables can significantly enhance the health, productivity, and resilience of your garden. By considering the unique characteristics and needs of each vegetable type, you can create thriving, symbiotic relationships between your plants and cultivate a more prosperous and sustainable garden ecosystem. Remember to rotate your crops each year to prevent the build-up of diseases and pests and maintain healthy soil fertility.

BRASSICA FAMILY NON-COMPANION PLANTS

As previously mentioned there are certain vegetable plants that you should avoid companion planting with the Brassica "Cabbage" Family, as they may compete for resources, attract similar pests, or inhibit each other's growth. Here are some types of vegetable plants not to companion plant with brassicas:

Nightshades (Tomatoes, Peppers, and Eggplants): Nightshade family members, including tomatoes, peppers, and eggplants, should not be planted near brassicas. These plants can compete for nutrients, and their proximity may increase the risk of disease spreading between them. Additionally, tomatoes can inhibit the growth of brassicas, making it essential to keep these plants separate in your garden.

Strawberries: Strawberries should be kept away from brassicas, as they can inhibit each other's growth. Moreover, planting strawberries near brassicas may increase the risk of pests like slugs, which could damage both types of plants.

Potatoes: Potatoes should not be planted near brassicas, as they can compete for nutrients and share common pests, such as flea beetles and aphids. Keeping potatoes and brassicas apart in your garden can help reduce the risk of pest infestations and ensure both types of plants have access to the necessary nutrients for healthy growth.

Mustard Greens: Mustard greens are another brassica family member, but they should not be planted near other brassicas, as they can attract pests like cabbage worms and flea beetles. Planting mustard greens in a different area of your garden can help prevent the spread of pests and diseases between brassicas.

Beans (for Kale and Collard Greens): While beans can be beneficial companions for some brassicas, they should not be planted near kale or collard greens. These plants can compete for nutrients and attract similar pests, making it essential to keep them separate in your garden.

When planning your garden layout, it's crucial to consider the compatibility of different vegetable plants to ensure a harmonious and productive garden ecosystem. By avoiding planting incompatible plants near brassicas, you can promote healthier growth and reduce the risk of pests and diseases affecting your garden. Remember to practice crop rotation each year to maintain soil fertility and prevent the build-up of pests and diseases.

THE RIGHT SOIL FOR BRASSICA FAMILY VEGETABLES

The right soil conditions are essential for the successful growth of different Brassica family vegetables and their compatible companion plants. Understanding the specific soil requirements for each brassica vegetable and ensuring compatibility with their companion plants helps gardeners create a thriving and productive garden ecosystem.

In the following paragraphs, we will discuss the ideal soil conditions for different Brassica family vegetables and how these conditions affect companion planting with compatible companion vegetables.

Cabbage (Brassica oleracea var. capitata): Cabbage prefers well-draining, fertile loamy soil with a pH between 6.0 and 7.0. This soil type provides the necessary moisture retention and nutrient availability for healthy cabbage growth. When companion planting with cabbage, it's essential to select plants that thrive in similar soil conditions, such as aromatic herbs like dill and mint or leafy greens like lettuce and spinach. Ensuring compatible soil requirements for both cabbage and its companion plants will promote a harmonious and productive garden ecosystem.

Broccoli (Brassica oleracea var. italica): Broccoli thrives in well-draining, nutrient-rich loamy or sandy loam soil with a pH between 6.0 and 7.0. This soil type promotes strong root development and provides the consistent moisture and nutrients that broccoli needs for optimal growth. Companion plants like onions, garlic, and legumes, such as beans and peas, also prefer similar soil conditions, making them suitable partners for broccoli in a companion planting system.

CHAPTER 3

Cauliflower (Brassica oleracea var. botrytis): Cauliflower requires well-draining, fertile loamy soil with a pH between 6.0 and 7.0 for the best growth. This soil type allows for adequate moisture retention and nutrient availability, which is crucial for cauliflower's development. When companion planting with cauliflower, select plants like oregano, sage, and chamomile that also thrive in similar soil conditions. This compatibility will ensure that both cauliflower and its companion plants can grow healthily together.

Kale (Brassica oleracea var. acephala): Kale prefers well-draining, loamy or sandy loam soil with a pH between 6.0 and 7.5. This soil type provides the necessary moisture and nutrient availability for healthy kale growth. Companion plants like basil, dill, and parsley also thrive in similar soil conditions, making them suitable partners for kale in a companion planting system. Root vegetables like beets and carrots can also be planted alongside kale, as they occupy different soil layers and do not compete for nutrients.

Brussels sprouts (Brassica oleracea var. gemmifera): Brussels sprouts grow best in well-draining, fertile loamy soil with a pH between 6.0 and 7.0. This soil type supports strong root development and provides the consistent moisture and nutrients necessary for optimal Brussels sprouts growth. When companion planting with Brussels sprouts, choose plants like mint, sage, and rosemary that also prefer similar soil conditions. Additionally, legumes like peas can be planted nearby to improve soil fertility through nitrogen fixation.

Collard greens (Brassica oleracea var. acephala): Collard greens thrive in well-draining, loamy, or sandy loam soil with a pH between 6.0 and 7.5. This soil type offers adequate moisture retention and nutrient availability for healthy collard greens growth. Aromatic herbs like dill, mint, and thyme can be excellent companion plants for collard greens, as they also prefer similar soil conditions and can help deter pests.

Kohlrabi (Brassica oleracea var. gongylodes): Kohlrabi grows best in well-draining, fertile loamy soil with a pH between 6.0 and 7.5. This soil type promotes strong root development and provides the consistent moisture and nutrients that kohlrabi needs for optimal growth. When companion planting with kohlrabi, select plants like sage, oregano, and marjoram that also thrive in similar soil conditions, ensuring a harmonious and productive garden ecosystem.

Understanding the ideal soil conditions for the different Brassica family vegetables and their impact on companion planting with compatible companion vegetables is essential for creating a flourishing garden ecosystem. By selecting compatible companion plants and providing the right soil conditions for each Brassica vegetable, gardeners can cultivate a thriving and productive garden with Brassica family vegetables and their companions. Remember to practice crop rotation and incorporate organic matter regularly to maintain soil fertility and prevent the build-up of diseases and pests.

CHAPTER 3

SOWING BRASSICA FAMILY VEGETABLES

CORRECT SEASON TO SOW BRASSICA VEGETABLE PLANTS

Sowing vegetables in the Brassica, or cabbage family in the correct season is vitally important for companion planting. This family includes a range of cool-season crops like cabbage, broccoli, kale, cauliflower, and Brussels sprouts. These plants typically prefer cooler temperatures and can often withstand light frosts, making them perfect for planting in early spring or late summer for a fall harvest.

Planting Brassicas during the appropriate seasons ensures they grow during their optimal climate conditions, which can lead to healthier plants, better yields, and fewer pest and disease problems. In addition, when you sow Brassicas in the correct season, you can more effectively coordinate their growth with that of their companion plants. Proper timing allows these companion plants to provide maximum benefits, whether deterring pests, providing shade, or improving soil health. Therefore, understanding the seasonal preferences of your Brassica vegetables is a crucial aspect of successful companion planting. In the following paragraphs, we will discuss the best seasons to sow different Brassica family vegetables.

Cabbage (Brassica oleracea var. capitata): Cabbage can be grown as both a spring and fall crop, with seeds sown indoors 6-8 weeks before the last expected frost for the spring planting and 12-14 weeks before the first anticipated frost for the fall planting. Transplant seedlings outdoors when they are about 4-6 weeks old and have at least two sets of true leaves. Cabbage thrives in cooler temperatures, and planting in the appropriate season helps to avoid bolting or poor head formation due to heat stress.

Broccoli (Brassica oleracea var. italica): Broccoli is a cool-season crop, best grown in early spring or fall. For spring planting, start seeds indoors 6-8 weeks before the last expected frost and transplant seedlings outdoors when they have at least two sets of true leaves. For fall planting, sow seeds outdoors 85-100 days before the first expected frost, allowing the plants to mature in cooler weather for optimal flavor and texture.

Cauliflower (Brassica oleracea var. botrytis): Cauliflower prefers cooler temperatures and can be grown in spring and fall. Start seeds indoors 6-8 weeks before the last expected frost for a spring crop and 12-14 weeks before the first expected frost for a fall crop. Transplant seedlings outdoors when they are 4-6 weeks old, ensuring they have enough time to mature before temperature extremes set in.

Kale (Brassica oleracea var. acephala): Kale is a hardy, cool-season vegetable that can be grown in spring, fall, and even winter in milder climates. For spring planting, sow seeds indoors 6-8 weeks before the last expected frost or directly outdoors 3-5 weeks before the last frost date. For fall planting, sow seeds outdoors 10-12 weeks before the first expected frost. Kale's flavor improves after exposure to frost, making it an excellent choice for extending the growing season.

Brussels sprouts (Brassica oleracea var. gemmifera): Brussels sprouts are a cool-season crop best suited for fall harvesting. Sow seeds indoors 12-14 weeks before the first expected frost and transplant seedlings outdoors when they are 4-6 weeks old. Brussels sprouts require a long growing season and should be planted early enough to mature before temperatures drop below freezing.

Collard greens (Brassica oleracea var. acephala): Collard greens are a cool-season crop that can be grown in spring and fall. Sow seeds indoors 6-8 weeks before the last expected frost for a spring crop and 10-12 weeks before the first expected frost for a fall crop. Transplant seedlings outdoors when they are 4-6 weeks old. Collard greens are frost-tolerant and can continue to produce leaves even after light frosts.

Kohlrabi (Brassica oleracea var. gongylodes): Kohlrabi grows best in cooler temperatures and can be sown in spring and fall. For spring planting, sow seeds indoors 4-6 weeks before the last expected frost or directly outdoors 2-4 weeks before the last frost date. For fall planting, sow seeds outdoors 8-10 weeks before the first expected frost. Kohlrabi has a relatively short growing season, making it a suitable choice for multiple plantings throughout the year.

Grasping the perfect season to sow various Brassica Cabbage Family vegetables is key to their flourishing growth and evolution. By aligning their planting to the prime growing seasons, garden enthusiasts can amplify germination, growth, and harvest yields, while reducing the threat of bolting or subpar crop quality due to temperature stress. Don't forget to keep an eye on local weather patterns and tweak planting schedules as needed to guarantee the best outcomes.

PLANTING NEEDS & REQUIREMENTS

Germinating the different brassica vegetable plants from seeds to seedlings requires careful planning, attention to temperature, and proper timing. In the following, we will discuss the steps to germinate different Brassica family vegetables, the ideal temperatures for germination, and when seedlings are ready to be transplanted.

Step 1: Sowing seeds indoors: For most brassica vegetables, start by sowing seeds indoors 4-8 weeks before the last expected frost (for spring planting) or 10-14 weeks before the first expected frost (for fall planting). Fill seed trays or small pots with a high-quality seed-starting mix or peat pellets, and sow seeds according to the recommended depth and spacing for each vegetable type. Gently press the seeds into the soil and cover them lightly with the soil mix.

Step 2: Providing moisture and warmth: Brassica seeds require consistent moisture and warmth to germinate successfully. Water the soil mix gently but thoroughly, ensuring it remains consistently moist but not waterlogged. Cover the seed trays or pots with a plastic dome or plastic wrap to maintain humidity. Place the containers in a warm location, ideally between 65-75°F (18-24°C), as this is the optimal temperature range for brassica seed germination. Using a heat mat can help maintain consistent soil temperature during germination.

Step 3: Monitoring germination: Brassica seeds typically germinate within 5-10 days, depending on the specific vegetable type and germination conditions. Check the seeds daily and remove the plastic covering once seedlings begin to emerge. At this point, move the seedlings to a well-lit area, such as a sunny windowsill or under grow lights, to encourage strong growth and prevent legginess.

Step 4: Thinning and hardening off: Once seedlings have developed at least two sets of true leaves, thin them out by removing weaker seedlings and leaving the strongest ones to continue growing. About 1-2 weeks before transplanting, gradually expose the seedlings to outdoor conditions by placing them outside for a few hours each day, gradually increasing the time spent outdoors. This process, known as hardening off, helps the seedlings acclimate to outdoor conditions and reduces transplant shock.

Step 5: Transplanting seedlings: Brassica seedlings are typically ready to be transplanted when they are 4-6 weeks old and have developed a robust root system. Choose a planting location with well-draining, fertile soil and total sun exposure. Space the seedlings according to the recommended spacing for each vegetable type, and plant them at the same depth they were growing in their containers. Water the transplants thoroughly to help them establish themselves in their new environment.

Fostering the diverse brassica vegetable plants from tiny seeds to thriving seedlings demands meticulous planning, temperature vigilance, and perfect timing. By adhering to these steps, green thumbs can cultivate sturdy and vibrant brassica seedlings that are eager to take root in the garden and flourish throughout the growing season. Don't forget to keep a watchful eye on local weather patterns and tweak planting schedules as necessary to guarantee the best yield for each unique brassica vegetable variety.

SPACING & MEASUREMENTS

Spacing and measurements when transplanting brassica vegetable seedlings are particularly important in vegetable companion planting, as it ensures the harmonious coexistence of various plant species while maximizing their mutual benefits. Proper spacing allows each plant to receive adequate sunlight, air circulation, and access to nutrients, promoting strong growth and reducing competition for resources.

This is essential in companion planting, where different plant species have varying growth patterns, resource requirements, and potential interactions with neighboring plants. Furthermore, appropriate spacing helps prevent the spread of diseases and pests by limiting the areas where they can thrive, which is crucial in mixed plantings where multiple species may be susceptible to the same threats.

By adhering to the recommended spacing and measurements for each brassica vegetable type in a companion planting setup, gardeners can optimize the benefits of this gardening technique, such as improved nutrient uptake, enhanced pest control, and better pollination, ultimately leading to a thriving and productive garden ecosystem. In the following, we will discuss the recommended spacing and measurements for different Brassica family vegetables.

Cabbage (Brassica oleracea var. capitata): When transplanting cabbage seedlings, space them 18-24 inches apart within rows and maintain a distance of 24-36 inches between rows. This spacing allows each plant to develop fully without competing for sunlight, air circulation, and nutrients, resulting in well-formed heads and a more bountiful harvest.

Broccoli (Brassica oleracea var. italica): Broccoli seedlings should be spaced 18-24 inches apart within rows, with 24-36 inches between rows. This spacing provides enough room for the development of large, healthy heads and ensures that each plant has access to adequate sunlight and nutrients while minimizing the risk of diseases and pests.

Cauliflower (Brassica oleracea var. botrytis): When planting cauliflower seedlings, space them 18-24 inches apart within rows and maintain a distance of 24-36 inches between rows. This spacing promotes proper airflow and sunlight exposure, allowing each plant to produce large, tightly-packed curds and reducing the risk of diseases and pests.

Kale (Brassica oleracea var. acephala): Kale seedlings should be spaced 12-18 inches apart within rows and 18-24 inches between rows. This spacing ensures that each plant has sufficient room to grow and produce leaves without competing for resources, resulting in a more abundant and continuous harvest throughout the season.

Brussels sprouts (Brassica oleracea var. gemmifera): When transplanting Brussels sprouts seedlings, space them 18-24 inches apart within rows and maintain a distance of 24-36 inches between rows. This spacing allows for proper development of the sprouts along the plant's stem and ensures that each plant receives adequate sunlight, air circulation, and nutrients.

Collard greens (Brassica oleracea var. acephala): Collard greens seedlings should be spaced 12-18 inches apart within rows and 18-24 inches between rows. This spacing allows for optimal leaf production while minimizing competition for sunlight, water, and nutrients, resulting in a more generous and continuous harvest throughout the growing season.

Kohlrabi (Brassica oleracea var. gongylodes): When planting kohlrabi seedlings, space them 6-8 inches apart within rows and maintain a distance of 12-18 inches between rows. This spacing accommodates the rapid growth and development of the enlarged stem, ensuring each plant has sufficient room to grow without competing for resources and resulting in a more uniform and bountiful harvest.

Understanding the desired spacing and measurements when planting various brassica vegetable seedlings is essential for promoting healthy growth, maximizing productivity, and preventing diseases and pests. By following the recommended spacing guidelines for each brassica vegetable type, gardeners can optimize their garden space and ensure a successful and plentiful harvest.

MAINTAINING BRASSICA VEGETABLE PLANTS

Maintaining your Brassica Vegetable Plants is essential in vegetable companion gardening to ensure the harmonious coexistence and mutual benefits of various plant species within the garden ecosystem. Proper maintenance practices, such as regular watering, fertilizing, and pruning, contribute to the overall health and productivity of each plant, allowing them to thrive and support their neighboring plants.

In a companion planting setup, different plant species often provide specific benefits to one another, such as enhanced pest control, improved nutrient uptake, or better pollination. Diligent maintenance helps maximize these advantages by ensuring that each plant remains healthy and capable of contributing positively to the garden ecosystem. In summary, consistent care and maintenance of brassica vegetable plants are crucial for creating a thriving and productive vegetable companion garden, leading to a successful and rewarding gardening experience.

PRUNING AND THINNING BRASSICA VEGETABLE PLANTS

Pruning and thinning vegetable plants within the brassica family are especially important in vegetable companion planting. Proper pruning and thinning ensure that each plant has adequate space to grow and develop without competing for resources such as sunlight, water, and nutrients. This is particularly crucial in companion planting, as different plant species have varying growth patterns and resource requirements.

By providing enough space for each plant, gardeners can maximize the benefits of companion planting. Furthermore, pruning and thinning help maintain optimal air circulation and sunlight exposure, reducing the risk of diseases and pests that can spread more easily in mixed plantings. Diligent pruning and thinning of brassica vegetables in companion planting are essential for creating a harmonious and productive garden ecosystem, ensuring that each plant species thrives and contributes to the overall success of the garden.

When companion planting with brassica vegetables, it is essential to know the appropriate times and methods for pruning and thinning during their various growth stages. Here we discuss the best practices for pruning and thinning different brassica vegetables in a companion planting setup throughout their growth cycle.

Cabbage (Brassica oleracea var. capitata): Thinning cabbage seedlings should be done approximately 2-3 weeks after germination when the plants have developed at least two true leaves. Remove the weaker seedlings, leaving one healthy plant every 18-24 inches. Pruning is not typically required for cabbage plants; however, removing any yellow or damaged leaves throughout the growing season can help maintain good airflow and reduce the risk of diseases.

Broccoli (Brassica oleracea var. italica): Broccoli seedlings should be thinned once they have reached a height of 2-3 inches, leaving one healthy plant every 18-24 inches. As broccoli grows, prune by cutting off the lower leaves once the central head has been harvested. This encourages the growth of side shoots, providing a continuous harvest throughout the season.

Cauliflower (Brassica oleracea var. botrytis): Thinning cauliflower seedlings should be done when the plants have at least two true leaves, leaving one healthy plant every 18-24 inches. During the growing season, prune cauliflower by removing any yellow or damaged leaves to maintain good air circulation and prevent diseases.

Kale (Brassica oleracea var. acephala): Kale seedlings should be thinned when they reach a height of 3-4 inches, leaving one healthy plant every 12-18 inches. As kale grows, prune by removing the lower, older leaves as the plant grows, allowing the plant to focus its energy on producing new leaves at the top.

Brussels sprouts (Brassica oleracea var. gemmifera): Thinning Brussels sprouts seedlings should be done when the plants are 2-3 inches tall, leaving one healthy plant every 18-24 inches. Throughout the growing season, prune by removing the lower leaves as the plant grows, which encourages the development of sprouts along the stem.

Collard greens (Brassica oleracea var. acephala): Collard greens seedlings should be thinned when they reach a height of 3-4 inches, leaving one healthy plant every 12-18 inches. As collard greens grow, prune by removing the lower, older leaves throughout the growing season, allowing the plant to focus its energy on producing new leaves at the top.

Kohlrabi (Brassica oleracea var. gongylodes): Thinning kohlrabi seedlings should be done when they have developed two true leaves, leaving one healthy plant every 6-8 inches. Kohlrabi does not require extensive pruning during its growth stages, but removing any yellow or damaged leaves can help maintain good air circulation and prevent diseases.

Comprehending the appropriate timing and methods for pruning and thinning brassica family vegetables during their growth stages is crucial for sustaining a healthy and fruitful companion planting garden. By adhering to these directives, horticulturists can ensure each plant has adequate space and resources needed for growth, while maximizing companion planting benefits such as increased nutrient absorption, superior pest resistance, and improved pollination.

WATERING BRASSICA VEGETABLE PLANTS

Watering your brassica vegetable plants is a crucial aspect of successful companion planting. Adequate and consistent moisture is necessary for these vegetables to grow strong root systems, absorb essential nutrients, and produce bountiful harvests. In a companion planting setup, various plants work together to provide mutual benefits, such as improved nutrient uptake, enhanced pest control, and better pollination.

By ensuring that each brassica plant receives sufficient water, gardeners can facilitate these beneficial interactions and create a thriving ecosystem within their garden. Furthermore, proper watering helps to prevent common issues such as bolting, cracking, or the development of diseases, which can significantly impact the overall health and productivity of the brassica plants and their companions.

When companion planting with brassica vegetables, it is essential to know the appropriate times and methods for watering each plant to ensure a healthy and productive garden. In the following paragraphs, we will discuss the best practices for watering different brassica vegetables in a companion planting setup.

Cabbage (Brassica oleracea var. capitata): Cabbage requires consistent moisture throughout its growing season. Water the plants deeply once or twice a week, providing about 1-1.5 inches of water per week. Avoid overhead watering to prevent diseases and focus on watering at the base of the plant. During hot weather or dry spells, increase the frequency of watering to keep the soil evenly moist but not soggy.

Broccoli (Brassica oleracea var. italica): Broccoli also needs consistent moisture for optimal growth. Water the plants deeply once or twice a week, providing about 1-1.5 inches of water per week. As with cabbage, water at the base of the plant to minimize the risk of diseases. Ensure that the soil remains evenly moist, especially during the head formation stage.

CHAPTER 3

Cauliflower (Brassica oleracea var. botrytis): Cauliflower has similar watering requirements to broccoli and cabbage. Provide about 1-1.5 inches of water per week, watering deeply once or twice a week. Focus on watering at the base of the plant and maintain even soil moisture, particularly during the head formation stage, to prevent issues such as buttoning or uneven head development.

Kale (Brassica oleracea var. acephala): Kale prefers consistent soil moisture for optimal growth. Water the plants deeply once or twice a week, providing about 1 inch of water per week. During hot weather or dry spells, increase the frequency of watering to keep the soil evenly moist. Water at the base of the plant to minimize the risk of diseases.

Brussels sprouts (Brassica oleracea var. gemmifera): Brussels sprouts require consistent moisture to produce a healthy crop. Provide about 1-1.5 inches of water per week, watering deeply once or twice a week. Water at the base of the plant to reduce the risk of diseases and maintain even soil moisture, especially during the sprout development stage.

Collard greens (Brassica oleracea var. acephala): Collard greens thrive with consistent moisture. Water the plants deeply once or twice a week, providing about 1 inch of water per week. During hot weather or dry spells, increase the frequency of watering to keep the soil evenly moist. As with other brassicas, water at the base of the plant to minimize disease risks.

Kohlrabi (Brassica oleracea var. gongylodes): Kohlrabi needs even soil moisture for proper bulb development. Water the plants deeply once or twice a week, providing about 1 inch of water per week. Increase the frequency of watering during hot weather or dry spells to maintain evenly moist soil. Water at the base of the plant to minimize the risk of diseases.

Grasping the correct methods and timing to water the diverse vegetables in the brassica family is vital for sustaining a healthy and fruitful companion planting garden. By adhering to these rules, gardening enthusiasts can guarantee that each plant gets adequate hydration. This knowledge aids them in maximizing the benefits of companion planting. Employing the right watering strategies will play a significant role in the comprehensive success of your companion planting garden.

ORGANIC FERTILISATION FOR BRASSICA VEGETABLE PLANTS

Organic fertilization plays a vital role in the health and productivity of brassica vegetable plants when companion planting. Utilizing organic fertilizers, such as compost, well-rotted manure, or worm castings, provides essential nutrients to the plants while also improving the soil structure, moisture retention, and beneficial microorganism populations.

These factors contribute to a thriving garden ecosystem, where brassicas and their companion plants can mutually benefit from each other's presence. Organic fertilization promotes strong root systems, increased nutrient uptake, and enhanced resistance to pests and diseases, all of which are crucial for successful companion planting. Moreover, using organic fertilizers aligns with the principles of sustainable and environmentally friendly gardening practices, minimizing the reliance on synthetic fertilizers that may have adverse effects on soil health and the surrounding ecosystem.

When companion planting with brassica vegetables, it is essential to know the appropriate types of organic fertilizers each plant requires and the best times to apply them. In the following, we will discuss the ideal organic fertilizers for different brassica vegetables in a companion planting setup and when to fertilize each plant.

Cabbage (Brassica oleracea var. capitata): Cabbage thrives on rich, well-draining soil with plenty of organic matter. Amend the soil with compost or well-rotted manure before planting, and side-dress with additional compost or aged manure when the plants are about half their mature size. Another option is to use a balanced organic granular fertilizer or liquid fish emulsion during the early growth stage and again when the heads begin to form.

Broccoli (Brassica oleracea var. italica): Broccoli benefits from high levels of nitrogen and phosphorus, which promote healthy growth and head formation. Before planting, amend the soil with compost or aged manure. Apply an organic granular fertilizer, such as one with a 4-6-4 ratio, when transplanting seedlings into the garden. Side-dress with additional compost or aged manure halfway through the growing season, or use a liquid fish emulsion or seaweed extract every 3-4 weeks.

Cauliflower (Brassica oleracea var. botrytis): Cauliflower requires a rich, well-draining soil with sufficient organic matter to support its growth and head development. Amend the soil with compost or well-rotted manure before planting. Apply a balanced organic granular fertilizer or liquid fish emulsion during the early growth stage and again when the heads start to form. Side-dress with additional compost or aged manure a few weeks after transplanting.

Kale (Brassica oleracea var. acephala): Kale prefers nutrient-rich soil with ample organic matter. Amend the soil with compost or well-rotted manure before planting. Apply a balanced organic granular fertilizer, such as one with a 4-4-4 ratio, when transplanting seedlings into the garden. Side-dress with additional compost or aged manure halfway through the growing season, or use a liquid fish emulsion or seaweed extract every 3-4 weeks.

Brussels sprouts (Brassica oleracea var. gemmifera): Brussels sprouts need consistent nutrients to support their long growing season and sprout development. Before planting, amend the soil with compost or aged manure. Apply a balanced organic granular fertilizer, such as one with a 4-6-4 ratio, when transplanting seedlings into the garden. Side-dress with additional compost or aged manure halfway through the growing season, or use a liquid fish emulsion or seaweed extract every 3-4 weeks.

Collard greens (Brassica oleracea var. acephala): Collard greens thrive in nutrient-rich soil with adequate organic matter. Amend the soil with compost or well-rotted manure before planting. Apply a balanced organic granular fertilizer, such as one with a 4-4-4 ratio, when transplanting seedlings into the garden. Side-dress with additional compost or aged manure halfway through the growing season, or use a liquid fish emulsion or seaweed extract every 3-4 weeks.

Kohlrabi (Brassica oleracea var. gongylodes): Kohlrabi benefits from fertile, well-draining soil with plenty of organic matter. Amend the soil with compost or well-rotted manure before planting. Apply a balanced organic granular fertilizer, such as one with a 4-4-4 ratio, when transplanting seedlings into the garden. Side-dress with additional compost or aged manure halfway through the growing season, or use a liquid fish emulsion or seaweed extract every 3-4 weeks.

Understanding the specific organic fertilizers required by the diverse vegetables in the brassica family and the optimal timing for their application is crucial for preserving a healthy and bountiful companion planting garden. By adhering to these directives, home gardeners can ensure each plant receives the vital nutrients needed for robust growth.

PROTECTING BRASSICA VEGETABLE PLANTS

Extreme Temperatures

Protecting brassica vegetables from extreme temperatures is crucial for their health and productivity when companion planting. Here we will discuss various strategies to shield different brassica vegetables from temperature extremes in a companion planting setup.

Mulching: One of the most effective ways to protect brassica plants from both hot and cold temperature extremes is by applying a layer of organic mulch around the base of the plants. Mulch helps regulate soil temperature, keeping it cooler in the summer and warmer in the winter. It also aids in retaining moisture and suppressing weeds. Use materials such as straw, shredded leaves, or wood chips for effective insulation.

Shade cloth: During hot summer months, using shade cloth can help protect brassica plants from intense heat and sun exposure. Install a shade cloth over your brassica vegetable garden, ensuring that it is suspended above the plants to allow for air circulation. Choose a shade cloth with a 30-50% shade rating to provide adequate protection while still allowing sufficient sunlight for photosynthesis.

Row covers: To protect brassica plants from cold temperatures, frost, and wind, use floating row covers made from lightweight fabric. Row covers can be draped directly over the plants or supported by hoops or wireframes. These covers allow light, air, and water to penetrate while providing insulation against cold temperatures. Be sure to secure the edges of the row cover to the ground to trap warmth effectively.

Cold frames: Cold frames are structures with transparent tops that create a microclimate around the plants, protecting them from low temperatures, wind, and frost. They can be constructed from various materials, such as wood, metal, or plastic, and covered with glass or clear plastic. Place cold frames over your brassica plants during fall and early winter to extend the growing season and shield them from harsh weather conditions.

Companion plants: Selecting appropriate companion plants can also help protect brassicas from extreme temperatures. For instance, taller plants or those with broad leaves can provide shade and shelter for heat-sensitive brassicas during hot weather. Examples include sunflowers, corn, or pole beans. Conversely, low-growing plants like marigolds or nasturtiums can help insulate the soil and maintain more stable temperatures around brassicas during colder periods.

Proper watering: Ensuring that brassica plants receive consistent and adequate water is vital for their resilience against temperature extremes. Water the plants deeply and regularly, particularly during hot weather or dry spells. Properly hydrated plants are better equipped to handle both high and low temperatures.

Employing various strategies to protect vegetables in the brassica family from extreme temperatures when companion planting is essential for maintaining a healthy and productive garden. By combining these techniques, such as mulching, using shade cloth or row covers, constructing cold frames, selecting appropriate companion plants, and ensuring proper watering, growers can help their brassica plants withstand temperature fluctuations and thrive throughout the growing season.

PROTECTING BRASSICA VEGETABLES FROM PEST

Protecting brassica vegetables from pests is a crucial aspect of successful companion planting. In the following paragraphs, we will discuss various strategies to safeguard brassica vegetables from pests in a companion planting setup.

Companion planting for pest control: One of the primary benefits of companion planting is its ability to naturally deter pests. By strategically selecting and placing companion plants, you can create an environment that is less hospitable to pests. For example, planting garlic, onions, or chives near brassicas can help repel aphids, cabbage worms, and other pests. Similarly, marigolds produce a scent that deters pests like cabbage moths and nematodes. Planting herbs like basil, mint, or dill can also attract beneficial insects that prey on common brassica pests.

Crop rotation: Practicing crop rotation is essential for preventing pest infestations in your brassica vegetable garden. Rotate brassica crops with plants from different families yearly to disrupt the life cycles of pests and diseases that target brassicas. This practice helps reduce the build-up of pests and pathogens in the soil, ultimately leading to healthier plants and fewer pest issues.

Physical barriers: Using physical deterrents like floating row covers or insect netting can effectively protect brassica plants from various pests, such as cabbage moths and flea beetles. These lightweight materials allow sunlight, air, and water to pass through while keeping pests at bay. Be sure to secure the edges of the row cover or netting to the ground to prevent pests from crawling underneath.

Hand-picking and traps: Regularly inspecting your brassica plants for signs of pests and hand-picking them off can be an effective method of controlling small infestations. For caterpillars like cabbage worms or loopers, hand-picking and dropping them into a bucket of soapy water is an efficient control method. Additionally, using pheromone traps or yellow sticky traps can help monitor and catch various flying pests like cabbage moths and whiteflies.

Biological control: Introducing beneficial insects that prey on brassica pests is another effective way to protect your plants. For example, ladybugs and lacewings are natural predators of aphids, while parasitic wasps help control caterpillar populations. You can attract these beneficial insects by planting flowers and herbs like yarrow, dill, fennel, or cosmos, which provide nectar and pollen for predators.

Maintaining garden hygiene: Keeping your garden clean and free of debris is essential for preventing pest infestations. Remove any dead or diseased plant material promptly, as it can harbor pests and diseases. Regularly weed your garden, as weeds can serve as hosts for pests and compete with your brassica plants for nutrients and water.

Harnessing a variety of strategies to shield the brassica family vegetables from pests during companion planting is key to cultivating a vibrant and fruitful garden. By integrating these tactics - from companion planting for pest deterrent, rotating crops, employing physical barriers, hand-picking pests, introducing biological control, to upkeeping garden cleanliness, green thumbs can keep pesky issues at bay and guarantee a flourishing brassica vegetable garden.

PROTECTING BRASSICA VEGETABLES FROM DISEASES

Various diseases can affect brassica vegetables, and it's crucial to identify them and take appropriate organic measures to protect your plants when companion planting. In the following paragraphs, we will discuss common diseases that affect different brassica vegetables, how to identify them, and organic strategies for protection in a companion planting setup.

Clubroot: Clubroot is a soil-borne disease caused by the fungus Plasmodiophora brassicae. It affects the roots of brassica plants, causing them to become swollen and distorted. Infected plants may exhibit stunted growth, yellowing leaves, and wilting. To manage clubroot organically, practice crop rotation, use disease-resistant varieties, and avoid moving infected soil between garden beds. Additionally, liming the soil to increase pH levels can help suppress the fungus.

Black rot: Black rot is a bacterial disease caused by Xanthomonas campestris pv. campestris. It causes V-shaped yellow lesions on the margins of the leaves that eventually turn black and necrotic. To manage black rot organically, practice crop rotation, use disease-resistant varieties, and avoid overhead watering. Remove any infected plant material from the garden to prevent the spread of the bacteria. Planting companions like garlic, onions, or chives can help deter the growth of the bacteria due to their antimicrobial properties.

Downy mildew: Downy mildew is a fungal disease that causes yellow spots on the upper surface of leaves and a grayish-white mold on the underside. It thrives in cool, wet conditions. To manage downy mildew organically, ensure proper spacing and pruning, avoid overhead watering, and encourage good air circulation by planting brassicas with companions that do not overcrowd the area. Applying an organic fungicide, such as copper-based products, can help control downy mildew when used according to label instructions.

White mold (Sclerotinia): White mold is a fungal disease that causes water-soaked lesions on the stems and leaves of brassica plants. These lesions eventually become covered in a white, cottony mold. To manage white mold organically, maintain proper plant spacing, prune lower leaves, and remove infected plant material from the garden. Companion planting with disease-resistant plants or those with antimicrobial properties can help discourage the growth of white mold.

Alternaria leaf spot: Alternaria leaf spot is a fungal disease that causes dark brown to black spots on brassica leaves. These spots may have concentric rings and can eventually lead to leaf drop. To manage Alternaria leaf spot organically, practice crop rotation, use disease-resistant varieties, and avoid overhead watering. Remove any infected plant material from the garden to prevent the spread of the fungus. Apply organic fungicides, such as neem oil or potassium bicarbonate, according to label instructions to help control the disease.

Cabbage yellows (Fusarium wilt): Cabbage yellows is a soil-borne fungal disease caused by Fusarium oxysporum f. sp. conglutinans. It affects primarily cabbage and cauliflower plants, causing yellowing and wilting of the lower leaves. In severe cases, it can lead to plant death. To manage cabbage yellows organically, practice crop rotation, use disease-resistant varieties, and maintain proper soil drainage. Adding organic matter like compost or well-rotted manure can help improve soil structure and drainage.

Understanding the diseases that impact the diverse vegetables in the brassica family and the organic methods to identify and protect them during companion planting is crucial for sustaining a healthy and productive garden. By adhering to these directives and employing organic strategies like crop rotation, correct spacing and pruning, suitable watering techniques, and removal of diseased plant material, horticulturists can reduce disease incidents and ensure a flourishing brassica vegetable garden. Further, choosing appropriate companion plants and utilizing organic fungicides when required can boost disease prevention measures, fostering a more robust and eco-friendly garden ecosystem.

HARVESTING BRASSICA VEGETABLE PLANTS

The time it takes for various brassica vegetables to be ready for harvest can vary depending on the specific plant and growing conditions. In the following paragraphs, we will discuss the approximate time it takes for different brassica vegetables to reach maturity when companion planting and how to harvest each vegetable plant.

Cabbage (Brassica oleracea var. capitata): The time to harvest cabbage largely depends on the variety being grown. Generally, it takes between 60 to 100 days from transplanting for cabbage heads to reach maturity. To harvest cabbage, use a sharp knife or prunes to cut the head off at its base, leaving a few outer leaves attached to protect it. Early varieties may be ready in as little as 60-70 days, while late-season varieties can take up to 100 days or more.

Broccoli (Brassica oleracea var. italica): Broccoli typically takes about 60-85 days from transplanting to reach maturity. Harvest broccoli when the central head is fully developed, compact, and dark green in color before the florets begin to separate or turn yellow. Use a sharp knife or prunes to cut the main stem about 5-6 inches below the head. After harvesting the central head, side shoots may continue to develop, providing additional smaller harvests.

Cauliflower (Brassica oleracea var. botrytis): Cauliflower usually takes between 55-100 days from transplanting to reach maturity, depending on the variety. Harvest cauliflower when the heads are compact, firm, and white or the desired color for colored varieties. Cut the main stem with a sharp knife or prunes about 1-2 inches below the head, leaving some outer leaves attached for protection.

Kale (Brassica oleracea var. acephala): Kale can be harvested at various stages of growth, depending on your preference. Baby kale leaves can be harvested as early as 25-30 days after planting, while mature leaves can be picked around 50-65 days after planting. To harvest kale, simply use a sharp knife or prunes to cut the outer leaves at their base, allowing the center of the plant to continue producing new leaves.

Brussels sprouts (Brassica oleracea var. gemmifera): Brussels sprouts have a relatively long growing season, generally taking about 90-110 days from transplanting to reach maturity. Harvest the sprouts when they are firm, green, and about 1-2 inches in diameter. Use a sharp knife or prunes to remove the sprouts from the bottom of the stalk upwards as these sprouts mature first.

Collard greens (Brassica oleracea var. acephala): Collard greens can be harvested at various stages of growth. Young, tender leaves can be picked around 30-40 days after planting, while mature leaves can be harvested around 60-75 days after planting. To harvest collard greens, use a sharp knife or prunes to cut the outer leaves at their base, allowing the center of the plant to continue producing new leaves.

Kohlrabi (Brassica oleracea var. gongylodes): Kohlrabi typically takes about 50-60 days from transplanting to reach maturity. Harvest kohlrabi when the swollen stem is approximately 2-3 inches in diameter for the best flavor and texture. Use a sharp knife or prunes to cut the kohlrabi stem at the soil level, taking care not to damage the roots of neighboring plants.

The time it takes for various brassica vegetables to be ready for harvest depends on the specific plant, variety, and growing conditions. When companion planting, it's essential to monitor each plant's progress and harvest them at the appropriate stage for the best flavor and quality. By understanding the approximate time frames for each brassica vegetable and knowing how to harvest them properly, gardeners can better plan their harvests and enjoy a continuous supply of fresh, homegrown produce.

CROP ROTATION FOR BRASSICA VEGETABLE PLANTS

Crop rotation is an essential agricultural practice that involves growing different types of crops in the same area in sequential seasons. This method offers numerous benefits, such as improved soil fertility, reduced pest and disease pressure, and enhanced overall garden health. In the following paragraphs, we will discuss the process of crop rotation and how it works for brassica vegetables when companion planting.

The Importance Of Crop Rotation For Brassicas

Brassica vegetables, including cabbage, broccoli, cauliflower, kale, and Brussels sprouts, are susceptible to several pests and diseases that can persist in the soil for extended periods. By rotating brassicas with plants from different families, you can disrupt the life cycles of these pests and diseases, reducing their impact on your garden. Additionally, crop rotation helps maintain soil fertility by preventing the depletion of specific nutrients and promoting a more balanced nutrient profile.

Planning Crop Rotation For Brassicas

When planning a crop rotation schedule for brassicas, it's essential to consider the plant families involved. Ideally, you should follow a rotation plan that involves at least a three or four-year cycle, ensuring that brassicas are not planted in the same location for consecutive years. Divide your garden into sections and assign each section to a different plant family. In the following year, rotate the families so that each section hosts a different family. This way, you avoid growing brassicas in the same spot for multiple years.

CHAPTER 3

Incorporating Companion Planting

Companion planting can be integrated into your crop rotation plan by selecting suitable companions for brassicas that belong to different plant families. For instance, you can plant brassicas alongside alliums (onions, garlic, and chives), which help repel pests like aphids and cabbage worms. In the following season, you can plant legumes (beans, peas) or Solanaceae (tomatoes, potatoes, peppers) in the area previously occupied by brassicas. These plant families have different nutrient requirements and can help balance soil fertility.

Cover Crops and Green Manure

Integrating cover crops or green manure into your crop rotation plan can further enhance soil health and fertility. After harvesting brassicas, consider planting a cover crop like clover, vetch, or rye in the same area. These plants help fix nitrogen in the soil, suppress weeds, and prevent soil erosion. Before planting the next season's crops, incorporate the cover crops into the soil as green manure, allowing them to decompose and release valuable nutrients back into the soil.

Record-Keeping and Observation

Keeping detailed records of your crop rotation plan, including planting dates, harvest times, and any pest or disease issues, can help you refine your approach over time. Regularly observe your garden and note any changes in plant health, growth patterns, or pest pressure. This information can be invaluable in fine-tuning your crop rotation and companion planting strategies to optimize your garden's productivity and health.

Implementing crop rotation for brassica vegetables when companion planting is crucial for maintaining soil health, reducing pest and disease pressure, and ensuring a thriving and productive garden. By planning a crop rotation schedule that incorporates different plant families, integrating companion planting, and utilizing cover crops and green manure, gardeners can create a more resilient and sustainable growing environment for brassicas and other vegetable crops. Remember to keep detailed records and regularly observe your garden to continually improve your crop rotation and companion planting practices.

CHAPTER 4
ALLIUM "ONION" FAMILY COMPANION PLANTING

The Allium family, commonly referred to as the onion family, holds a prominent position in the world of vegetable companion planting due to their distinct attributes and advantageous properties. Encompassing an array of species such as onions, garlic, chives, leeks, and shallots, Alliums are celebrated not only for their culinary versatility but also for their capacity to promote the well-being and growth of surrounding plants in the garden. When strategically incorporated into a companion planting layout, these aromatic, resilient, and adaptable vegetables can effectively repel pests, attract beneficial insects, and foster a more diverse, robust, and fruitful garden ecosystem.

Incorporating companion plants alongside the Allium family in your garden can yield numerous benefits, contributing to a vibrant, sustainable, and flourishing ecosystem. One key advantage of pairing Alliums with companion plants is their natural ability to deter various pests, such as aphids, slugs, and cabbage worms, through their strong scent and sulfur compounds. This organic pest control method reduces the need for chemical interventions, promoting a healthier environment for both plants and gardeners.

Additionally, Alliums attract beneficial insects like bees, ladybugs, and hoverflies, which not only help with pollination but also aid in controlling harmful pests. Furthermore, when planted strategically, companion plants can enhance soil fertility by fixing nitrogen or adding essential nutrients, creating optimal growing conditions for the Alliums and other neighboring plants. In turn, this fosters stronger growth and improved overall plant health, ultimately leading to a bountiful and thriving garden.

ALLIUM FAMILY VEGETABLE PLANTS

The Allium onion family is a diverse and valuable group of vegetables that can significantly contribute to a successful vegetable companion planting strategy. In this group, several key vegetables stand out for their unique properties and advantages when integrated into your garden.

CHAPTER 4

Onions are perhaps the most widely recognized members of the Allium family, known for their distinct flavor and aroma. As companion plants, onions can be grown alongside various veggies, such as tomatoes, lettuce, and carrots, to help repel pests like aphids, spider mites, and cabbage worms. Onions' pungent smell confuses these pests, making it difficult for them to locate their preferred host plants. However, it's essential to avoid planting onions near beans and peas, as they can inhibit their growth.

Garlic is another popular Allium vegetable, prized for its potent flavor and numerous health benefits. In the context of companion planting, garlic can be an effective deterrent against pests like Japanese beetles, root maggots, and even larger animals like deer and rabbits. Moreover, garlic can help prevent fungal diseases, such as late blight in tomatoes, by producing natural fungicidal compounds. Good garlic companions include tomatoes, peppers, spinach, and brassicas like kale and broccoli.

Chives are a versatile culinary herb and an excellent addition to any companion planting scheme. They not only deter pests like aphids and carrot rust flies but also attract beneficial insects, such as bees and hoverflies. Chives can be planted alongside a variety of vegetables, including tomatoes, carrots, and members of the Brassica family, to enhance their growth and protect them from pests. Furthermore, chive blossoms add an aesthetic appeal to the garden with their beautiful purple flowers.

Leeks are a flavorful Allium vegetable that can be used in soups, stews, and other dishes. When incorporated into a companion planting strategy, leeks can help repel carrot rust flies and onion maggots, thanks to their strong aroma. Leeks form a successful partnership with carrots, as they both deter each other's pests, leading to healthier growth for both plants. However, leeks should not be planted near beans or peas, as they can adversely affect their development.

Shallots, often considered a gourmet ingredient, are another member of the Allium family that can thrive in a companion planting setup. Like other Alliums, shallots can help repel pests such as aphids and spider mites due to their pungent smell. Compatible companions for shallots include lettuce, tomatoes, and beets. Avoid planting them near beans and peas, as they may hinder their growth.

To summarize, the Allium onion family provides a variety of vegetables that can boost your garden's yield and overall vitality through companion planting. By gaining knowledge about the unique advantages and compatibility of each Allium vegetable, you can establish a varied, robust, and fruitful garden ecosystem.

ALLIUM FAMILY COMPANION VEGETABLES

Companion planting with the Allium "Onion" family can significantly enhance your garden's productivity and resilience, as these vegetables offer unique advantages and synergies when paired with other suitable plants. By carefully selecting the best companion plants for Alliums, you can create a thriving garden ecosystem that benefits from natural pest control, improved soil fertility, and increased biodiversity.

Tomatoes are an excellent companion for many Allium vegetables, especially onions and garlic. The strong scent of Alliums helps repel common tomato pests like aphids, spider mites, and whiteflies. Additionally, garlic can help protect tomatoes from fungal diseases due to its natural fungicidal properties. In return, tomatoes provide shade for onion bulbs, helping them retain moisture and develop better flavor.

Carrots can also benefit from being planted alongside Alliums, particularly onions and leeks. The pungent aroma of Alliums repels carrot rust flies and carrot root maggots, while carrots help deter onion maggots in return. This mutually beneficial relationship leads to healthier growth for both plants. To maximize the benefits, interplant carrot and Allium seedlings close together, ensuring that their scents mingle effectively to confuse pests.

Lettuce is another suitable companion plant for Alliums, mainly onions and shallots. Lettuce has shallow roots that do not compete with the deeper roots of Alliums for nutrients and water. Moreover, the scent of Alliums can help deter pests like aphids and slugs that often target lettuce. Planting lettuce between rows of onions or shallots can make efficient use of garden space and promote healthy growth for both vegetables.

Peppers pair well with garlic, as the strong scent of garlic can help protect peppers from pests like aphids, spider mites, and Japanese beetles. Additionally, garlic may help improve the flavor of pepper plants when grown in close proximity. Plant garlic cloves near the base of pepper plants, ensuring that they do not compete for sun exposure and have enough space to grow.

Brassicas, such as kale, cabbage, and broccoli, can also benefit from Alliums' companionship, particularly chives and garlic. Alliums help deter common Brassica pests like cabbage worms and cabbage loopers through their strong scent. Chives also attract beneficial insects like hoverflies and ladybugs, which prey on aphids and other pests that may target Brassicas. Intersperse chives or garlic among Brassica plants to create a diverse and pest-resistant planting arrangement.

When selecting companion plants for your Alliums family vegetables, consider the following tips:

- Research the specific needs and growth habits of both the Alliums and their potential companion plants to ensure compatibility in terms of soil, water, and sunlight requirements.
- Be aware of any allelopathic effects or antagonistic relationships between certain Alliums and other plants, such as onions inhibiting the growth of beans and peas.
- Experiment with different plant combinations and observe the results, adjusting your garden layout as needed to optimize the benefits of companion planting.

In summary, companion planting with the Allium "Onion" family can lead to a more productive and resilient garden by leveraging each plant's unique strengths and synergies. By carefully selecting the best companion plants for your Alliums and applying strategic planting techniques, you can cultivate a diverse, healthy, and bountiful garden ecosystem.

CHAPTER 4

ALLIUM FAMILY NON-COMPANION PLANTS

While the Allium "Onion" family offers numerous benefits when paired with compatible plants in a companion planting strategy, it is essential to be aware of certain vegetable plants that do not thrive well when grown alongside Alliums. By identifying and avoiding these incompatible pairings, you can prevent potential issues and ensure the overall health and productivity of your garden.

Beans are one type of vegetable plant that should not be planted near Alliums, particularly onions and garlic. The strong scent of Alliums can inhibit the growth of beans by suppressing their ability to fix nitrogen, a process essential for healthy bean development. Moreover, beans have shallow roots that may compete with Alliums for nutrients and water, leading to reduced growth and yield for both plants. To avoid these issues, maintain a reasonable distance between bean plants and Alliums in your garden layout.

Peas share a similar incompatibility with Alliums as beans do. Like beans, peas are legumes that rely on nitrogen fixation for their growth. The presence of Alliums, especially onions and garlic, can hinder this process, resulting in stunted growth and reduced yields for pea plants. Additionally, peas and Alliums may compete for soil nutrients and moisture. Therefore, it is advisable to keep peas separated from Alliums in the garden to ensure optimal growth for both plant types.

Asparagus is another vegetable that may not fare well when planted near Alliums. Asparagus has a long growing season and can remain productive for many years, making it more susceptible to the negative impacts of incompatible neighbors. Alliums, particularly onions and garlic, can inhibit asparagus growth by competing for essential nutrients and water.

Furthermore, the strong scent of Alliums may repel beneficial insects that are necessary for asparagus pollination. To protect your asparagus plants, designate a separate area in your garden for them, away from Alliums.

Sage is an herb that does not pair well with Alliums, particularly onions. Although not a vegetable, sage may be grown in many vegetable gardens for its culinary and medicinal uses. The strong scent of onions may stunt the growth of sage plants, while sage can also inhibit onion bulb formation. To ensure that both plants can grow to their full potential, it is best to plant them in separate areas of your garden.

Potatoes can also encounter issues when planted near Alliums, specifically garlic. Garlic can increase the risk of potato blight, a fungal disease that can devastate potato crops. To prevent this issue, avoid planting garlic near your potato plants and maintain proper crop rotation practices to minimize disease transmission between seasons.

While the Allium "Onion" family can provide numerous benefits in a companion planting strategy, it is crucial to identify and avoid incompatible vegetable plants to maintain a healthy and productive garden. By carefully planning your garden layout and respecting the unique requirements of each plant, you can cultivate a diverse and thriving garden ecosystem.

THE RIGHT SOIL FOR ALLIUM FAMILY VEGETABLES

Optimal soil conditions play a crucial role in the successful cultivation of Allium family vegetables and their companion plants. By understanding the specific soil requirements for various Alliums and their compatible companions, you can create a thriving garden ecosystem where both types of plants can grow together harmoniously and support each other's growth.

Onions prefer well-draining, loamy soil with a pH between 6.0 and 7.0. Sufficient drainage is essential to prevent root rot and ensure proper bulb formation. Moreover, onions benefit from soil that is rich in organic matter, which provides essential nutrients and promotes healthy growth.

When companion planting with onions, it's crucial to select compatible vegetables, such as tomatoes, lettuce, and carrots, that share similar soil preferences. This ensures that both the onions and their companions receive the necessary nutrients and growing conditions to flourish.

Garlic thrives in fertile, well-draining soil with a pH between 6.0 and 7.0. Soil enriched with organic matter, such as compost or well-rotted manure, can provide garlic plants with the nutrients they need for robust growth.

Maintaining proper soil fertility and pH is vital when companion planting garlic with compatible vegetables like tomatoes, peppers, and brassicas, as it allows both the garlic and its companions to grow strong and healthy while naturally repelling pests and diseases.

Chives are relatively adaptable but perform best in well-draining, loamy soil with a pH between 6.0 and 7.0. They also benefit from the addition of organic matter, which helps improve soil fertility and structure.

When companion planting chives with vegetables like tomatoes, carrots, and brassicas, it's essential to ensure that the soil conditions meet the needs of both chives and their companion plants. This will promote healthy growth and enable the chives to effectively deter pests and attract beneficial insects.

Leeks require well-draining soil with a pH between 6.0 and 7.5, and they benefit from the addition of organic matter to improve fertility and soil structure. Leeks have a relatively shallow root system, which makes proper soil preparation and drainage even more critical.

When planting leeks alongside compatible companions like carrots, maintaining optimal soil conditions is vital to ensure that both plants can grow strong and healthy while protecting each other from pests.

Shallots favor well-draining, loamy soil with a pH between 6.0 and 7.0. They also benefit from fertile soil rich in organic matter, as it provides essential nutrients for healthy growth. When companion planting shallots with vegetables such as lettuce, tomatoes, and beets, it's crucial to maintain appropriate soil conditions that cater to the needs of both shallots and their companion plants. This helps promote strong growth and allows shallots to effectively repel pests with their pungent aroma.

Understanding and maintaining the right soil conditions for various Allium family vegetables and their compatible companion plants is essential for creating a successful and productive garden ecosystem. By ensuring proper soil drainage, fertility, and pH, you can support the growth of both Alliums and their companion plants, allowing them to flourish and provide mutual benefits through their natural interactions.

CHAPTER 4

SOWING ALLIUM FAMILY VEGETABLES

CORRECT SEASON TO SOW ALLIUM VEGETABLE PLANTS

Sowing vegetables in the Allium, or onion family, in the correct season is crucial for successful companion planting. This family includes onions, garlic, leeks, and shallots, which have specific growing seasons that can greatly impact their health and productivity.

These plants are typically planted in the fall or early spring, depending on the specific variety and your climate. Planting Alliums in the appropriate season ensures that they grow during their optimal climate conditions, leading to healthier plants and better yields. Moreover, sowing Alliums in the correct season allows for effective coordination with their companion plants. For example, planting onions next to carrots can help deter pests like carrot flies, but this benefit would be lost if the two crops are not growing at the same time.

Therefore, understanding the seasonal preferences of your Allium vegetables and aligning their growth with their companion plants is a key part of successful vegetable companion planting.

Onions can be started from seeds, transplants, or sets, with each method having its own ideal sowing time. In general, onions are a cool-season crop and can tolerate light frosts. If starting from seeds, sow them indoors 8-10 weeks before the last spring frost date.

Transplant seedlings outdoors when they are about the size of a pencil, typically 4-6 weeks before the last frost. If using onion sets, plant them directly outdoors 4 weeks before the last spring frost. In regions with mild winters, onions can also be planted in the fall for a late-spring harvest.

Garlic is typically planted in the fall, as it requires a period of cold temperatures to initiate bulb formation. In most regions, garlic cloves should be planted 4-6 weeks before the ground freezes, usually between September and November. This allows the roots to establish before winter sets in, and the plants will resume growth in early spring. In warmer climates with mild winters, garlic can be planted in late winter or early spring for a late-summer harvest.

Chives can be sown from seeds or transplanted from divisions. To start chives from seeds, sow them indoors 6-8 weeks before the last spring frost date, then transplant the seedlings outdoors when the soil has warmed up and all danger of frost has passed. If dividing established chive plants, transplant the divisions directly outdoors in early spring or fall. Chives are perennials and will return year after year, providing a continuous supply of fresh leaves and blossoms.

Leeks are typically started from seeds and can be sown indoors 8-10 weeks before the last spring frost date. Transplant leek seedlings outdoors when they are about the size of a pencil, usually around the same time as onion seedlings, 4-6 weeks before the last frost. In mild winter climates, leeks can also be planted in the fall for a late-spring or early-summer harvest.

Shallots are usually grown from bulbs, known as sets, which should be planted outdoors in the fall or early spring. In areas with cold winters, plant shallot sets 4-6 weeks before the ground freezes, typically around the same time as garlic.

In milder climates, plant shallot sets in late winter or early spring as soon as the soil can be worked. Shallots require a period of cold temperatures to initiate bulb formation, so planting at the appropriate time is crucial for a successful harvest.

Understanding the appropriate sowing season for diverse vegetables in the Allium onion family is essential for guaranteeing their robust growth and optimizing yields. By meticulously planning your planting timetable based on each Allium's distinct preferences, you can cultivate a flourishing garden that offers a consistent supply of these tasty and adaptable vegetables.

PLANTING NEEDS & REQUIREMENTS

Germinating Allium vegetable plants from seeds to seedlings requires careful planning and attention to detail. By following the appropriate steps for each type of Allium, you can ensure successful germination and healthy growth. Understanding the optimal temperatures for germination and when seedlings are ready to be transplanted is also essential for a thriving garden.

Onions can be started from seeds indoors approximately 8-10 weeks before the last spring frost date. To germinate onion seeds, plant them in seed trays or small pots filled with moist, well-draining seed-starting mix. Sow seeds about 1/4 inch deep and keep the soil consistently moist but not soggy.

Onion seeds germinate best at temperatures between 60-70°F (15-21°C). Seedlings should emerge within 7-10 days. When onion seedlings have reached the size of a pencil and have at least two sets of true leaves, they are ready to be transplanted outdoors, typically 4-6 weeks before the last frost.

Garlic is typically grown from cloves rather than seeds. However, if you choose to grow garlic from seeds, known as bulbils, start them indoors in late winter. Plant bulbils in seed trays filled with moist, well-draining seed-starting mix and maintain a consistent temperature of 50-60°F (10-15°C).

Keep the soil moist, and the garlic seedlings should emerge within 2-3 weeks. Transplant the seedlings outdoors when they have developed several sets of true leaves, usually in early spring.

Chives can be sown from seeds indoors 6-8 weeks before the last spring frost date. Plant chive seeds in seed trays or small pots filled with moist, well-draining seed-starting mix, covering them lightly with soil.

Chive seeds germinate best at temperatures between 60-70°F (15-21°C). Seedlings should emerge within 10-14 days. Once chive seedlings have at least two sets of true leaves and are 3-4 inches tall, they can be transplanted outdoors after all danger of frost has passed.

Leeks can be started from seeds indoors 8-10 weeks before the last spring frost date. Sow leek seeds in seed trays or small pots filled with moist, well-draining seed-starting mix, planting them 1/4 inch deep. Maintain a consistent temperature of 60-70°F (15-21°C) for optimal germination.

Leek seedlings should emerge within 7-14 days. When they are about the size of a pencil and have at least two sets of true leaves, leek seedlings can be transplanted outdoors, typically 4-6 weeks before the last frost.

Shallots are generally grown from bulbs, known as sets, rather than seeds. However, if you choose to grow shallots from seeds, start them indoors in late winter or early spring. Plant shallot seeds in seed trays or small pots filled with moist, well-draining seed-starting mix, covering them lightly with soil. Maintain a consistent temperature of 60-70°F (15-21°C) for optimal germination.

Shallot seedlings should emerge within 7-14 days. Transplant the seedlings outdoors when they have developed several sets of true leaves, usually in early spring or fall, depending on your region's climate.

In summary, successfully germinating various Allium vegetable plants from seeds to seedlings requires careful planning, attention to detail, and an understanding of each plant's specific needs. By following the appropriate steps, maintaining optimal germination temperatures, and transplanting seedlings at the right time, you can cultivate a thriving garden filled with flavorful and versatile Allium vegetables.

SPACING & MEASUREMENTS

Spacing and measurements play a crucial role in the success of vegetable companion planting, particularly when transplanting Allium vegetable seedlings. Proper spacing ensures that each plant has adequate room to grow, access to sunlight, and sufficient nutrients from the soil. It also helps prevent overcrowding, which can lead to poor air circulation and increased risk of pests and diseases. In the context of companion planting, correct spacing allows Alliums and their compatible companions to effectively support each other's growth and provide mutual benefits.

For example, the optimal distance between plants enables the strong scent of Alliums to repel pests from their companions while preventing competition for resources. Additionally, proper spacing promotes biodiversity within the garden, attracting beneficial insects and improving overall garden health. By paying close attention to spacing and measurements when transplanting Allium vegetable seedlings, you can maximize the advantages of companion planting and cultivate a thriving, productive garden ecosystem.

Proper spacing and measurements are essential for the healthy growth of various Allium vegetable seedlings. By providing each plant with adequate space, you can ensure they receive enough sunlight, nutrients, and water while minimizing the risk of pests and diseases. Here's a guide to the desired spacing and measurements when planting different Allium vegetable seedlings:

Onions: When transplanting onion seedlings, space them approximately 4-6 inches apart in rows that are 12-18 inches apart. This spacing allows for adequate air circulation and sunlight exposure while preventing competition for nutrients and water. If you plan to harvest some onions as green onions or scallions, you can space them closer together (about 2-3 inches apart) and thin them out as they grow.

Garlic: Plant garlic cloves with the pointed end facing up, about 2-4 inches apart in rows that are 12-18 inches apart. This spacing ensures that each garlic plant has sufficient room to develop healthy bulbs without competing for resources. Proper spacing also helps to reduce the risk of fungal diseases, which can be more prevalent in crowded garlic plantings.

Chives: Chive seedlings should be spaced 6-12 inches apart in rows that are 12-18 inches apart. This spacing allows chives to form clumps and spread out as they mature while ensuring they have access to necessary resources. Chives are relatively low-maintenance and adaptable, but providing adequate spacing will help promote healthy growth and prevent competition with neighboring plants.

Leeks: When transplanting leek seedlings, space them 6 inches apart in rows that are 12-18 inches apart. Leeks have a shallow root system, making proper spacing even more critical. This spacing allows leeks to grow large, robust stalks without competing for nutrients and water. Adequate spacing also helps improve air circulation, reducing the risk of pests and diseases.

Shallots: Plant shallot sets or seedlings about 4-6 inches apart in rows that are 12-18 inches apart. This spacing allows shallots to develop healthy bulbs and minimizes competition for resources. Proper spacing also promotes better air circulation, reducing the risk of fungal diseases that can affect shallot plants.

Understanding the desired spacing and measurements when planting various Allium vegetable seedlings is crucial for ensuring their healthy growth and development. By providing each plant with adequate space, you can minimize competition for resources, improve air circulation, and reduce the risk of pests and diseases. This results in a thriving garden with an abundant harvest of flavorful and versatile Allium vegetables.

MAINTAINING ALLIUM VEGETABLE PLANTS

Maintaining your Allium vegetable plants is essential in vegetable companion gardening for several reasons. First, properly cared-for Alliums can effectively support the growth and health of their companion plants by providing natural pest control, thanks to their strong scent that repels harmful insects. This reduces the need for chemical pesticides and creates a healthier garden ecosystem. Second, well-maintained Alliums can attract beneficial insects like pollinators and predatory insects, further promoting the overall health and productivity of the garden.

Third, by ensuring that your Allium plants grow strong and healthy, you minimize competition for resources like nutrients, water, and sunlight, enabling both the Alliums and their companions to thrive. Finally, regular maintenance, such as pruning, weeding, and proper watering, can prevent the spread of diseases and pests that might otherwise affect both the Alliums and their companion plants. In summary, maintaining your Allium vegetable plants is crucial for maximizing the benefits of companion gardening, leading to a more productive, sustainable, and harmonious garden.

PRUNING AND THINNING ALLIUM VEGETABLE PLANTS

Pruning and thinning vegetable plants within the Allium family is vital in vegetable companion planting for several reasons. First, these practices help maintain the optimal balance between Alliums and their companion plants, ensuring that each plant receives adequate access to sunlight, nutrients, and water without competing for resources.

This promotes healthier growth and higher yields for both Alliums and their companions. Second, pruning and thinning can improve air circulation around the plants, reducing the risk of fungal diseases and pest infestations that thrive in damp, overcrowded conditions. This contributes to a healthier garden ecosystem and reduces the need for chemical interventions. Third, selectively removing weaker or damaged plants during the thinning process allows the remaining plants to grow stronger and more resilient, further enhancing the overall health of the garden.

Finally, pruning and thinning Allium plants, such as chives or onion tops, can encourage bushier growth and stimulate the production of essential oils, which in turn enhances their pest-repelling properties. In conclusion, regular pruning and thinning of Allium vegetables are vital practices in companion planting, ensuring a harmonious and productive garden environment.

Pruning and thinning the various vegetables within the Allium family during their growing stages when companion planting require careful timing and technique to ensure the plants' health and productivity. Here's a guide on when and how to prune and thin different Allium vegetables in a companion planting setup.

Onions: Thinning onion seedlings is essential for their proper growth, as overcrowded plants compete for resources. When onion seedlings are about 3-4 inches tall and have at least two sets of true leaves, it's time to thin them. Gently remove weaker or smaller seedlings, leaving the stronger ones spaced 4-6 inches apart.

You can harvest the thinned seedlings as green onions. Pruning onion tops is not typically necessary, but if the plants become too tall or top-heavy, you can trim the leaves back to one-third of their length to encourage stockier growth.

Garlic: Garlic plants do not generally require pruning or thinning. However, it's essential to remove the garlic scapes (flower stalks) as they appear, usually in late spring or early summer. Cutting the scapes redirects the plant's energy into bulb development, resulting in larger and more flavorful garlic bulbs. Use a sharp pair of scissors or pruning shears to cut the scape at its base, taking care not to damage the main stem.

Chives: To encourage bushy growth and stimulate the production of essential oils in chives, regular pruning is necessary. Use prunes to trim the tips of the leaves, cutting back to about 2 inches above the soil level. Begin pruning when the chive plants are 6 inches tall and continue throughout the growing season, removing spent flower heads as well. Chives do not require thinning, as they naturally form clumps and spread out over time.

Leeks: Leeks do not require pruning, but thinning is essential to prevent overcrowding and ensure proper growth. When leek seedlings are about the size of a pencil and have at least two sets of true leaves, it's time to thin them. Gently remove weaker or smaller seedlings, leaving the stronger ones spaced 6 inches apart. The removed seedlings can be transplanted elsewhere in the garden or used in cooking.

Shallots: Shallots typically do not require pruning or thinning when grown from sets. However, if you're growing shallots from seeds, thin the seedlings when they reach 3-4 inches tall, leaving the strongest plants spaced 4-6 inches apart. If shallot plants produce flower stalks, remove them to direct the plant's energy into bulb development.

Understanding when and how to prune and thin the different vegetables within the Allium family during their growing stages is crucial for successful companion planting. By implementing these practices at the appropriate times and using the correct techniques, you can promote healthy growth, maximize yields, and maintain a harmonious and productive garden.

CHAPTER 4

WATERING ALLIUM VEGETABLE PLANTS

Watering your Allium vegetable plants is crucial when companion planting to ensure their optimal growth and development, as well as that of their neighboring plants. Alliums, like most vegetables, require consistent moisture to prevent stress and promote healthy root systems and foliage. Adequate watering helps Allium plants produce the essential oils responsible for their pest-repelling properties, enhancing their effectiveness in protecting companion plants from harmful insects.

Furthermore, proper hydration supports the overall health of the garden ecosystem by fostering strong, disease-resistant plants that can better withstand environmental challenges. By maintaining consistent and appropriate watering practices, you create a harmonious and productive companion planting environment where Alliums and their neighboring plants can mutually benefit and thrive together.

Onions: Onions have shallow root systems, so they require consistent watering to ensure adequate moisture levels. Water them once or twice a week, providing about an inch of water each time. Be careful not to overwater, as this can lead to bulb rot.

In the early stages of growth, water near the base of the plants to encourage root development. As the bulbs begin to form, switch to a more gentle watering method, such as using a soaker hose, to avoid dislodging the soil around the bulbs.

Garlic: Garlic prefers well-drained soil and requires moderate watering throughout the growing season. Water the plants deeply once a week, providing about an inch of water each time. Be cautious not to overwater, as soggy soil can cause bulb rot. As the garlic plants approach maturity and the lower leaves begin to turn yellow, gradually reduce watering to allow the bulbs to harden off before harvest.

Chives: Chives thrive in consistently moist soil, so regular watering is crucial. Water the plants deeply once or twice a week, ensuring that the soil remains evenly moist but not waterlogged. During hot or dry spells, you may need to increase the frequency of watering to prevent the soil from drying out. A layer of mulch around the chive plants can help conserve moisture and maintain consistent soil temperatures.

Leeks: Leeks have similar watering requirements as onions. Water them deeply once or twice a week, providing about an inch of water each time. Monitor the soil moisture regularly, as leeks prefer consistently moist soil but do not tolerate waterlogged conditions. Using a soaker hose or drip irrigation system can help provide even and consistent moisture without disturbing the soil around the plants.

Shallots: Shallots require steady watering throughout their growing season to support healthy growth. Water the plants once a week, providing about an inch of water each time. Ensure that the soil remains consistently moist but not waterlogged. As with onions and garlic, be cautious not to overwater, as this can lead to bulb rot.

Through understanding how and when to water the different vegetables in the Allium family when companion planting, gardeners can promote healthy growth, diseases prevention, and maximize the benefits to neighboring plants. By implementing proper watering practices and monitoring soil moisture levels, you can maintain a harmonious and productive garden environment where both Alliums and their companions can thrive.

CHAPTER 4

ORGANIC FERTILISATION FOR ALLIUM VEGETABLE PLANTS

Organic fertilization is vital for Allium vegetable plants when companion planting, as it provides essential nutrients to support their growth and development while promoting a healthy and sustainable garden environment. Organic fertilizers, such as compost, aged manure, or worm castings, release nutrients slowly and steadily over time, ensuring that Alliums receive the necessary nourishment without the risk of nutrient burn or imbalance.

Furthermore, organic fertilization enhances soil structure and fertility by introducing beneficial microorganisms that improve nutrient availability and water retention. This, in turn, fosters strong root systems, which are crucial for Alliums to absorb water and nutrients effectively. In addition, organic fertilization supports the production of essential oils in Allium plants, enhancing their pest-repelling properties and bolstering their protective role within a companion planting setup. Ultimately, using organic fertilizers for Alliums when companion planting contributes to a harmonious and productive garden ecosystem, where both Alliums and their neighboring plants can mutually benefit and flourish.

Organic fertilizers play a significant role in providing the necessary nutrients for the various vegetables in the Allium family when companion planting. Here's a guide on the type of organic fertilizers each Allium plant requires and when to fertilize them in a companion planting setup.

Onions: Onions benefit from a balanced organic fertilizer, such as compost or well-aged manure, which provides essential nutrients like nitrogen, phosphorus, and potassium.

Apply fertilizer at the time of planting by mixing it into the soil, and then side-dress with additional compost or aged manure once the onions have established and are growing vigorously. This ensures that the plants receive a consistent supply of nutrients throughout their growth cycle, promoting healthy bulb development and optimal yields.

Garlic: Garlic thrives when provided with a slow-release organic fertilizer high in phosphorus and potassium, such as bone meal or rock phosphate. Mix the fertilizer into the soil at the time of planting, ensuring that the nutrients are available to support root development and bulb growth. Additionally, top-dress the garlic plants with compost or aged manure in early spring to provide a boost of nitrogen, which is essential for vigorous leaf growth.

Chives: Chives require a balanced organic fertilizer, such as compost or aged manure, to support their growth and essential oil production. Apply fertilizer at the time of planting by incorporating it into the soil, and then add a layer of compost or aged manure as a top-dressing each spring to replenish nutrients and encourage bushy growth. Regularly applying organic liquid fertilizer, such as fish emulsion or seaweed extract, can also provide chives with a steady supply of nutrients during the growing season.

Leeks: Leeks benefit from a balanced organic fertilizer that provides a steady supply of nitrogen, phosphorus, and potassium. Incorporate compost or aged manure into the soil at the time of planting to support strong root development and vigorous growth. Once the leeks are well-established, side-dress them with additional compost or aged manure to ensure consistent nutrient availability throughout their growth cycle.

Shallots: Shallots require a balanced organic fertilizer, such as compost or aged manure, which provides essential nutrients for healthy bulb formation. Mix the fertilizer into the soil at the time of planting, and then top-dress the shallot plants with additional compost or aged manure in early spring to provide a boost of nitrogen for leaf growth. A slow-release organic fertilizer high in phosphorus and potassium, like bone meal or rock phosphate, can also be beneficial for promoting robust bulb development.

Understanding the type of organic fertilizers the various vegetables in the Allium family require and when to fertilize each plant is essential for successful companion planting. By providing the appropriate nutrients at the right times, you can ensure that your Allium plants grow strong and healthy, maximizing their benefits to neighboring plants and contributing to a productive and harmonious garden ecosystem.

PROTECTING ALLIUM VEGETABLE PLANTS

EXTREME TEMPERATURES

Protecting vegetables in the Allium family from extreme temperatures when companion planting is essential for ensuring their optimal growth and development, as well as the overall health of the garden ecosystem. Here are some strategies to safeguard your Allium plants from temperature extremes.

Mulching: Applying a layer of organic mulch, such as straw, shredded leaves, or wood chips, around your Allium plants can help insulate the soil, maintaining consistent temperatures and protecting the plants' shallow root systems from extreme heat or cold. Mulch also helps conserve soil moisture, reduces weed competition, and gradually decomposes, providing additional nutrients to the soil over time.

Shade Protection: During periods of intense heat, providing shade for your Allium plants can help prevent heat stress and minimize the risk of bolting. You can use shade cloth, umbrellas, or temporary structures to create dappled shade over your Alliums and their companion plants. Alternatively, strategic placement of taller companion plants, such as sunflowers or corn, can provide natural shade for your more heat-sensitive Alliums.

Frost Protection: If frost is a concern for your Allium plants, you can use various methods to protect them from freezing temperatures. Floating row covers, cloches, or cold frames can be employed to shield your plants from frost and extend the growing season. It's essential to monitor weather forecasts and install these protective measures before the arrival of frost to prevent damage to your Alliums and their companions.

Proper Plant Spacing: Adequate spacing between your Allium plants and their companions is crucial for promoting good air circulation, which can help prevent temperature-related stress. Properly spaced plants can better dissipate heat during hot spells and reduce humidity levels around the foliage, decreasing the risk of fungal diseases that may thrive in damp conditions.

Water Management: Ensuring consistent and appropriate watering practices is vital for helping your Allium plants cope with extreme temperatures. During hot spells, increase watering frequency to maintain adequate soil moisture, as Alliums require sufficient water to prevent heat stress and support healthy growth. Conversely, in cold weather, avoid overwatering to prevent root rot and other cold-related issues.

Plant Selection: When companion planting, it's essential to choose plant varieties that are well-suited to your region's climate conditions. This includes selecting Allium varieties with appropriate temperature tolerance levels and pairing them with compatible companion plants that can withstand similar temperature extremes.

Protecting vegetables in the Allium family from extreme temperatures when companion planting requires a combination of proactive measures and careful planning. By implementing strategies such as mulching, shade protection, frost protection, proper plant spacing, water management, and plant selection, you can create a resilient garden environment where both your Alliums and their companion plants can thrive despite challenging temperature fluctuations.

PROTECTING ALLIUM VEGETABLES FROM PEST

Protecting the various vegetables in the Allium family from pests when companion planting is essential for maintaining a healthy and productive garden. Here are some strategies to safeguard your Allium plants from common pests:

Companion Planting: One of the primary benefits of companion planting is the natural pest control it offers. Alliums, with their pungent odor and essential oil production, can repel many pests, such as aphids, spider mites, and cabbage worms. In turn, Alliums benefit from being planted near companions that deter pests specific to them, such as carrot fly and onion maggot. Good companion plants for Alliums include carrots, beets, tomatoes, and chamomile.

Beneficial Insects: Encouraging populations of beneficial insects in your garden can help keep pest populations in check. Ladybugs, lacewings, and predatory mites are natural predators of many common pests that affect Allium plants. Planting flowers such as marigolds, calendula, and yarrow can attract these beneficial insects and provide them with a habitat to thrive in.

Physical Barriers: Installing physical barriers can prevent pests from reaching your Allium plants. Floating row covers can protect your plants from flying insects, while collars made from plastic or cardboard can be placed around the base of each plant to deter soil-dwelling pests like onion maggots. Additionally, fine mesh netting can be used to exclude pests like aphids and whiteflies without inhibiting sunlight or air circulation.

Trap Cropping: Planting trap crops can be an effective way to lure pests away from your Allium plants and their companions. Trap crops are plants that are more attractive to pests than the main crops you want to protect. For example, planting nasturtiums near your Alliums can attract aphids away from your main crops, reducing the risk of infestation.

Regular Monitoring: Regularly inspecting your Allium plants and their companions for signs of pests is crucial for early detection and intervention. By monitoring your garden closely, you can identify and address pest issues before they escalate. When you spot pests, remove them manually or use a strong spray of water to dislodge them from the plants.

Organic Pest Control: If pest infestations persist despite your preventative efforts, consider using organic pest control methods. Insecticidal soap, neem oil, or diatomaceous earth can be applied to affected plants to target specific pests without harming beneficial insects or introducing harsh chemicals into your garden ecosystem.

Protecting the different vegetables in the Allium family from pests when companion planting requires a multifaceted approach. By employing these strategies, you can create a harmonious and resilient garden environment where both your Alliums and their companion plants can thrive.

PROTECTING ALLIUM VEGETABLES FROM DISEASES

Several diseases can affect vegetable plants in the Allium family, impacting their growth and productivity. When companion planting, it is crucial to identify these diseases early and protect your Alliums organically to maintain a healthy garden ecosystem. Here are some common diseases that affect Allium plants, along with tips for identification and organic protection:

White Rot: White rot is a soil-borne fungal disease caused by Sclerotium cepivorum. It affects all members of the Allium family, causing yellowing and wilting of leaves, white fluffy growth on the base of the plant, and black sclerotia on the roots. To manage white rot organically, practice crop rotation, avoid overwatering, and remove and dispose of infected plants promptly. Solarizing the soil by covering it with clear plastic during hot weather can help reduce the presence of the fungus in the soil.

Downy Mildew: Downy mildew is a fungal disease caused by Peronospora destructor that affects onions, garlic, and leeks. It presents as yellow or pale green patches on the upper leaf surfaces and grayish-purple fuzzy growth on the underside of leaves. To combat downy mildew, ensure proper plant spacing for good air circulation, avoid overhead watering, and remove infected plant material from the garden. Applying an organic fungicide, such as copper-based products or potassium bicarbonate, can help control the spread of downy mildew.

Onion Smudge: Onion smudge is a fungal disease caused by Colletotrichum circinans that affects onion bulbs. It appears as black, sooty spots on the outer scales of the bulb. To prevent onion smudge, practice crop rotation, maintain a balanced soil pH, and avoid injuring the bulbs during harvesting and storage. Treat seeds with hot water before planting to reduce the risk of introducing the fungus to your garden.

Rust: Rust is a fungal disease that affects Allium plants, particularly garlic and leeks. It manifests as orange or yellow pustules on the leaves, which release spores and can spread rapidly. To manage rust organically, maintain good air circulation through proper plant spacing, remove infected leaves, and avoid overhead watering. Applying organic fungicides like sulfur or neem oil can help control rust infestations.

Botrytis Leaf Blight: Botrytis leaf blight is a fungal disease caused by Botrytis spp. that affects onions, garlic, and other Alliums. It presents as small, white flecks on the leaves that develop into larger, water-soaked lesions with a gray moldy appearance. To protect your Alliums from botrytis leaf blight, practice crop rotation, ensure adequate plant spacing, and remove infected plant material from the garden. Organic fungicides containing copper or Bacillus subtilis can be applied to prevent the spread of the disease.

Identifying and protecting the vegetable plants in the Allium family from diseases organically when companion planting involves vigilance, preventative measures, and the use of

CHAPTER 4

organic treatments. By implementing these strategies, you can safeguard your Alliums and their companion plants from common diseases and maintain a thriving and resilient garden ecosystem.

HARVESTING ALLIUM VEGETABLE PLANTS

The vegetables within the Allium family all have different growth durations and harvesting techniques. When companion planting, it is essential to know when each Allium plant is ready for harvest and how to collect them properly to ensure optimal yield and quality. Here's a guide on the harvesting timeline and techniques for different Allium vegetables in a companion planting setup.

Onions: Onions typically take 100-120 days to reach maturity, depending on the variety. You'll know they're ready for harvest when the tops begin to yellow and fall over. At this point, gently loosen the soil around each onion bulb with a garden fork, being careful not to damage the bulb. Lift the bulbs out of the ground and let them cure in a well-ventilated, shaded area for 2-3 weeks before trimming the tops and roots and storing them in a cool, dry place.

Garlic: Garlic usually takes 180-210 days to mature, depending on the variety and planting time. Harvest garlic when the lower leaves turn yellow, and the upper leaves are still green. Carefully loosen the soil around the base of the plant with a garden fork and lift the bulbs out of the ground. Allow the garlic to cure in a shaded, well-ventilated area for 2-4 weeks before trimming the tops and roots and storing the bulbs in a cool, dry place.

Chives: Chives can be harvested continually throughout the growing season, beginning about 60 days after planting. To harvest chives, use scissors or a sharp knife to cut the leaves about 1-2 inches above the soil line, leaving some foliage to encourage new growth. Regularly harvesting chives will promote bushy growth and prevent flowering, ensuring a continuous supply of fresh leaves.

Leeks: Leeks generally take 100-120 days to mature, depending on the variety. They can be harvested once they reach a desirable size, typically when the stems are about 1 inch in diameter. To harvest leeks, use a garden fork to loosen the soil around each plant, then gently lift the leeks from the ground. Trim the roots and remove any damaged outer leaves before washing and storing them in the refrigerator.

Shallots: Shallots usually reach maturity within 90-120 days after planting. Harvest them when the tops begin to yellow and fall over, similar to onions. Gently loosen the soil around each cluster of shallots with a garden fork and lift them out of the ground. Allow the shallots to cure in a well-ventilated, shaded area for 2-3 weeks before trimming the tops and roots and storing them in a cool, dry place.

CHAPTER 4

CROP ROTATION FOR ALLIUM VEGETABLE PLANTS

Crop rotation is an essential agricultural practice that involves growing different types of crops in the same area in sequential seasons. This method helps prevent soil depletion, disrupts the life cycle of pests and diseases, and promotes a healthy and sustainable garden ecosystem.

When companion planting with Allium vegetables, implementing crop rotation can be particularly beneficial in maintaining soil fertility and reducing the risk of pest and disease infestations. Here's a guide on the process of crop rotation for Allium vegetables when companion planting.

Understanding Crop Families: The first step in planning a crop rotation for your Allium vegetables is to familiarize yourself with the different plant families. Grouping plants by their botanical family helps ensure that similar crops are not grown consecutively in the same area, as this can deplete the soil of specific nutrients and increase the risk of soil-borne diseases and pests. Allium vegetables belong to the Amaryllidaceae family, which includes onions, garlic, leeks, shallots, and chives.

Establishing a Rotation Plan: Develop a crop rotation plan that spans at least three to four years to maximize its benefits. In each growing season, rotate your Allium vegetables and their companion plants to a different location within your garden. Ideally, avoid planting Alliums or their close relatives in the same area more than once every three to four years.

Incorporating Different Plant Families: When rotating Alliums and their companions, consider incorporating plants from various families to balance nutrient demands and provide natural pest control. For example, follow a planting of Alliums with legumes (Fabaceae family), such as beans or peas, which can fix nitrogen in the soil and replenish this essential nutrient for subsequent crops.

Other plant families to include in your rotation plan are the Brassicaceae (cabbage, kale, broccoli), Solanaceae (tomatoes, peppers, eggplants), and Cucurbitaceae (squash, cucumbers, melons) families.

Managing Soil Fertility: Crop rotation can help maintain soil fertility by balancing nutrient demands and reducing the need for chemical fertilizers. Be sure to amend your soil with organic matter, such as compost or aged manure, at the beginning of each growing season to replenish nutrients and improve soil structure. This practice is particularly important when rotating Alliums, which have shallow root systems and require consistent nutrient availability for healthy growth.

Controlling Pests and Diseases: Crop rotation can help break the life cycle of pests and diseases specific to Allium vegetables, reducing their impact on your garden. By rotating your Alliums and their companion plants, you can minimize the risk of soil-borne diseases, such as white rot, and pests like onion maggots from becoming established in your garden. Furthermore, companion planting with other plant families can attract beneficial insects and provide additional natural pest control.

Implementing crop rotation for Allium vegetables when companion planting is a vital practice for maintaining soil fertility, controlling pests and diseases, and promoting a healthy garden ecosystem. By understanding crop families, establishing a rotation plan, incorporating different plant families, managing soil fertility, and controlling pests and diseases, you can ensure the long-term success and sustainability of your Allium companion garden.

CHAPTER 5
CUCURBITACEAE "SQUASH" FAMILY COMPANION PLANTING

The Cucurbitaceae family, commonly known as the squash family, is a diverse and essential group of plants for vegetable companion planting. Comprising various species such as squash, cucumbers, melons, and pumpkins, these versatile vegetables not only offer a wide range of culinary uses but also provide numerous benefits to the garden ecosystem. When incorporated into a companion planting strategy, Cucurbitaceae plants can enhance soil fertility, attract pollinators, suppress weeds, and even deter pests through natural pest control methods, such as repelling harmful insects with aromatic plants or attracting beneficial predatory insects.

By understanding the unique characteristics and needs of the squash family, growers can harness their full potential and create a thriving, harmonious garden that promotes the growth and productivity of both Cucurbitaceae plants and their companions.

CUCURBITACEAE FAMILY VEGETABLE PLANTS

The Cucurbitaceae squash family comprises a diverse range of vegetables that are well-suited for companion planting. These plants offer various benefits to the garden ecosystem while providing an abundance of flavors and textures for culinary use. Here's an in-depth look at some of the most popular vegetables within the Cucurbitaceae family.

Summer Squash: Summer squash, which includes zucchini, yellow squash, and pattypan squash, is known for its tender flesh and short growing season. These fast-growing plants thrive when paired with companions like nasturtiums, marigolds, and borage, which can deter pests like squash bugs and cucumber beetles.

Additionally, summer squash benefits from being planted alongside corn and beans as part of the "Three Sisters" planting method, where each plant supports and complements the others.

Winter Squash: Winter squash varieties, such as butternut, acorn, and spaghetti squash, have a longer growing season and develop a hard rind, allowing for extended storage. Like summer squash, winter squash can benefit from companion planting with corn and beans, as well as aromatic herbs like dill and oregano, which can repel pests. Planting winter squash with sunflowers can also provide additional support for their sprawling vines and attract pollinators to the garden.

Cucumbers: Cucumbers are a popular garden staple prized for their refreshing taste and versatility in salads, pickles, and other dishes. When companion planting cucumbers, consider partnering them with radishes, which can help deter cucumber beetles.

Other beneficial companions include beans, peas, and lettuce, which can improve soil fertility and provide shade to keep the soil cool and moist. Planting flowers like calendula and chamomile near cucumbers can also attract beneficial insects and enhance pollination.

Melons: Melons, such as cantaloupe and honeydew, are cherished for their sweet, juicy flesh. When companion planting melons, consider partnering them with corn, which can provide support and shade for the melon vines while benefiting from the nutrients that melons add to the soil. Other good companions for melons include sunflowers, which attract pollinators, and nasturtiums, which can repel pests like aphids and squash bugs.

Pumpkins: Pumpkins, known for their vibrant orange color and versatility in both sweet and savory dishes, are another essential member of the Cucurbitaceae family.

Like other squash varieties, pumpkins benefit from companion planting with corn and beans, as well as aromatic herbs like oregano and catnip, which can deter pests. Planting pumpkins near flowers such as marigolds and zinnias can also attract pollinators and enhance the overall health of your garden.

The Cucurbitaceae squash family presents an extensive assortment of vegetables that can significantly profit from the practice of companion planting. By choosing the appropriate plant companions, you can establish a flourishing garden ecosystem that fosters robust growth, boosts soil fertility, repels pests, and encourages pollination.

Implementing this comprehensive gardening strategy enables you to relish the abundant yield of these delectable and adaptable vegetables while preserving a sustainable and harmonious garden habitat.

CUCURBITACEAE FAMILY COMPANION VEGETABLES

Companion planting with the Cucurbitaceae squash family can significantly enhance the health and productivity of your garden by promoting a balanced ecology. Choosing the right companion plants for squash, cucumbers, melons, and pumpkins involves considering their unique growth habits, nutrient requirements, and pest challenges. Here are some types of vegetable plants to companion plant with the Cucurbitaceae family and tips on selecting the best companions.

Legumes: Legumes, such as beans and peas, make excellent companions for Cucurbitaceae vegetables due to their ability to fix nitrogen in the soil. This process replenishes essential nutrients that squash and other Cucurbitaceae plants require for healthy growth. When selecting legumes as companion plants, opt for bush varieties that won't compete with the squash family's sprawling vines for space and support.

Corn: Corn is a traditional companion plant for the squash family, especially when using the "Three Sisters" planting method. This Native American technique involves planting corn, beans, and squash together, where each plant supports and complements the others. Corn provides support for the climbing beans and shade for the Cucurbitaceae plants, while the beans fix nitrogen in the soil, and the squash's large leaves help suppress weeds and conserve soil moisture.

Leafy Greens: Leafy greens, such as lettuce, spinach, and Swiss chard, can be beneficial companions for Cucurbitaceae vegetables because they provide ground cover, shading the soil and helping to retain moisture.

Additionally, their shallow root systems will not compete with the deeper roots of squash plants, allowing both types of vegetables to access nutrients without hindering each other's growth.

Radishes: Radishes make excellent companions for Cucurbitaceae plants, particularly cucumbers, as they can help deter cucumber beetles and other pests. The pungent smell of radishes can act as a natural repellent, while their fast-growing nature ensures they won't compete with the squash family plants for nutrients and space.

Aromatic Herbs: Aromatic herbs like basil, dill, oregano, and parsley can make good companion plants for the Cucurbitaceae family. These herbs not only repel pests with their strong scents but also attract beneficial insects that help control pests and enhance pollination.

When selecting aromatic herbs as companion plants, consider the specific pest challenges your squash family plants may face and choose herbs known to deter those pests effectively.

Flowering Plants: Flowering plants such as marigolds, nasturtiums, sunflowers, and zinnias are excellent companions for the Cucurbitaceae family. These flowers attract pollinators like bees and butterflies, which are essential for the successful fruit set of squash, cucumbers, melons, and pumpkins. Additionally, some flowering plants, like marigolds and nasturtiums, can repel pests with their strong scents or even act as trap crops, drawing pests away from your Cucurbitaceae plants.

To sum it up, picking the ideal companion plants for your Cucurbitaceae family vegetables requires a thoughtful analysis of their growth patterns, nutritional needs, and pest issues. By weaving in a varied assortment of companion plants - legumes, corn, leafy greens, radishes, aromatic herbs, and blooming flora, you can nurture a bustling garden ecosystem that champions robust growth, bolsters soil richness, wards off pests, and fosters pollination.

This all-encompassing gardening strategy lets you relish the plentiful harvest of these tasty and flexible vegetables while preserving an eco-friendly and harmonious garden ambiance.

CUCURBITACEAE FAMILY NON-COMPANION PLANTS

While companion planting with the Cucurbitaceae squash family can yield numerous benefits, it's crucial to be aware of certain vegetable plants that should not be paired with these crops. Some plants may compete for resources, attract pests, or even inhibit the growth of squash, cucumbers, melons, and pumpkins. Here are several types of vegetable plants to avoid when companion planting with the Cucurbitaceae family:

Potatoes: Potatoes and the Cucurbitaceae family should not be planted together, as they share common pests, such as cucumber beetles, which can transmit bacterial wilt and other diseases. Additionally, both potatoes and squash family plants have high water requirements, leading to competition for this essential resource, which could negatively impact the growth and productivity of both crops.

Tomatoes: Although tomatoes and Cucurbitaceae vegetables do not have a direct negative impact on each other, they tend to compete for sunlight, nutrients, and water due to their similar growing habits. Tomatoes can grow quite large and bushy, potentially overshadowing the sprawling vines of squash family plants. This competition can lead to reduced growth and productivity of both types of vegetables.

Peppers: Like tomatoes, peppers are part of the Solanaceae family and have similar growth habits and nutrient requirements. Planting peppers near Cucurbitaceae plants can result in competition for sunlight, water, and nutrients, potentially affecting the overall health and productivity of your garden. Additionally, peppers and squash family plants can share common pests, increasing the risk of infestations and disease transmission.

Melons and Watermelons: Although melons and watermelons are part of the Cucurbitaceae family, planting different varieties too close together can lead to cross-pollination, affecting the fruit quality and flavor. To maintain the integrity of your melon and watermelon varieties, it's best to separate them by a reasonable distance or plant them in different areas of your garden.

Other Squash Family Plants: Planting different types of squash family plants too close together can increase the risk of pests and diseases spreading among your crops. For example, powdery mildew and squash vine borers can easily infest multiple plants when they are in close proximity. To minimize these risks, it's essential to provide adequate spacing between different types of Cucurbitaceae plants and practice proper crop rotation.

While the practice of companion planting with the Cucurbitaceae squash family can work wonders for your garden, it's paramount to keep an eye out for certain vegetable plants that could potentially compete for resources, lure pests, or stunt growth.

By giving a wide berth to potatoes, tomatoes, peppers, and closely related Cucurbitaceae plants, you can cultivate a garden oasis that fosters robust growth and productivity across all your crops. In addition to this, adopting appropriate spacing methods and crop rotation practices can significantly boost the prosperity and longevity of your garden.

THE RIGHT SOIL FOR CUCURBITACEAE FAMILY VEGETABLES

Each Cucurbitaceae family vegetable has specific soil requirements that contribute to their successful growth and productivity. By providing the right soil conditions for each type of squash family plant, you can create a thriving garden environment that supports both your Cucurbitaceae vegetables and their companion plants. Here's an overview of the ideal soil conditions for various Cucurbitaceae family vegetables and their effect on companion planting with compatible companion vegetables.

Summer Squash: Summer squash, including zucchini, yellow squash, and pattypan squash, prefer well-drained, fertile soil with a pH between 6.0 and 6.8. These plants thrive in loose, loamy soil rich in organic matter, which supports their rapid growth and fruit production.

Ensuring optimal soil conditions for summer squash not only promotes their overall health but also benefits companion plants like beans, corn, and marigolds, which can access the same nutrient-rich soil.

Winter Squash: Winter squash varieties, such as butternut, acorn, and spaghetti squash, require similar soil conditions to their summer counterparts. They grow best in well-drained, fertile soil with a pH between 6.0 and 6.8.

Providing ample organic matter in the form of compost or aged manure contributes to a healthy soil structure that supports both winter squash and their companion plants, like corn, beans, and sunflowers, by ensuring a consistent supply of nutrients.

Cucumbers: Cucumbers thrive in well-drained, fertile soil with a slightly acidic pH between 6.0 and 6.5. They prefer a light, airy soil structure that allows their roots to penetrate easily and access water and nutrients.

Ensuring the right soil conditions for cucumbers not only promotes their vigorous growth but also benefits companion plants such as radishes, peas, and lettuce, which can take advantage of the same fertile soil and optimal pH.

Melons: Melons, including cantaloupe and honeydew, require well-drained, nutrient-rich soil with a pH between 6.0 and 6.5 for optimal growth. These plants benefit from the addition of organic matter, which helps to retain moisture and provide essential nutrients.

By maintaining the right soil conditions for melons, you can also support the growth and health of companion plants like corn, sunflowers, and nasturtiums, which can access the same fertile soil and thrive alongside your melon plants.

Pumpkins: Pumpkins, like other Cucurbitaceae family vegetables, grow best in well-drained, fertile soil with a slightly acidic to neutral pH between 6.0 and 6.8. They prefer a loose, friable soil structure that allows their extensive root systems to access water and nutrients easily.

Ensuring the right soil conditions for pumpkins not only supports their robust growth but also benefits companion plants such as beans, corn, and marigolds, which can share the same nutrient-rich environment.

Tailoring the soil conditions to suit each variety of Cucurbitaceae family vegetable is a cornerstone for fruitful companion planting with compatible veggies.

By nurturing a well-drained, nutrient-dense soil with just the right pH balance and texture, you can foster a vibrant garden habitat that bolsters the health and productivity of both your squash family plants and their plant partners. Regular soil upkeep and enriching amendments can significantly amplify the prosperity and longevity of your garden.

SOWING CUCURBITACEAE FAMILY VEGETABLES

CORRECT SEASON TO SOW CUCURBITACEAE VEGETABLE PLANTS

Planting vegetables in the Cucurbitaceae, or squash family, in the right season is vital for successful companion planting. This family includes warm-season crops such as squash, cucumbers, melons, and pumpkins. These plants thrive in warmer temperatures and are often planted after the risk of frost has passed in the spring.

Planting Cucurbitaceae in the appropriate season ensures they grow during their optimal climate conditions, leading to healthier plants, better yields, and reduced susceptibility to pests and diseases. Additionally, when you sow these plants in the correct season, it allows for effective synchronization with their companion plants.

For instance, planting squash with corn and beans, known as the "Three Sisters" method, provides mutual benefits: the corn provides a structure for beans to climb, the beans fix nitrogen in the soil for the other plants, and the squash leaves shade the soil, reducing evaporation and deterring weeds.

However, these benefits can only be realized if all three crops are growing together, highlighting the importance of correct seasonal planting in successful companion planting strategies. Here's an overview of the correct season to sow the different vegetables in the Cucurbitaceae squash family.

Summer Squash: Summer squash varieties, including zucchini, yellow squash, and pattypan squash, should be sown in the late spring or early summer when soil temperatures have warmed to at least 60°F (15°C). These fast-growing plants have a shorter growing season compared to their winter counterparts and typically reach maturity within 50-65 days of planting. In regions with mild climates, summer squash can be sown successively every few weeks throughout the summer for a continuous harvest.

Winter Squash: Winter squash varieties, such as butternut, acorn, and spaghetti squash, have a longer growing season and should be sown in the late spring or early summer as well.

However, they require more time to mature, usually between 80-110 days from planting. To ensure a successful harvest before the first frost, it's crucial to calculate the number of days required for your specific winter squash variety to mature and plan your planting date accordingly.

Cucumbers: Cucumbers are best sown in the late spring or early summer when soil temperatures have reached at least 60°F (15°C) and there's no risk of frost. These plants thrive in warm weather and typically take 50-70 days to reach maturity, depending on the variety. In areas with long growing seasons, cucumbers can be sown successively every few weeks for a continuous harvest throughout the summer months.

Melons: Melons, such as cantaloupe and honeydew, should be sown in the late spring or early summer when soil temperatures are consistently above 65°F (18°C). These warm-season crops typically take 70-100 days to reach maturity, depending on the variety. In regions with short growing seasons, melon seeds can be started indoors several weeks before the last expected frost date and transplanted outdoors once the soil has warmed.

Pumpkins: Pumpkins are best sown in the late spring or early summer when soil temperatures have reached at least 60°F (15°C) and there's no risk of frost. These plants require a relatively long growing season, typically between 90-120 days, depending on the variety. To ensure a successful harvest before the first frost, it's essential to calculate the number of days required for your specific pumpkin variety to mature and plan your planting date accordingly.

Grasping the ideal sowing season for different vegetables in the Cucurbitaceae squash family is pivotal for yielding a successful harvest. By timing the planting of each squash family plant during their prime sowing period, you can unlock their maximum growth potential, guarantee timely fruiting, and reap a plentiful harvest. Don't forget to weigh factors like your area's climate, frost dates, and the unique needs of each Cucurbitaceae vegetable when crafting your planting timetable.

PLANTING NEEDS & REQUIREMENTS

Bringing the different Cucurbitaceae vegetable plants to life, from tiny seeds to thriving seedlings, requires meticulous adherence to particular steps and creating the optimal conditions for each plant type. Let's embark on a journey through the stages of germinating different Cucurbitaceae vegetables, exploring the temperatures at which they spring to life, and pinpointing when these sprouting seedlings are primed for transplanting.

Summer Squash: To germinate summer squash seeds, such as zucchini, yellow squash, and pattypan squash, sow seeds directly into the garden or start them indoors in seed trays or peat pots. Plant seeds 1 inch deep and maintain a consistent soil temperature of 70-85°F (21-29°C).

Seeds should germinate within 7-10 days. If starting indoors, transplant seedlings outdoors when they have two sets of true leaves and all danger of frost has passed. Harden off seedlings by gradually exposing them to outdoor conditions for a week before transplanting.

Winter Squash: Winter squash varieties, including butternut, acorn, and spaghetti squash, can be sown directly into the garden or started indoors. Plant seeds 1 inch deep and maintain a soil temperature of 70-85°F (21-29°C) for optimal germination, which should occur within 7-10 days.

If starting seeds indoors, transplant seedlings outdoors after they develop two sets of true leaves and when there's no risk of frost. Acclimate seedlings to outdoor conditions by hardening them off for a week prior to transplanting.

Cucumbers: Cucumber seeds can be sown directly into the garden or started indoors approximately 3-4 weeks before the last expected frost date. Plant seeds 1 inch deep and maintain a soil temperature of 70-85°F (21-29°C); germination should occur in 7-10 days.

Transplant cucumber seedlings outdoors when they have two sets of true leaves and all danger of frost has passed. Gradually expose seedlings to outdoor conditions over a week before transplanting to reduce transplant shock.

Melons: Melon seeds, including cantaloupe and honeydew, should be sown directly into the garden or started indoors 3-4 weeks before the last expected frost date. Plant seeds 1 inch deep and provide a consistent soil temperature of 75-85°F (24-29°C) for optimal germination, which typically takes 7-10 days.

Transplant melon seedlings outdoors when they have two sets of true leaves and the soil temperature is consistently above 65°F (18°C). Harden off seedlings for a week before transplanting to help them acclimate to outdoor conditions.

Pumpkins: Pumpkin seeds can be sown directly into the garden or started indoors 2-4 weeks before the last frost date. Plant seeds 1 inch deep and maintain a soil temperature of 70-85°F (21-29°C); germination should occur within 7-10 days.

Transplant pumpkin seedlings outdoors when they have two sets of true leaves, and there's no risk of frost. Acclimate seedlings to outdoor conditions by gradually exposing them to sunlight and cooler temperatures for a week before transplanting.

The journey from seeds to seedlings for the different Cucurbitaceae vegetable plants demands adherence to particular steps and tailoring the conditions to suit each type of plant.

By keeping a keen eye on maintaining the perfect soil temperatures, vigilantly tracking the emergence of true leaves, and diligently preparing seedlings for the outside world before transplanting, you can lay a strong foundation for your squash family vegetable garden.

SPACING & MEASUREMENTS

Proper spacing and measurements when transplanting Cucurbitaceae vegetable seedlings play a crucial role in successful vegetable companion planting. Adequate spacing ensures that each plant receives the necessary sunlight, nutrients, and water required for optimal growth and productivity.

It also helps maintain healthy air circulation, reducing the risk of diseases and pest infestations that can spread rapidly in crowded conditions. Furthermore, appropriate spacing allows companion plants to work together more effectively, whether by repelling pests, attracting beneficial insects, or enhancing nutrient availability.

Ultimately, adhering to the recommended spacing and measurements when transplanting Cucurbitaceae vegetable seedlings and their companion plants contributes to a healthier, more productive, and harmonious garden ecosystem.

The desired spacing and measurements when planting various Cucurbitaceae vegetable seedlings depend on the specific type of plant and its growth habits. Here's an overview of the recommended spacing and measurements for Cucurbitaceae vegetable seedlings.

Summer Squash: Summer squash varieties, including zucchini, yellow squash, and pattypan squash, should be spaced 18-24 inches (45-60 cm) apart within rows, with rows spaced 3-4 feet (90-120 cm) apart. These plants have a bush-like growth habit and require ample space to spread their large leaves and produce abundant fruits without competing for resources.

Winter Squash: Winter squash varieties, such as butternut, acorn, and spaghetti squash, are vining plants that typically require more space than summer squash. Space individual plants 3-4 feet (90-120 cm) apart within rows, with rows spaced 8-10 feet (240-300 cm) apart. This spacing allows the vines to spread without crowding and ensures adequate air circulation, reducing the risk of diseases.

Cucumbers: Cucumbers can be grown as either bush or vining varieties. Bush cucumbers should be spaced 2-3 feet (60-90 cm) apart within rows, with rows spaced 3-4 feet (90-120 cm) apart.

Vining cucumbers, which can be trained to climb a trellis or other support structure, should be spaced 1-2 feet (30-60 cm) apart within rows, with rows spaced 5-6 feet (150-180 cm) apart. Proper spacing promotes healthy growth, reduces disease pressure, and makes it easier to harvest the cucumbers.

Melons: Melons, including cantaloupe and honeydew, require ample space to grow their sprawling vines. Space individual melon plants 2-3 feet (60-90 cm) apart within rows, with rows spaced 6-8 feet (180-240 cm) apart.

This spacing allows the vines to spread without competing for resources and ensures adequate air circulation, which can help prevent diseases and pest infestations.

Pumpkins: Pumpkins are large vining plants that require substantial space to grow and produce fruit. Space individual pumpkin plants 3-5 feet (90-150 cm) apart within rows, with rows spaced 8-12 feet (240-360 cm) apart.

By providing ample space between plants, you can ensure healthy growth, minimize competition for resources, and reduce the risk of diseases and pests.

To sum it up, sticking to the suggested spacing and measurements when planting assorted Cucurbitaceae vegetable seedlings can unlock their ultimate growth, productivity, and overall vitality. By gifting each plant with ample space to stretch out and ensuring a breeze can easily waft through, you can nurture a flourishing garden habitat that paves the way for a successful cultivation of your squash family vegetables.

MAINTAINING CUCURBITACEAE VEGETABLE PLANTS

Maintaining your Cucurbitaceae vegetable plants is essential in vegetable companion gardening because it ensures the overall health and productivity of both the squash family plants and their companion plants. Proper maintenance practices, such as pruning, watering, fertilizing, and pest control, help create a balanced and thriving garden ecosystem.

By keeping your Cucurbitaceae plants healthy, you enable them to effectively contribute to the benefits of companion planting, such as repelling pests, attracting beneficial insects, and improving nutrient availability. Furthermore, well-maintained plants are more resistant to diseases and pests, reducing the likelihood of these issues spreading to neighboring companion plants.

Ultimately, diligent care and maintenance of your Cucurbitaceae vegetable plants are crucial for maximizing the advantages of companion gardening and ensuring a bountiful harvest from your garden.

PRUNING AND THINNING CUCURBITACEAE VEGETABLE PLANTS

and thinning vegetable plants within the Cucurbitaceae family are important practices in vegetable companion planting because they help maintain a healthy garden environment and promote overall plant vigor. By selectively removing excess foliage, damaged leaves, and overcrowded growth, pruning allows for better air circulation and sunlight penetration, reducing the risk of diseases and pest infestations that can spread to nearby companion plants.

Thinning, or removing weaker seedlings, ensures that the remaining plants have adequate space and resources to grow and thrive without competing with one another. This practice also benefits companion plants by allowing them to access sufficient nutrients, water, and sunlight without being overshadowed or outcompeted by the squash family plants. Ultimately, proper pruning and thinning of Cucurbitaceae vegetables contribute to a more productive, harmonious, and disease-resistant companion garden.

Pruning and thinning the various vegetables within the Cucurbitaceae family during their growing stages are essential practices to ensure healthy growth and successful companion planting. Here's a guide on when and how to prune and thin different Cucurbitaceae vegetables during their growing stages.

Summer Squash: Summer squash, including zucchini, yellow squash, and pattypan squash, typically require minimal pruning. However, you may need to remove any damaged or diseased leaves as soon as they are noticed to prevent the spread of infections. Thinning is more important for these bush-like plants; when seedlings reach 3-4 inches (7-10 cm) in height, thin them to one healthy plant every 18-24 inches (45-60 cm) to prevent overcrowding and competition for resources.

Winter Squash: Winter squash varieties, such as butternut, acorn, and spaghetti squash, benefit from occasional pruning during their growing stages. Remove any damaged, diseased, or yellowing leaves to improve air circulation and reduce disease risk.

Additionally, trimming back some of the long vines can encourage more fruit production. When thinning winter squash seedlings, leave one healthy plant every 3-4 feet (90-120 cm) to ensure ample space for vine growth.

Cucumbers: Both bush and vining cucumber varieties can benefit from selective pruning. Remove any damaged or diseased leaves to promote air circulation and reduce disease pressure. For vining cucumbers, you may also prune back some lateral branches to encourage vertical growth when using a trellis or support structure. Thinning cucumber seedlings is crucial; leave one healthy plant every 1-2 feet (30-60 cm) for vining types or 2-3 feet (60-90 cm) for bush types to prevent overcrowding.

Melons: Melons, including cantaloupe and honeydew, require careful pruning and thinning during their growing stages. Prune off any damaged or diseased leaves to promote air circulation and reduce disease risk.

You may also trim back some secondary vines to encourage fruit production on the main vine. Thin melon seedlings to one healthy plant every 2-3 feet (60-90 cm) to allow sufficient space for the sprawling vines.

Pumpkins: Pumpkins are vigorous vining plants that benefit from occasional pruning. Remove any damaged, diseased, or yellowing leaves to improve air circulation and reduce the risk of diseases. Pruning back some of the vine tips can encourage bushier growth and more fruit production.

Thinning pumpkin seedlings is essential; leave one healthy plant every 3-5 feet (90-150 cm) to ensure adequate space for vine growth and fruit development.

Prompt and appropriate pruning and thinning of diverse vegetables within the Cucurbitaceae family during their growth stages form the backbone of successful companion planting. By striking the right balance in plant density, fostering healthy growth patterns, and keeping diseases and pests at bay, you can cultivate a fruitful and balanced garden habitat that nurtures both Cucurbitaceae vegetables and their companion plants.

WATERING CUCURBITACEAE VEGETABLE PLANTS

Watering your Cucurbitaceae vegetable plants is essential when companion planting, as it ensures the overall health, growth, and productivity of both the squash family vegetables and their companion plants. Cucurbitaceae plants, such as squash, cucumbers, melons, and pumpkins, are particularly water-demanding, requiring consistent moisture to produce quality fruits and prevent issues like blossom end rot.

Adequate watering also helps companion plants thrive, enabling them to contribute effectively to the benefits of companion planting, such as repelling pests, attracting beneficial insects, and improving nutrient availability. Furthermore, well-watered plants are more resistant to diseases and pests, reducing the likelihood of these issues spreading to neighboring companion plants.

Ultimately, proper watering of your Cucurbitaceae vegetable plants plays a crucial role in maximizing the advantages of companion gardening and ensuring a bountiful harvest from your garden.

Watering the different vegetables in the Cucurbitaceae family correctly is essential when companion planting to ensure optimal growth, health, and productivity. Here's a guide on how and when to water different Cucurbitaceae vegetables during their growing stages.

Summer Squash: Summer squash varieties, including zucchini, yellow squash, and pattypan squash, require consistent moisture throughout their growing season. Water your summer squash plants deeply once or twice a week, providing 1-1.5 inches (2.5-3.8 cm) of water per week.

Aim to water the plants early in the morning to give the leaves time to dry before the evening, reducing the risk of fungal diseases. Use drip irrigation or soaker hoses to deliver water directly to the root zone, minimizing water contact with the foliage.

Winter Squash: Winter squash plants, such as butternut, acorn, and spaghetti squash, have similar watering needs as summer squash. Provide 1-1.5 inches (2.5-3.8 cm) of water per week, watering deeply once or twice a week.

Watering in the morning and using drip irrigation or soaker hoses can help prevent the spread of diseases by keeping the foliage dry. As fruits begin to mature, gradually reduce the frequency of watering to encourage the development of a hard outer shell.

Cucumbers: Cucumbers have high water requirements, especially during fruit production. Water cucumber plants consistently, providing 1-2 inches (2.5-5 cm) of water per week, depending on weather conditions and soil type. Water the plants deeply and evenly, avoiding wetting the foliage to minimize disease risk. Drip irrigation or soaker hoses are the best methods for watering cucumbers in a companion planting setup.

Melons: Melons, including cantaloupe and honeydew, require consistent moisture throughout their growing season. Provide 1-2 inches (2.5-5 cm) of water per week, depending on weather conditions and soil type.

Water your melon plants deeply and evenly, using drip irrigation or soaker hoses to minimize water contact with the foliage and reduce disease risk. As fruits begin to ripen, reduce watering frequency to encourage the development of sweet, flavorful fruits.

Pumpkins: Pumpkins are thirsty plants that require ample water, particularly during fruit development. Water pumpkin plants deeply and consistently, providing 1-2 inches (2.5-5 cm) of water per week.

Use drip irrigation or soaker hoses to deliver water directly to the root zone, avoiding wetting the leaves to minimize disease risk. As pumpkins approach maturity, gradually reduce the frequency of watering to help harden the outer shell.

Mastering the art of when and how to water the diverse vegetables in the Cucurbitaceae family is key to triumphant companion planting. By delivering a steady supply of just-right moisture, you can fuel healthy growth and productivity for both the squash family vegetables and their companion plants. Not to mention, proper watering techniques act as a shield against diseases and pests, contributing to a balanced and flourishing garden ecosystem.

ORGANIC FERTILISATION FOR CUCURBITACEAE VEGETABLE PLANTS

Organic fertilization is important for Cucurbitaceae vegetable plants when companion planting because it provides essential nutrients for healthy growth, fruit development, and overall plant vigor while maintaining a balanced and sustainable garden ecosystem. Organic fertilizers, such as compost, aged manure, or worm castings, release nutrients slowly and steadily, ensuring a consistent supply for both the squash family plants and their companion plants.

This promotes strong root systems, robust foliage, and an abundant harvest. Moreover, organic fertilizers contribute to improved soil structure, increased moisture retention, and enhanced microbial activity, which ultimately benefits all plants in the companion planting setup. Additionally, organic fertilization practices support the principles of sustainable gardening by reducing reliance on synthetic chemical fertilizers, which can cause nutrient imbalances, harm beneficial soil organisms, and contribute to environmental pollution.

In summary, organic fertilization plays a crucial role in nurturing Cucurbitaceae vegetable plants and their companion plants while fostering a productive and eco-friendly garden environment.

The various vegetables in the Cucurbitaceae family have different nutrient requirements for optimal growth and fruit production. When companion planting, it is essential to provide appropriate organic fertilizers at the right time to ensure a healthy and productive garden. Here are some guidelines for the type of organic fertilizers needed and when to fertilize each plant.

Summer Squash: Summer squash varieties, such as zucchini, yellow squash, and pattypan squash, benefit from an initial application of compost or well-aged manure mixed into the planting hole. This provides a slow-release source of nutrients throughout the growing season.

Additionally, side-dress the plants with compost or aged manure when the first flowers appear and again when the fruits begin to develop. This ensures a consistent supply of nutrients during their rapid growth and fruiting stages.

Winter Squash: Winter squash plants, including butternut, acorn, and spaghetti squash, require similar organic fertilization as summer squash. Mix compost or aged manure into the planting hole at the time of planting. Side-dress the plants with additional compost or aged manure when the first flowers appear and once more when the fruits start to develop.

Winter squash plants have a longer growing season, so consider adding a slow-release organic fertilizer, such as alfalfa meal or feather meal, to provide sustained nutrients throughout the season.

Cucumbers: Cucumbers have high nutrient demands, particularly during fruit production. Before planting, amend the soil with compost or aged manure to provide a slow-release source of nutrients.

As cucumber plants begin to flower and set fruit, side-dress them with additional compost or aged manure to support their rapid growth. You can also supplement with a balanced organic liquid fertilizer, such as fish emulsion or seaweed extract, every 2-3 weeks during the fruiting stage to ensure adequate nutrient availability.

Melons: Melons, including cantaloupe and honeydew, require rich, fertile soil for optimal growth and fruit development. Incorporate compost or aged manure into the planting hole to provide a slow-release source of nutrients.

As melon plants start to flower, side-dress them with additional compost or aged manure to support their nutrient demands during fruiting. Consider using a balanced organic liquid fertilizer, such as fish emulsion or seaweed extract, every 2-3 weeks during the fruiting stage to ensure consistent nutrient supply.

Pumpkins: Pumpkins are heavy feeders, requiring ample nutrients throughout their growing season. Before planting, mix compost or aged manure into the planting hole to provide a slow-release source of nutrients.

Side-dress pumpkin plants with additional compost or aged manure when the first flowers appear and again when the fruits begin to develop. Supplement with a slow-release organic fertilizer, such as alfalfa meal or feather meal, to provide sustained nutrients throughout their long growing season.

Offering the right variety and timing of organic fertilizers for the assorted veggies in the Cucurbitaceae family plays a pivotal role in successful companion planting. By securing a constant and sufficient nutrient supply, you can foster robust growth, plentiful harvests, and a harmonious garden ecosystem that nurtures both the squash family vegetables and their companion plants. Moreover, organic fertilization practices propagate sustainable gardening by lessening dependence on synthetic chemical fertilizers and enhancing soil well-being.

PROTECTING CUCURBITACEAE VEGETABLE PLANTS

EXTREME TEMPERATURES

Protecting vegetables in the Cucurbitaceae family from extreme temperatures is essential when companion planting to ensure healthy growth and bountiful harvests. Extreme heat or cold can stress plants, hinder growth, and reduce fruit production. Here are some strategies to protect Cucurbitaceae vegetables and their companion plants from extreme temperatures.

Mulching: Applying a layer of organic mulch, such as straw, wood chips, or shredded leaves, around the base of the plants can help regulate soil temperature and moisture levels.

In hot weather, mulch helps keep the soil cooler and reduces evaporation, ensuring consistent moisture for your plants. In cold conditions, mulch acts as insulation, protecting plant roots from freezing temperatures. Mulching also suppresses weed growth and contributes to improved soil structure over time.

Shade Cloth: During periods of extreme heat, using a shade cloth can protect Cucurbitaceae vegetables and their companion plants from scorching sun and heat stress. Install a shade cloth with a 30-50% shade rating above your plants to filter sunlight and lower air temperatures. Be sure to allow for adequate airflow to prevent humidity buildup and avoid creating an environment conducive to diseases.

Row Covers: Row covers made of lightweight fabric can be used to protect plants from both extreme heat and cold. During hot weather, row covers can provide shade and reduce heat stress. In cold conditions, row covers can be used as a protective barrier against frost, trapping heat near the plants and preventing damage from freezing temperatures. Ensure proper ventilation and monitor the temperature under the row covers to avoid overheating or excessive humidity.

Windbreaks: Wind can exacerbate the effects of extreme temperatures, causing increased evaporation in hot weather and intensifying the chill factor in cold conditions. Installing windbreaks, such as trellises with climbing plants, tall perennial plants, or temporary barriers like burlap or plastic fencing, can help protect your Cucurbitaceae vegetables and companion plants from the damaging effects of wind. Windbreaks also create a microclimate that can moderate temperature fluctuations in your garden.

Proper Watering: Consistent and appropriate watering is crucial for helping plants cope with extreme temperatures. During hot weather, water your Cucurbitaceae vegetables and companion plants deeply and consistently to ensure they have sufficient moisture to withstand the heat.

Watering early in the morning or late in the evening can reduce evaporation and help plants absorb water more efficiently. In cold conditions, avoid overwatering, as excess moisture can make plants more susceptible to frost damage.

Gradual Acclimatization: When transplanting seedlings or young plants into the garden, gradually acclimate them to outdoor conditions to minimize shock from extreme temperatures. This process, known as hardening off, involves exposing the plants to outdoor conditions for increasing periods each day, allowing them to adapt to temperature fluctuations and other environmental factors before being permanently planted in the garden.

Protecting Cucurbitaceae vegetables and their companion plants from extreme temperatures is vital for maintaining a healthy and productive garden. By adopting these strategies, you can create a supportive, growing environment that allows your plants to thrive even in challenging weather conditions.

PROTECTING CUCURBITACEAE VEGETABLES FROM PEST

Protecting the various vegetables in the Cucurbitaceae family from pests is crucial for ensuring healthy growth and a bountiful harvest when companion planting. Implementing integrated pest management strategies can help you maintain a balanced garden ecological unit and minimize the impact of pests on your plants. Here are some tactics to protect Cucurbitaceae vegetables and their companion plants from pests.

Companion Planting: One of the primary benefits of companion planting is its ability to naturally deter pests. Select companion plants that repel common pests of Cucurbitaceae vegetables, such as aphids, squash bugs, and cucumber beetles.

For example, marigolds, nasturtiums, and calendula can repel many pests, while plants like dill, fennel, and parsley attract beneficial insects that prey on pests. Planting a diverse mix of companions can confuse pests and reduce the likelihood of infestations.

Crop Rotation: Practicing crop rotation can help prevent the buildup of pests and diseases in the soil. Avoid planting Cucurbitaceae vegetables or their close relatives in the same garden location for at least two to three years. This disrupts the life cycles of pests and diseases that specifically target these plants, reducing their prevalence in your garden.

Physical Barriers: Using physical barriers can help protect your Cucurbitaceae vegetables from pests. Floating row covers made from lightweight fabric can be used to shield plants from pests like cucumber beetles and squash bugs while still allowing light, air, and water to penetrate.

Be sure to remove row covers during flowering to allow pollinators access to the plants. Collars made from cardboard or plastic can be placed around the base of seedlings to deter cutworms and other soil-dwelling pests.

Hand Picking: Regularly inspect your Cucurbitaceae vegetables and their companion plants for signs of pests. Hand-picking larger pests, such as squash bugs or cucumber beetles, can be an effective method of controlling their populations. Dispose of the pests by dropping them into a bucket of soapy water. Be sure to check the undersides of leaves and other hiding spots during your inspections.

Beneficial Insects: Encourage beneficial insects, such as ladybugs, lacewings, and parasitic wasps, to take up residence in your garden. These insects prey on common pests of Cucurbitaceae vegetables, providing natural pest control. Plant a variety of flowering plants that attract these beneficial insects, and provide a source of water and shelter for them in your garden.

Organic Pesticides: If pest infestations become severe, consider using organic pesticides as a last resort. Neem oil, insecticidal soap, and diatomaceous earth are all safe, organic options that can help control pests without harming beneficial insects or the environment. Always follow label instructions and apply these treatments judiciously to minimize any potential negative effects on your garden ecosystem.

Safeguarding the diverse vegetables in the Cucurbitaceae family from pests is a cornerstone of successful companion planting. By deploying a mix of these tactics, you can cultivate a balanced garden ecosystem that encourages vigorous plant growth and curtails pest impacts. This approach not only paves the way for a plentiful harvest but also advances sustainable gardening practices that are a boon for your garden and the environment alike.

PROTECTING CUCURBITACEAE VEGETABLES FROM DISEASES

Various diseases can affect vegetable plants in the Cucurbitaceae family, impacting their growth, health, and productivity. Recognizing these diseases and implementing organic control measures are essential when companion planting to maintain a thriving garden system. Here are some common diseases affecting Cucurbitaceae vegetables, how to identify them, and organic strategies for protection.

Powdery Mildew: Powdery mildew is a fungal disease that affects many Cucurbitaceae plants, including squash, cucumbers, melons, and pumpkins. It appears as white, powdery spots on the leaves, stems, and fruit surfaces, eventually causing leaves to yellow, wither, and drop.

To manage powdery mildew organically, ensure proper spacing between plants for good air circulation, water plants at the base to avoid wetting the foliage, and remove infected plant material promptly. Applying a homemade or commercially available organic fungicide, such as a baking soda solution or sulfur-based spray, can help prevent and control the spread of powdery mildew.

Downy Mildew: Downy mildew is another fungal disease that affects Cucurbitaceae vegetables, characterized by yellowish, irregular-shaped spots on the upper surface of leaves and a grayish-white, fuzzy growth on the underside. Downy mildew thrives in cool, damp conditions and can cause significant defoliation and reduced yields.

To protect your plants organically, practice proper plant spacing, water early in the day, and avoid overhead watering. Remove infected plant material and use organic fungicides, such as copper-based sprays, to prevent and control the disease.

Bacterial Wilt: Bacterial wilt is a devastating disease that primarily affects cucumbers and melons, caused by the bacterium Erwinia tracheiphila. It is transmitted by cucumber beetles, which introduce the bacteria into the plant as they feed. Infected plants initially exhibit wilting leaves, followed by rapid wilting and death of the entire plant.

To manage bacterial wilt organically, focus on controlling cucumber beetle populations using companion planting, physical barriers, or organic pesticides like neem oil. Remove and dispose of infected plants promptly to prevent the spread of the disease.

Fusarium Wilt: Fusarium wilt is a soil-borne fungal disease that affects various Cucurbitaceae vegetables, causing yellowing and wilting of the leaves, often on one side of the plant. As the disease progresses, the entire plant may wilt and die.

To protect your plants organically, practice crop rotation, maintain a balanced soil pH, and avoid overwatering. Adding organic matter and beneficial microbes to the soil can help improve its health and suppress the growth of Fusarium fungi.

Anthracnose: Anthracnose is a fungal disease that affects many Cucurbitaceae vegetables, causing small, water-soaked spots on leaves, stems, and fruits. These spots eventually enlarge, darken, and become sunken, leading to defoliation and fruit rot.

To manage anthracnose organically, practice proper plant spacing, water at the base of the plants, and remove infected plant material. Apply organic fungicides, such as copper-based sprays, or biological controls, like Bacillus subtilis, to prevent and control the disease.

Understanding the diseases that trouble the diverse veggies in the Cucurbitaceae family and applying organic defense tactics is indispensable for companion planting. By preserving a vigorous garden atmosphere and embracing eco-friendly practices, you can mitigate the effect of these diseases and foster a flourishing garden ecosystem that showers benefits on both Cucurbitaceae vegetables and their companion plants.

HARVESTING CUCURBITACEAE VEGETABLE PLANTS

The duration from planting to harvest varies for different vegetables within the Cucurbitaceae family. When companion planting, it is important to know when each vegetable is ready for harvest and how to harvest them properly to ensure the best quality and flavor. Here is a guide on the approximate time to harvest and proper harvesting techniques for various Cucurbitaceae vegetables.

Summer Squash: Summer squash varieties, including zucchini, yellow squash, and pattypan squash, typically take 40 to 60 days from planting to reach harvest maturity. Harvest summer squash when they are young and tender, as their flavor and texture are best at this stage.

Zucchini and yellow squash should be harvested when they are 6 to 8 inches (15 to 20 cm) long, while pattypan squash should be picked when they are 2 to 3 inches (5 to 7.5 cm) in diameter. Use a sharp knife or pruning shears to cut the squash from the vine, leaving a short stub of the stem attached to the fruit.

Winter Squash: Winter squash plants, such as butternut, acorn, and spaghetti squash, have a longer growing season than summer squash, generally taking 80 to 110 days from planting to reach harvest maturity. Harvest winter squash when the rind has hardened and developed a deep, uniform color. The stem should be dry and slightly shriveled. Use a sharp knife or pruning shears to cut the squash from the vine, leaving about 1-2 inches (2.5-5 cm) of stem attached to the fruit. This helps prevent rot and extends storage life.

Cucumbers: Cucumbers are usually ready for harvest 50 to 70 days after planting, depending on the variety. Pick cucumbers when they reach their desired size and before they become overripe, as they can become bitter and develop tough seeds.

Slicing cucumbers should be harvested when they are 6 to 8 inches (15 to 20 cm) long while pickling cucumbers should be picked at 3 to 4 inches (7.5 to 10 cm) long. Use a sharp knife or pruning shears to cut the cucumbers from the vine, taking care not to damage the plant.

Melons: Melons, including cantaloupe and honeydew, typically take 70 to 100 days from planting to reach harvest maturity. Harvest cantaloupe when the fruit easily separates from the vine with a slight twist, indicating that it is ripe. The melon should have a sweet, musky aroma and a slightly soft blossom end.

Honeydew melons should be harvested when they develop a creamy white or yellowish color and the blossom end becomes somewhat soft. Use a sharp knife or pruning shears to cut the melons from the vine, leaving a short stub of the stem attached to the fruit.

Pumpkins: Pumpkins are usually ready for harvest 90 to 120 days after planting, depending on the variety. Harvest pumpkins when the rind has hardened, developed a deep, uniform color, and the stem is dry and slightly shriveled.

The pumpkin should sound hollow when tapped. Use a sharp knife or pruning shears to cut the pumpkin from the vine, leaving 3-4 inches (7.5-10 cm) of stem attached to the fruit. This helps prevent rot and extends storage life.

Understanding the perfect timing for harvesting the vegetables in the Cucurbitaceae family and mastering the art of proper harvesting is vital in companion planting. By plucking your homegrown veggies at the right moments and employing appropriate techniques, you can guarantee quality, delectable flavor, and extended storage life. This, in turn, leads to a fruitful and triumphant garden bounty.

CROP ROTATION FOR CUCURBITACEAE VEGETABLE PLANTS

Crop rotation is the practice of planting different types of crops in a specific order and location within the garden over several seasons. This method helps maintain soil fertility, reduce the buildup of pests and diseases, and promote a balanced, healthy garden ecosystem.

When companion planting with Cucurbitaceae vegetables, incorporating proper crop rotation techniques is essential for ensuring long-term garden success. Here's a guide on how crop rotation works for Cucurbitaceae vegetables when companion planting.

Maintaining Soil Fertility: Different types of plants have varying nutrient requirements and contribute to soil fertility in unique ways. By rotating Cucurbitaceae vegetables with crops that have different nutrient needs or that add nutrients back into the soil, such as legumes, you can prevent the depletion of specific nutrients from the soil. For example, after growing heavy feeders like squash or pumpkins, plant nitrogen-fixing legumes like beans or peas to replenish nitrogen levels in the soil naturally.

Reducing Pest and Disease Buildup: Many pests and diseases are specific to certain plant families, including the Cucurbitaceae family. By practicing crop rotation, you can disrupt the life cycles of these pests and diseases, reducing their prevalence in your garden. Avoid planting Cucurbitaceae vegetables or their close relatives in the same garden location for at least two to three years. This helps prevent the buildup of soil-borne pathogens and pests, such as Fusarium wilt, bacterial wilt, and cucumber beetles, which can target these plants.

Promoting Biodiversity: Crop rotation encourages biodiversity in the garden, which contributes to a more balanced and resilient ecosystem. By rotating Cucurbitaceae vegetables with different plant families, you can create a diverse environment that supports various beneficial insects, pollinators, and soil microorganisms. This diversity helps create a more stable garden ecosystem that can better withstand pest infestations, disease outbreaks, and other challenges.

Implementing Crop Rotation With Companion Planting: When companion planting with Cucurbitaceae vegetables, consider the nutrient requirements, pest, and disease susceptibilities of both the squash family plants and their companions. Plan your garden layout and planting schedule to ensure that you are rotating crops from different plant families in each garden bed or area over time.

For example, after growing a Cucurbitaceae companion planting group, such as cucumbers with beans and marigolds, you might follow it with a brassica companion planting group, like cabbage with onions and calendula. This approach ensures that you are effectively rotating crops while still benefiting from the advantages of companion planting.

To sum up, integrating crop rotation with Cucurbitaceae vegetables in your companion planting strategy is key to nurturing a vibrant and fruitful garden. By adhering to these guidelines, you can supercharge soil fertility, keep pest and disease woes at bay, and foster a balanced garden ecosystem. This not only paves the way for the triumph of your Cucurbitaceae veggies and their companion plants, but it also bolsters eco-friendly gardening practices that are a boon for your garden and Mother Nature.

CHAPTER 6
LEGUMINOSAE "PEA" FAMILY COMPANION PLANTING

The Leguminosae family, also known as Fabaceae, is a diverse and essential group of plants that play a crucial role in vegetable companion planting. Among the many members of this family, peas are a popular and highly valued garden crop, offering numerous benefits for both gardeners and fellow plants.

As nitrogen-fixing legumes, peas have the remarkable ability to convert atmospheric nitrogen into a form that can be readily absorbed by plants, enriching the soil and promoting healthy growth of their companions. By incorporating peas into your companion planting strategy, you can support a thriving garden ecosystem, improve soil fertility, and enjoy a bountiful harvest of delicious, nutrient-rich vegetables.

Incorporating companion plants from the Leguminosae family into your garden can offer a multitude of benefits that contribute to a healthy and productive ecosystem. As nitrogen-fixing plants, members of this family, such as peas, beans, and lentils, have symbiotic relationships with bacteria in their root nodules, which enables them to convert atmospheric nitrogen into a form that is readily available for other plants.

This natural process enriches the soil, reducing the need for synthetic fertilizers and promoting vigorous growth among neighboring plants. Additionally, Leguminosae companions provide valuable habitat and support for beneficial insects, such as ladybugs, lacewings, and parasitic wasps, which help control pest populations.

Moreover, these companion plants can act as living mulch, shading the soil, conserving moisture, and suppressing weed growth. By integrating plants from the Leguminosae family into your garden, you can harness their unique qualities to create a flourishing, sustainable environment that benefits both your plants and the surrounding ecosystem.

LEGUMINOSAE FAMILY VEGETABLE PLANTS

The Leguminosae family, also known as Fabaceae or the pea family, is a diverse group of plants that offer numerous benefits for vegetable companion planting. These nitrogen-fixing legumes are well known for their ability to enrich the soil and promote healthy growth among neighboring plants. Here are some of the most popular vegetables within the Leguminosae family that can be used for companion planting.

Peas: Peas are a versatile and delicious legume that thrive in cooler temperatures, making them an ideal early-season crop. They come in various types, such as snow peas, snap peas, and garden peas, each with unique characteristics and flavors.

Peas are excellent companions for plants like cucumbers, carrots, radishes, and brassicas, as they help improve soil fertility and provide natural support for climbing plants. Additionally, peas can be interplanted with leafy greens like lettuce and spinach, which benefit from the shade provided by the taller pea plants.

Beans: Beans are another popular vegetable within the Leguminosae family, offering a wide range of varieties, including green beans, pole beans, bush beans, and dried beans. Like peas, beans contribute to soil fertility by fixing nitrogen, making them beneficial companions for heavy feeders like corn, tomatoes, and squash.

Beans also provide habitat and support for beneficial insects, helping to control pests like aphids and spider mites. When planted with aromatic herbs like basil, rosemary, or marigolds, beans can benefit from their pest-repellent properties and enhanced flavor.

Lentils: Lentils are a highly nutritious legume and an excellent choice for companion planting in the garden. They can be grown alongside plants like tomatoes, peppers, and eggplants, where they help improve soil fertility and provide a natural mulch that suppresses weeds and conserves moisture.

Lentils also attract beneficial insects like ladybugs and lacewings, which help control pest populations and maintain a balanced garden ecosystem.

Chickpeas: Chickpeas, also known as garbanzo beans, are another valuable member of the Leguminosae family. They can be grown in tandem with plants like kale, cabbage, and cauliflower, as they help enrich the soil with nitrogen and provide support for taller, heavier plants. Chickpeas also work well planted near aromatic herbs like parsley, cilantro, and dill, which repel pests and enhance the flavor of the chickpeas.

Soybeans: Soybeans are a versatile and protein-rich legume that can be used for companion planting in the garden. As nitrogen-fixers, they are beneficial when grown alongside crops like corn, potatoes, and squash, which have high nutrient demands. Soybeans can also be interplanted with small grains like wheat or barley to improve soil structure and suppress weeds.

The veggies nestled within the Leguminosae pea family bring a vibrant array of benefits to the table for companion planting. By weaving these nitrogen-boosting legumes into your garden tapestry, you can amp up soil fertility, champion beneficial insects, hold onto precious moisture, and keep weeds in check. This all culminates in a sustainable garden ecosystem that thrives season after season.

CHAPTER 6

LEGUMINOSAE FAMILY COMPANION VEGETABLES

Companion planting is an essential aspect of sustainable gardening, as it can promote plant health, prevent pests, and improve soil quality. When it comes to the Leguminosae family choosing the right companion plants is crucial for ensuring a thriving vegetable garden. Here are some excellent companion plants for Leguminosae family vegetables and tips on selecting the best ones.

Brassica Family: The Brassica family, which includes cabbage, broccoli, cauliflower, kale, and Brussels sprouts, makes excellent companions for Leguminosae plants. These vegetables are heavy feeders and require a lot of nutrients from the soil.

Legumes, on the other hand, are nitrogen-fixing plants, meaning they can convert atmospheric nitrogen into a form that is usable by plants. By planting Brassicas alongside Leguminosae vegetables, you can ensure that there is enough nitrogen in the soil for both types of plants to grow well.

Allium Family: Onions, garlic, leeks, and shallots belong to the Allium family, which can be beneficial when planted near Leguminosae vegetables. Allium plants have a strong scent that can deter pests such as aphids and spider mites, which can be harmful to legumes. In addition, their deep root systems help break up compacted soil, making it easier for legume roots to penetrate and access nutrients.

Root Vegetables: Root vegetables like carrots, radishes, and turnips can also make great companions for Leguminosae plants. These vegetables grow well in the same soil conditions as legumes, and their roots help to aerate the soil, improving drainage and nutrient uptake for all plants in the vicinity.

Additionally, the foliage of root vegetables can provide shade and ground cover for legumes, helping to conserve moisture and suppress weeds.

Marigolds: While not a vegetable, marigolds are a popular companion plant for many types of vegetables, including those in the Leguminosae family. Marigolds release chemicals that repel nematodes, microscopic worms that attack the roots of plants. Planting marigolds near your legumes can help protect them from these harmful pests.

When selecting companion plants for your Leguminosae family vegetables, consider the following tips:

Assess your garden's specific needs: Take note of any pest problems, soil conditions, or other factors that may impact the growth of your plants. Choose companion plants that can address these issues and support the overall health of your garden.

Plan your planting layout: Arrange your plants in a way that maximizes their benefits to one another. For example, plant taller vegetables like corn or sunflowers on the north side of your garden so they don't shade your legumes. Also, consider intercropping or planting different types of plants in alternating rows to encourage biodiversity and create a more resilient ecosystem.

Rotate your crops: To maintain soil health and prevent the build-up of pests and diseases, rotate your crops each year. Avoid planting the same type of plant in the same location for at least three years.

Companion planting with veggies from the Leguminosae family can work wonders for your garden, enhancing soil quality, warding off pests, and boosting overall plant vitality. By judiciously picking the perfect companion plants and deploying well-considered planting tactics, you can breathe life into a flourishing, sustainable vegetable haven.

LEGUMINOSAE FAMILY NON-COMPANION PLANTS

Companion planting, the practice of planting different species together to the benefit of one or both, is a popular strategy among gardeners. However, not every plant makes a good neighbor for every other. For plants in the Leguminosae family, which includes peas, beans, lentils, and peanuts, there are certain types of vegetables you may want to avoid planting nearby.

Allium: Firstly, plants from the Allium family, such as onions, garlic, leeks, and shallots, tend not to be compatible with legumes. Alliums can inhibit the growth of legumes, due to their strong aroma and the substances they release into the soil. They also compete for similar nutrients, which can result in stunted growth and reduced yields for your legumes.

Solanaceae: Secondly, members of the Solanaceae family, including tomatoes, peppers, eggplants, and potatoes, don't typically coexist well with legumes. These plants can compete for the same nutrients in the soil, making it harder for the legumes to thrive. Moreover, these plants often attract similar pests, which can lead to an increased risk of infestation in your garden.

Other Legumes: Another surprising group of plants that legumes do not get along with are other legumes. This may seem counterintuitive since they belong to the same family, but these plants actually compete for the same resources in the soil. Planting too many legumes together can lead to nutrient depletion and a less productive harvest.

Brassicaceae: Lastly, avoid companion planting legumes with vegetables from the Brassicaceae family, such as cabbage, broccoli, cauliflower, and kale. These plants are heavy feeders and require a lot of space to grow, which can crowd out legumes and limit their growth.

While companion planting can serve as a powerful ally in amplifying your garden's yield, it's crucial to be aware of the plant pairings that don't play well together. To secure a lavish harvest from your legumes, steer clear of planting them in close quarters with Alliums, Solanaceae, fellow legumes, and Brassicaceae.

THE RIGHT SOIL FOR LEGUMINOSAE FAMILY VEGETABLES

The Leguminosae family encompasses a variety of vegetables that each have unique soil requirements. Understanding these preferences can help you optimize your garden's productivity, particularly when employing companion planting strategies.

Peas: Peas thrive in well-drained, loamy soil with a pH level ranging from 6.0 to 7.5. This slightly acidic to neutral pH supports the symbiotic bacteria that allow peas to fix nitrogen in the soil, which benefits their companion plants. Peas are often grown with carrots, cucumbers, and potatoes, which all appreciate the enriched soil conditions.

Beans: Beans prefer a similar soil type to peas, leaning towards well-drained, sandy, or loamy soil. The pH should be slightly acidic to neutral, between 6.0 and 7.0. This soil condition supports the beans' nitrogen-fixing bacteria, which benefits companion plants like corn and squash.

The beans enrich the soil with nitrogen, the corn provides a trellis for the beans, and the squash acts as ground cover, conserving soil moisture.

Chickpeas: Chickpeas, another legume, prefer well-drained soil with a pH range of 6.0 to 7.0. They are drought-tolerant and can thrive in poor soil conditions, but they perform best in sandy, loamy soil. Chickpeas fix nitrogen in the soil, making them excellent companions for heavy feeders like broccoli and kale.

Soybeans: Soybeans thrive in well-drained, loamy soil with a neutral to slightly acidic pH. Like other legumes, soybeans are heavy feeders but also contribute to soil fertility by fixing nitrogen. They make good companions for corn, helping to keep the soil rich for this nutrient-demanding plant.

Lentils: Lentils, on the other hand, prefer sandy or silty soil with good drainage. The pH should be neutral, around 7.0. This soil condition helps lentils fix nitrogen, which can benefit leafy greens and root vegetables like radishes when used in a crop rotation system.

Gaining insights into the soil preferences of each member of the Leguminosae family, such as peas, beans, chickpeas, soybeans, and lentils, can significantly supercharge your companion planting endeavors. By tailoring the soil conditions to meet these plants' needs, you can pave the way for a more robust and bountiful garden.

SOWING LEGUMINOSAE FAMILY VEGETABLES

CORRECT SEASON TO SOW LEGUMINOSAE VEGETABLE PLANTS

Planting vegetables in the Leguminosae, or pea family, in the right season is essential for effective companion planting. This family includes cool-season crops like peas, lentils, and certain types of beans. These plants typically prefer cooler temperatures and can often withstand light frosts, making them ideal for planting in early spring or late summer for a fall harvest.

Planting Leguminosae in the appropriate season ensures they grow during their optimal climate conditions, leading to healthier plants, better yields, and fewer pest and disease problems. Moreover, when you sow these plants in the correct season, it allows for effective coordination with their companion plants. For example, planting peas next to carrots can help deter pests like carrot flies, but this benefit would be lost if the two crops are not growing at the same time.

Furthermore, legumes have the unique ability to fix nitrogen in the soil, which can benefit many other plants, but only if those plants are growing concurrently. Therefore, understanding the seasonal preferences of your Leguminosae vegetables and aligning their growth with their companion plants is a crucial component of successful vegetable companion planting.

Peas: Peas are cool-season crops and are typically one of the first vegetables planted in spring. They can be planted as soon as the soil can be worked, usually 4-6 weeks before the last spring frost. For a fall harvest, peas can also be sown 8-10 weeks before the first expected fall frost. Peas prefer cooler weather and will stop producing once temperatures exceed 70-75°F.

Beans: Beans, including green, lima, and snap varieties, are warm-season crops. They should be planted after the danger of frost has passed and the soil has warmed to at least 60°F, usually 1-2 weeks after the last spring frost. Beans do not tolerate frost, and their growth can be stunted by cool temperatures, so ensure the weather is reliably warm before planting.

Chickpeas: Chickpeas, also known as garbanzo beans, are typically sown in late spring. They prefer cooler weather than most legumes but should still be planted after the risk of frost has passed. Chickpeas are drought-tolerant and can be successfully grown in areas with hot, dry summers.

Soybeans: Soybeans are also warm-season crops and should be planted in late spring to early summer once soil temperatures reach 55-60°F. Soybeans require a long growing season and need to be planted early enough to mature before the first fall frost.

Lentils: Lentils, like peas, are cool-season crops and can tolerate light frosts. They can be sown in early spring as soon as the soil can be worked. In warmer regions, lentils can also be planted in late fall for a winter crop.

Grasping the ideal sowing seasons for each vegetable within the Leguminosae family is a surefire way to reap a successful harvest. By aligning your plantings with the rhythm of each plant's natural growth cycle, you can harness their full potential and cultivate a garden that brims with productivity and vitality.

PLANTING NEEDS & REQUIREMENTS

Germinating the different Leguminosae vegetable plants from seeds to seedlings correctly is a crucial step when companion planting. The germination process largely determines the initial health and vigor of these plants. Healthy seedlings are more likely to grow into strong, productive plants that can resist pests and diseases, ensuring a successful harvest.

Correct germination also guarantees that the plants start their life cycle at the right time, aligning with the growth patterns of their companion plants. This synchronization is essential in a companion planting setup, as the benefits of companion planting often depend on the simultaneous growth of different plants.

Germinating the different vegetables from the Leguminosae family from seeds to seedlings involves a few key steps. Understanding the optimal temperatures for germination and the right time for transplanting can significantly enhance your garden's success.

Peas: Starting with peas, begin by soaking the seeds in water for 24 hours to speed up germination. Sow the soaked seeds directly in the garden as soon as the soil can be worked in the spring, ideally when soil temperatures are around 45°F.

Plant the seeds about 1 inch deep and 2 inches apart. Pea seedlings are ready to be transplanted when they have at least two sets of true leaves, but they generally do best when sown directly where they will grow.

Beans: Beans should be sown directly into the garden after the danger of frost has passed and the soil has warmed to at least 60°F. Plant the seeds 1 inch deep and 2 to 4 inches apart. Beans typically germinate within 8 to 10 days under optimal conditions.

Like peas, beans do best when sown directly in their final growing location, but if necessary, they can be transplanted when they have developed their first set of true leaves.

Chickpeas: Chickpeas, or garbanzo beans, should also be planted directly in the garden after the last expected frost when soil temperatures reach 60°F. Sow the seeds 1-2 inches deep and 3-4 inches apart.

Chickpea seeds typically germinate within 7 to 14 days. They can be transplanted when they have at least one set of true leaves, but they prefer to be sown directly where they will grow.

Soybeans: Soybeans should be sown directly into the garden once soil temperatures reach 55-60°F, usually in late spring to early summer. Plant the seeds 1-2 inches deep and 2-4 inches apart. Soybeans usually germinate within 6 to 14 days. Soybean seedlings can be transplanted when they have developed their first set of true leaves, but they generally prefer direct sowing.

Lentils: Lentils should be sown directly into the garden as soon as the soil can be worked in early spring. Plant the seeds 1 inch deep and 1 to 2 inches apart. Lentils typically germinate within 7 to 10 days when soil temperatures are around 40°F. Like other legumes, lentils prefer to be sown directly where they will grow, but if needed, they can be transplanted when they have at least two sets of true leaves.

Getting to grips with the germination needs and transplantation stages of the Leguminosae family veggies can be the difference in creating a healthier, more fruitful garden. By adhering to these steps, you can guide your seeds on their journey to becoming robust, flourishing plants.

SPACING & MEASUREMENTS

Proper spacing and measurements when transplanting Leguminosae vegetable seedlings are crucial components of successful companion planting. Each plant in the Leguminosae family, from peas to lentils, requires a certain amount of space to grow and thrive. This space allows for adequate root development, ensures that each plant receives enough sunlight, and promotes good air circulation, which can help prevent the spread of diseases.

In a companion planting setup, correct spacing also plays a role in the symbiotic relationships between plants. For instance, some plants may provide ground cover or shade for others, and proper spacing is needed for these interactions to occur effectively.

Overcrowding can lead to competition for resources, hindering the growth and productivity of your plants. Therefore, adhering to recommended spacing guidelines when transplanting your legume seedlings can significantly enhance the health and yield of both your Leguminosae vegetables and their companion plants.

Peas: Peas should be sown about 1 inch deep and 2 inches apart in rows that are 18 to 24 inches apart. This allows enough room for the peas to grow without overcrowding, ensuring each plant gets enough sunlight and nutrients. When the seedlings emerge, thin them out if necessary to maintain this spacing.

Beans: Beans should be planted about 1 inch deep and 2 to 4 inches apart in rows that are 24 to 36 inches apart. This spacing gives the beans enough room to grow and ensures good air circulation, which can help prevent disease. If you're growing pole beans, which climb and need support, space the plants about 6 inches apart.

Chickpeas: For chickpeas, sow the seeds 1-2 inches deep and 3-4 inches apart in rows that are 18 to 24 inches apart. Chickpeas need plenty of space for air circulation to prevent fungal diseases. As the plants grow, they'll fill in the space between the rows.

Soybeans: Soybeans should be sown about 1-2 inches deep and 2-4 inches apart. The rows should be spaced about 24 to 30 inches apart. This spacing allows the soybean plants to spread out and ensures they get enough sunlight. Soybeans have a bushy growth habit, so they need plenty of space to grow.

Lentils: Lastly lentils should be sown about 1 inch deep and 1 to 2 inches apart in rows that are 12 to 18 inches apart. Like other legumes, lentils need adequate spacing for proper growth and disease prevention. They have a bushy growth habit and will fill in the space between rows as they grow.

Precision in spacing and measurements when embedding Leguminosae vegetable seedlings is key to providing each plant with ample room to stretch, as well as access to sunlight and nutrients. These handy guidelines can serve as your blueprint in designing your garden layout and squeezing out the maximum yield from your harvest.

MAINTAINING LEGUMINOSAE VEGETABLE PLANTS

Maintaining your Leguminosae vegetable plants is essential in vegetable companion gardening for several reasons. First, healthy legumes can enrich the soil with nitrogen, benefiting their companion plants. If the legumes are not well-maintained and become unhealthy, this beneficial nitrogen-fixing process can be compromised.

Second, proper maintenance, including correct watering, pest control, and pruning, can prevent diseases and pest infestations that could spread to nearby companion plants. Third, well-maintained legumes will be more productive, providing a better yield of peas, beans, chickpeas, soybeans, or lentils. This productivity can indirectly benefit companion plants by attracting more pollinators to the garden or by providing shade or support to other plants. Therefore, regular and attentive care of your Leguminosae vegetable plants is a key factor in the success of your vegetable companion garden.

PRUNING AND THINNING LEGUMINOSAE VEGETABLE PLANTS

Pruning and thinning vegetable plants within the Leguminosae family is an essential practice in vegetable companion planting. Pruning involves removing specific parts of a plant, such as dead or overgrown branches, to improve its overall health and productivity.

CHAPTER 6

This process allows the plant to focus its energy on growing fruit rather than unnecessary foliage. In a companion planting setup, pruning can help ensure that all plants receive adequate sunlight and aren't overshadowed by their neighbors. On the other hand, thinning is the process of removing excess plants to prevent overcrowding and competition for nutrients, water, and sunlight.

For legumes, this is particularly important as these plants fix nitrogen in the soil, benefiting their companions. Overcrowding can lead to a strain on this process and reduce the overall health and productivity of the garden. Therefore, regular pruning and thinning are integral to maintaining a balanced, healthy, and productive vegetable companion garden.

The Leguminosae family, also known as Fabaceae, is a diverse plant family that includes peas, beans, chickpeas, soybeans, and lentils. These vegetables are highly beneficial for companion planting, however to maximize the growth and productivity of these plants, it's essential to understand when and how to prune and thin them during their various growth stages.

Peas: Starting with peas, they generally do not require much pruning. However, if you notice the plant becoming too tall and overshadowing its companion plants, you can pinch off the tops to encourage more lateral growth. Thinning of pea plants should occur around 2 weeks after germination, leaving approximately 2-4 inches between each plant. This allows enough space for peas to grow without competing for resources.

Beans: Beans, both bush and pole types, need minimal pruning. But if you're growing pole beans and they reach the top of their supports, pinching off the tops can promote bushier growth and higher yields. Thinning of bean plants should be done about 2-3 weeks after planting, ensuring there's about 6 inches of space between each plant.

Chickpeas: Chickpeas, like other legumes, do not require much pruning. Any diseased or damaged parts should be removed promptly to prevent the spread of disease. Thinning chickpeas should occur when the plants are about 1-2 inches tall, leaving about 4-5 inches between plants.

Soybeans: Soybeans are another legume that doesn't typically need extensive pruning. However, if the plants become too dense, light pruning can help improve air circulation and sunlight penetration. Thinning is not usually necessary for soybeans since they naturally spread out as they grow.

Lentils: Lastly, we have lentils. These plants also don't need much pruning, but any diseased or damaged parts should be removed as soon as possible. Lentils should be thinned when they're about 1-2 inches tall, leaving 4-5 inches between plants.

In all cases, when companion planting, always consider the needs and habits of the companion plants. Make sure your legumes are not overshadowing or crowding them. The goal is to create a harmonious growing environment where each plant has access to sufficient sunlight, air, and nutrients.

Always use clean, sharp tools when pruning or thinning to minimize damage and prevent the spread of diseases. With proper care and attention, your Leguminosae vegetables and their companions can thrive together, leading to a bountiful and healthy garden.

CHAPTER 6

WATERING LEGUMINOSAE VEGETABLE PLANTS

Watering is a crucial aspect of gardening, especially when it comes to companion planting with the Leguminosae family of vegetables. These vegetables, like all living organisms, need water to survive and thrive. Water aids in nutrient absorption from the soil and is essential for photosynthesis, the process by which plants convert sunlight into chemical energy.

In a companion planting setup, consistent and proper watering ensures that all plants receive the moisture they need without any one species dominating the water supply. It helps maintain the balance of the ecosystem and promotes healthy growth for all plants involved. Over or underwatering can lead to various plant diseases, hinder growth, or even result in plant death. Thus, understanding the specific watering needs of your legumes and their companion plants is key to creating a successful, productive garden.

Peas, for instance, require consistent moisture, especially during the flowering and pod development stages. They prefer deep watering to shallow, frequent watering as it encourages deeper root growth. The soil should be allowed to dry slightly between waterings to prevent waterlogging.

Aim for about 1 to 1.5 inches of water per week, depending on the weather conditions. Early morning is the best time to water peas to minimize evaporation and allow the foliage to dry throughout the day.

Beans, both bush and pole varieties, also need regular watering, but the soil should not be waterlogged. A good rule of thumb is to provide about 1 inch of water per week, but this may need to be increased during hot, dry spells. Water the beans in the early morning at the base of the plant to avoid wetting the foliage, which can lead to disease.

Chickpeas are relatively drought-tolerant and do not require as much water as other legumes. However, they do need a consistent supply of water, especially during their early growth stages and flowering period. Aim for about 1 inch of water per week, but let the top layer of soil dry out between waterings to prevent waterlogging.

Soybeans require regular watering, especially during the flowering and pod-filling stages. Provide about 1 inch of water per week, but increase this amount during dry periods. As with other legumes, water in the early morning at the base of the plant.

Lentils prefer evenly moist soil. They should be watered deeply and allowed to dry out slightly between watering sessions. Aim for about 1 inch of water per week, adjusting as needed based on weather conditions.

In all cases, when companion planting, consider the water needs of the companion plants as well. The goal is to create a watering schedule that meets the needs of all the plants in the garden. By understanding the specific watering needs of each plant and adjusting your watering practices accordingly, you can create a harmonious and productive garden.

ORGANIC FERTILISATION FOR LEGUMINOSAE VEGETABLE PLANTS

Organic fertilization is particularly important for the Leguminosae vegetable family when companion planting because it helps to nourish not only the legumes but also their companion plants.

CHAPTER 6

Leguminosae vegetables, including peas, beans, chickpeas, soybeans, and lentils, are known for their nitrogen-fixing abilities, thanks to a symbiotic relationship with bacteria in their root nodules. However, these plants also need other essential nutrients that organic fertilizers can provide, such as phosphorus, potassium, and a range of trace minerals.

Organic fertilizers improve the overall soil structure, making it more fertile and better at retaining water, which benefits all plants in the garden. They also promote a healthy, diverse ecosystem of beneficial microorganisms in the soil, which can help protect the plants against diseases and pests.

By using organic fertilizers, you're not just feeding the plants, you're enriching the entire soil ecosystem, leading to healthier, more productive plants.

Organic fertilization is crucial for the growth and development of the Leguminosae family of vegetables. Each of these plants has unique nutritional requirements that need to be met, especially when companion planting.

Peas are nitrogen-fixing plants, meaning they can take nitrogen from the atmosphere and convert it into a form that plants can use. However, they also require phosphorus and potassium for robust growth.

An organic fertilizer high in these nutrients, such as bone meal or rock phosphate for phosphorus and greensand or sulfate of potash for potassium, can be beneficial. Apply the fertilizer at planting time, mixing it into the soil.

Beans, both bush and pole types, also fix nitrogen but need phosphorus, potassium, and calcium for best results. Bone meal or rock phosphate can provide phosphorus, greensand, or sulfate of potash for potassium and dolomite lime for calcium. Fertilize at planting time and again when the plants begin to flower.

Chickpeas, like other legumes, are nitrogen-fixers but also need phosphorus and potassium. The same organic fertilizers recommended for peas and beans can be used for chickpeas. Fertilize at planting time and again when the plants start to flower.

Soybeans require a balanced nutrient supply. They benefit from a complete organic fertilizer that contains nitrogen, phosphorus, and potassium. Compost or well-rotted manure can also be beneficial. Fertilize at planting time and again when the plants begin to flower.

Lentils need a balanced supply of nutrients as well. A complete organic fertilizer or compost can meet their needs. Fertilize at planting time and again when the plants start to flower.

In every scenario of companion planting, it's essential to take into account the dietary needs of your companion plants. For instance, some plants may not tolerate high nitrogen levels, while others may have their own unique nutrient demands.

By getting to know the specific nutritional needs of each plant and tweaking your fertilizing routines to suit them, you can foster a garden that thrives in harmony and productivity.

CHAPTER 6

PROTECTING LEGUMINOSAE VEGETABLE PLANTS

EXTREME TEMPERATURES

Protecting vegetables in the Leguminosae family, from extreme temperatures is crucial for their survival and productivity. This becomes even more important when companion planting, as the plants are closely spaced and interdependent, making them more susceptible to shared stressors. Here are some strategies you can employ to shield these plants from both excessive heat and chilling cold.

Mulching: For protection against high temperatures, one of the most effective practices is mulching. Mulch serves multiple purposes: it cools the soil, retains moisture, suppresses weeds, and, as it breaks down, enriches the soil with organic matter.

Organic mulches such as straw, wood chips, or compost are excellent choices. During periods of extreme heat, early morning watering becomes crucial. By watering in the cool of the morning, you ensure that the water reaches the roots before it evaporates. For direct protection against the harsh sun, consider using shade cloths. These are especially useful for young plants that are not yet hardy enough to withstand intense sunlight.

Row Covers or Garden Fleece: To guard against cold temperatures, the use of row covers or garden fleece can be very beneficial. These coverings create a barrier against cold air, trapping heat from the soil and protecting plants from frost damage.

Additionally, watering the garden before a predicted frost can help protect your plants. This is because moist soil retains heat better than dry soil, releasing it slowly overnight and creating a warmer microclimate around the plants.

Companion Planting: Companion planting itself can offer some protection against temperature extremes. Taller plants can provide shade for shorter ones during hot weather and act as windbreaks in cold conditions. For example, planting beans at the base of corn allows the beans to climb and use the corn stalks for support, while the corn provides shade for the beans, helping to moderate temperature.

It's important to remember that each type of vegetable in the Leguminosae family has its own specific temperature preferences and tolerances. Peas, for example, are cool-season crops and can tolerate lower temperatures, while beans prefer warmer conditions.

Always take these preferences into account when planning your companion planting arrangement, and choose companion plants with similar temperature needs. By taking these steps, you can create a resilient and productive garden that can withstand temperature extremes.

PROTECTING LEGUMINOSAE VEGETABLES FROM PEST

The protection of vegetables in the Leguminosae family is critically important when companion planting. These plants can be susceptible to a variety of pests that can cause significant damage, impacting their growth, health, and yield. Pests can destroy leaves, stems, flowers, and pods and even transmit diseases. In a companion planting system, pests can easily spread from one plant to another due to the proximity of the plants.

However, companion planting can also offer pest management benefits, as certain plants can repel pests or attract beneficial insects that control pests. Therefore, the implementation of effective pest protection strategies is key to maintaining a healthy and productive Leguminosae vegetable garden. There are several strategies you can use to help keep these valuable plants pest-free.

One of the key benefits of companion planting is that it can naturally deter pests. Certain plants, when grown together, can repel insects that might otherwise damage their companions.

For instance, marigolds are known to deter nematodes and other garden pests, making them excellent companions for many legumes. Similarly, nasturtiums can repel aphids, a common pest for peas and beans.

Intercropping, or planting different crops in close proximity, can also confuse pests and make it harder for them to find their preferred host plants. This strategy can be particularly effective with legumes, which are often affected by pests like pea weevils and bean beetles. Planting them alongside unrelated crops can help to mask their presence and reduce pest numbers.

Another way to protect Leguminosae vegetables from pests is through regular monitoring and early intervention. Regularly check your plants for signs of pest activity, such as chewed leaves or the presence of larvae or eggs.

Early detection can allow you to manage a pest problem before it becomes an infestation. Physical removal of pests, use of organic insecticidal soaps, or introducing beneficial insects like ladybugs and lacewings can all be effective methods of control.

Plant health is another crucial factor in pest resistance. Healthy plants are more able to withstand pest attacks and less likely to attract pests in the first place. Ensuring your legumes have the right growing conditions, including adequate sunlight, well-drained soil, and sufficient nutrients, can go a long way toward keeping them healthy and pest-free.

Finally, crop rotation can be a useful strategy in pest management. Many garden pests are specific to certain plant families, and their eggs or larvae may overwinter in the soil. By changing what you plant in a particular area each year, you can disrupt the life cycles of these pests and reduce their populations.

By employing these strategies, you can protect your Leguminosae vegetables from pests and enhance the overall health and productivity of your garden.

PROTECTING LEGUMINOSAE VEGETABLES FROM DISEASES

Vegetables in the Leguminosae family are susceptible to several diseases that can impact their growth and productivity. However, with careful observation, early detection, and organic management techniques, it's possible to protect these plants and maintain a healthy garden, even when companion planting.

Powdery Mildew: One common disease that affects this family of plants is powdery mildew, a fungal disease characterized by white, powdery spots on leaves, stems, and pods.

This disease often occurs under conditions of high humidity and moderate temperatures.

To manage powdery mildew organically, ensure good air circulation around your plants and avoid overhead watering. Organic fungicides that contain sulfur or potassium bicarbonate can also be effective.

Fusarium Wilt: Fusarium wilt is another disease that can afflict legumes. This soil-borne fungus causes wilting and yellowing of leaves, stunted growth, and eventually plant death. To manage this disease organically, practice crop rotation to prevent the build-up of the fungus in the soil. Also, adding organic matter to the soil can help improve its structure and drainage, making conditions less favorable for the fungus.

Bean Rust: Bean rust is a disease-specific to beans, causing small, rust-colored spots on the undersides of leaves. The disease can lead to leaf drop and reduced yields. To manage bean rust organically, remove and destroy infected leaves or plants, and avoid working in the garden when it's wet, as this can spread the disease. Spraying with an organic copper-based fungicide can also help control the disease.

Anthracnose: Anthracnose, caused by the fungus Colletotrichum lindemuthianum, is another disease that particularly affects beans. It manifests as dark, sunken lesions on leaves, stems, and pods. Good sanitation practices, such as removing and destroying infected plant debris, combined with crop rotation, can help control Anthracnose organically. Spraying plants with compost tea can also boost their immunity and help them resist the disease.

Companion planting can be a useful strategy in disease management. Some plants have natural antifungal properties and can help reduce disease incidence when planted alongside legumes.

For example, garlic and onions can deter many types of fungal diseases. Similarly, marigolds can help suppress nematodes, microscopic worms that can cause root diseases.

In all cases, maintaining overall plant health is key to disease resistance. Healthy plants are more capable of resisting diseases and recovering from them. Ensuring your legumes have the right growing conditions, including adequate sunlight, well-drained soil, and proper nutrients, will go a long way toward keeping them healthy and disease-free.

By using these strategies, you can protect your Leguminosae vegetables from diseases and ensure a productive and vibrant garden.

HARVESTING LEGUMINOSAE VEGETABLE PLANTS

The Leguminosae family, or Fabaceae, includes a variety of vegetables that are highly nutritious and beneficial for the soil. When it comes to companion planting, these plants can share resources and protect each other from pests, potentially leading to healthier growth and an earlier harvest.

Chickpeas, also known as garbanzo beans, take around 100 to 110 days to mature after planting. When the leaves start to yellow and the pods become brown, it's time to harvest. You can either pick the individual pods or pull up the entire plant. After harvesting, let them dry in a well-ventilated place for a few weeks before threshing to remove the chickpeas.

Soybeans, another valuable legume, usually take between 90 to 150 days to mature, depending on the variety. Harvesting soybeans can be a bit tricky as they need to be picked at the right moisture content, ideally when the beans are at 13-14% moisture. The pods should be brown, and the seeds inside should be hard. Like chickpeas, the whole plant can be pulled up or cut at the base.

Beans, including varieties like green beans, kidney beans, and black beans, typically take between 45 to 75 days to reach maturity. The pods should be firm and crisp but not bulging with seeds. To harvest beans, gently hold the plant with one hand and pluck the beans with the other to avoid damaging the plant.

Peas are usually ready to harvest within 60 to 70 days after planting. The pods should be plump and green. Harvesting is similar to beans; hold the vine with one hand and gently pluck the pod with the other. It's best to consume peas soon after harvesting as their sugar quickly turns to starch.

Lentils require about 80 to 110 days to mature. Unlike peas and beans, lentils are typically harvested for their seeds, not pods. Lentils are ready to harvest when the pods have turned brown but are not yet brittle. The whole plant can be cut at the base and left to dry in a well-ventilated area before threshing to remove the seeds.

CROP ROTATION FOR LEGUMINOSAE VEGETABLE PLANTS

Crop rotation is an essential agricultural practice that involves growing different types of crops in the same area in sequenced seasons. This method is beneficial for nutrient management, pest control, and preventing soil degradation, making it a vital tool for organic farming and gardening when applied to the vegetables in the Leguminosae family.

The Leguminosae family is well known for its ability to fix nitrogen from the atmosphere through a symbiotic relationship with bacteria in its root nodules. This process converts atmospheric nitrogen into a form that plants can use, effectively enriching the soil with this essential nutrient. Thus, legumes are often used in crop rotation plans to replenish nitrogen levels in the soil.

In a typical crop rotation cycle involving legumes, a nitrogen-fixing legume plant might be followed by a leafy vegetable that requires a high amount of nitrogen, like spinach or lettuce. After harvesting the leafy greens, a vegetable plant like tomatoes or peppers, which also need a fair amount of nitrogen but not as much as leafy greens, could be planted.

Finally, a root vegetable such as carrots or beets, which require less nitrogen, could be grown. This sequence takes advantage of the nitrogen added by the legumes and ensures balanced nutrient use over time.

Companion planting can be incorporated into this rotation scheme to further enhance its benefits. For example, beans (Leguminosae) could be companion planted with corn and

CHAPTER 6

squash, a trio often referred to as the "Three Sisters." The corn provides a natural trellis for the beans, the beans enrich the soil with nitrogen, and the squash acts as a living mulch, suppressing weeds and conserving soil moisture. After this trio, a leafy green could be grown in the same spot in the next season to utilize the nitrogen left by the beans.

It's important to remember that each garden is unique, and what works best may depend on specific local conditions and plant varieties. However, by understanding the principles of crop rotation and companion planting, gardeners can create a thriving, sustainable environment for growing the nutritious and diverse vegetables of the Leguminosae family.

CHAPTER 7
SOLANACEAE "NIGHTSHADE" FAMILY COMPANION PLANTING

The Solanaceae, commonly known as the "Nightshade" family, is a crucial aspect of vegetable companion planting, a practice that leverages the symbiotic relationships between different plant species to enhance growth and productivity. This family encompasses a wide array of familiar vegetables, including tomatoes, potatoes, peppers, and eggplants.

CHAPTER 7

Each of these plants brings unique characteristics to the table, from their nutrient requirements to their pest resistance, making them valuable players in a well-planned garden. However, it's worth noting that these nightshade vegetables, while beneficial, can also share common vulnerabilities to certain diseases and pests.

Therefore, understanding the specific needs and interactions of these plants within the Nightshade family is essential for effective companion planting. Proper placement can lead to improved soil health, better pest control, and, ultimately, a more bountiful harvest.

Implementing companion planting strategies with vegetables in the Solanaceae, or "Nightshade" family, can offer numerous benefits to your garden. For instance, tomatoes and basil not only complement each other flavor-wise but also in the garden; basil can repel insects harmful to tomatoes, while tomatoes provide a favorable microclimate for basil.

Similarly, planting marigolds near these vegetables can deter nematodes, which often plague members of the Solanaceae family. Moreover, companion planting increases biodiversity, fostering a healthier, more resilient garden ecosystem. This practice aids in improving soil quality, promoting beneficial insect activity, and maintaining a balanced nutrient cycle.

Additionally, it allows for efficient use of garden space, as certain plant pairings can maximize yield in a given area. However, it's important to remember that careful planning is necessary, as improper pairings within this family can result in shared vulnerabilities to pests and diseases.

SOLANACEAE FAMILY VEGETABLE PLANTS

The Solanaceae, or Nightshade family, encompasses a wide array of vegetables that are integral to many cuisines worldwide. These plants share common characteristics and growth requirements, making them suitable for companion planting.

Tomatoes are perhaps the most recognized member of the Solanaceae family. They thrive in warm, sunny conditions and well-draining soil enriched with organic matter.

Companion plants for tomatoes include basil, which is believed to enhance the flavor of tomatoes and repel pests, and marigolds, which can deter nematodes and other garden pests. Other good companions include carrots, onions, and nasturtiums.

Potatoes, another vital member of the Nightshade family, also benefit from companion planting. Beans, corn, and cabbage are good partners as they don't compete with potatoes for nutrients.

Horseradish planted at the corners of the potato patch can provide protection against the Colorado potato beetle. However, potatoes should be kept away from carrots, apples, and tomatoes to avoid disease cross-contamination.

Eggplants, like their Solanaceae cousins, enjoy warm conditions and rich, well-drained soil. They do well with beans, which can enrich the soil with nitrogen, and tarragon, which can repel harmful pests. Marigolds are also beneficial companions, providing a natural deterrent to nematodes and insects.

Peppers, both sweet and hot varieties, are also part of the Nightshade family. They prefer similar growing conditions as tomatoes and eggplants. Beneficial companions for peppers include onions, spinach, and basil. Basil not only repels pests but is also believed to improve the flavor of peppers.

Tomatillos, though less commonly grown, are also Nightshades. They're similar to tomatoes in their growth needs and benefit from companions like marigolds and basil. The tomatillo's distant cousin, the ground cherry, shares similar companion preferences.

The Solanaceae family boasts a diverse array of garden vegetables that can reap considerable rewards from skillful companion planting. By delving into their needs and likes, gardeners can weave together a nurturing and prosperous garden ecosystem.

SOLANACEAE FAMILY COMPANION VEGETABLES

The Solanaceae or "Nightshade" vegetable family is a significant part of many gardens. These plants can benefit greatly from companion planting, a practice that involves strategically placing plants together to support each other's growth, deter pests, and improve soil health.

Tomatoes, a staple in many gardens, have several ideal companions. Basil is often planted with tomatoes due to its ability to repel pests and enhance the flavor of tomato fruits.

Marigolds can also be beneficial, as they deter nematodes and other pests. Other good companions for tomatoes include carrots, which can help aerate the soil around tomato plants, and borage, which attracts beneficial insects and deters tomato hornworms.

Peppers, both sweet and hot varieties, also have several great companion options. Basil not only enhances the flavor of peppers but also repels pests like thrips and mosquitoes. Spinach can be planted under pepper plants to make use of the shade provided, effectively using space and helping to keep the soil moist. Onions are another good companion for peppers, as they can help deter certain pests.

Eggplant, another member of the Nightshade family, benefits from being planted with beans and peas, which can enrich the soil through nitrogen fixation. Tarragon can help repel harmful pests, while marigolds can deter nematodes.

Potatoes can thrive when planted with beans, corn, and cabbage family members, as these plants do not compete heavily for nutrients. Horseradish can be planted at the corners of a potato patch to ward off Colorado potato beetles. However, avoid planting potatoes near carrots, apples, and other Nightshade family members due to the risk of disease cross-contamination.

When selecting companion plants for the Solanaceae family, it's important to consider a few key factors. First, consider the growth habits and needs of the plants. Companion plants should ideally have complementary growth habits, such as one tall plant paired with a shorter, ground-covering plant, to maximize space usage.

Second, think about nutrient needs. Plants that enrich the soil with nutrients like nitrogen, such as beans and peas, can be beneficial companions for heavy feeders like tomatoes.

Finally, consider pest resistance. Plants that naturally repel common pests of the Nightshade family, or attract their predators, can be excellent choices for companion planting.

By carefully selecting companion plants, you can create a more harmonious and productive garden environment for your Solanaceae family vegetables.

CHAPTER 7

SOLANACEAE FAMILY NON-COMPANION PLANTS

While the Solanaceae or "Nightshade" family can benefit from many companion plants, there are certain vegetables that they should not be planted with. These plants may compete for resources, encourage disease, or attract pests that could harm your Nightshade vegetables.

Tomatoes, for instance, should not be planted with other members of the Nightshade family like potatoes, peppers, and eggplants. These plants share many of the same pests and diseases, so planting them together can increase the risk of problems spreading through your garden. Additionally, tomatoes should not be planted with corn, as the tomato fruitworm and corn earworm are the same pest and can easily move between these two crops.

Potatoes also have a few plants they should avoid. Carrots and apples, for instance, should not be planted near potatoes because they can encourage the spread of potato scab, a common potato disease. Similarly, sunflowers can inhibit potato growth and should be kept separate. Other crops to avoid planting with potatoes include other Nightshade family members and crops like beets and carrots that might compete for nutrients.

Peppers, both sweet and hot varieties, should not be planted with beans. Beans can inhibit pepper growth, leading to smaller yields. Fennel is another plant to avoid, as it can inhibit the growth of many plants, including peppers.

Eggplants should not be planted with fennel for the same reason. Additionally, like other Nightshades, they should not be planted with other members of the same family due to shared pests and diseases.

When planning your garden, it's important to consider not only what plants work well together but also which ones do not. Avoiding incompatible combinations can help prevent pest infestations, disease spread, and competition for resources, promoting healthier and more productive plants. Understanding these relationships can help you make the most of your garden space and enjoy a bountiful harvest from your Nightshade family vegetables.

THE RIGHT SOIL FOR SOLANACEAE FAMILY VEGETABLES

The Solanaceae, or "Nightshade" family, includes several popular vegetables like tomatoes, peppers, eggplants, and potatoes. Each of these has unique soil preferences that can significantly impact their growth and the success of companion planting.

Tomatoes thrive best in well-drained soil that is rich in organic matter. The soil pH should be slightly acidic, between 6.2 to 6.8, to promote optimal nutrient absorption. Tomatoes benefit from companion plants like basil, which prefers similar soil conditions. Basil not only enhances the flavor of tomatoes but also helps repel pests like aphids and spider mites.

Peppers require well-drained, fertile soil with a pH range of 6.2 to 7.0. Like tomatoes, they prefer a slightly acidic soil. Companion plants such as basil and parsley, which deter pests and share similar soil requirements, are excellent choices for peppers. Spinach, another good companion, provides ground cover to maintain soil moisture and suppress weed growth, contributing to the overall health of the pepper plants.

Eggplants, like their Nightshade cousins, prefer well-drained soil that's rich in organic matter. They thrive in a pH range of 6.0 to 7.5. Beans make good companions for eggplants because they enrich the soil with nitrogen, a nutrient eggplants require in large quantities. Additionally, tarragon, which repels harmful pests, prefers similar soil conditions, making it a beneficial partner for eggplants.

Potatoes prefer slightly acidic soil with a pH range of 4.8 to 5.5. They require well-drained, loose soil to allow their tubers to expand. Corn, a great companion for potatoes, provides shade to keep the soil cool and moist, enhancing the conditions for potato growth. However, avoid planting potatoes near carrots and apples, which prefer similar soil conditions but can encourage potato blight.

Grasping the unique soil preferences of each vegetable in the Solanaceae family is the cornerstone of fruitful growth and effective companion planting. By tailoring the soil conditions to their liking and matching them with compatible companions, you can boost your garden's health and harvest.

SOWING SOLANACEAE FAMILY VEGETABLES

CORRECT SEASON TO SOW SOLANACEAE VEGETABLE PLANTS

Sowing vegetables in the Solanaceae, or nightshade family, in the correct season is a crucial aspect of successful companion planting. This family includes warm-season crops such as tomatoes, potatoes, eggplants, and peppers. These plants thrive in warmer temperatures and are often planted after the risk of frost has passed in the spring. Planting Solanaceae in the appropriate season ensures they grow during their optimal climate conditions, which can lead to healthier plants, better yields, and reduced susceptibility to pests and diseases.

Moreover, when you sow these plants in the correct season, it allows for effective synchronization with their companion plants. For instance, planting tomatoes next to basil or marigolds can help deter pests, but this benefit would be lost if the two crops are not growing at the same time. Therefore, understanding the seasonal preferences of your Solanaceae vegetables and aligning their growth with their companion plants is a key part of successful vegetable companion planting.

Tomatoes are typically started indoors about 6-8 weeks before the last spring frost date. This gives the plants a head start and allows them to mature and fruit during the hottest part of the summer. Once the danger of frost has passed and the soil has warmed to at least 60°F (15°C), the seedlings can be transplanted outdoors. It's important to harden off tomato seedlings, gradually exposing them to outdoor conditions over a week or so to prevent shock.

Potatoes are a bit more versatile and can be planted in early spring as soon as the soil can be worked. However, they prefer soil temperatures of at least 45°F (7°C). Planting can continue until mid-spring, allowing for a staggered harvest throughout the summer and fall. Unlike tomatoes, potatoes are typically planted directly in the garden from seed potatoes, not started indoors from seeds.

Eggplants, like tomatoes, are sensitive to cold and should be started indoors 8-10 weeks before the last spring frost. The seedlings should not be transplanted outdoors until the soil has warmed to at least 70°F (21°C) and nighttime temperatures remain above 50°F (10°C). Eggplants need a long, warm growing season to produce well, so getting an early start indoors can be beneficial.

Peppers, both sweet and hot varieties, also require warm soil and air temperatures. They should be started indoors 8-10 weeks before the last spring frost date and transplanted outdoors when soil temperatures reach at least 65°F (18°C) and nighttime temperatures stay above 55°F (13°C).

While all these Nightshade family vegetables are warm-season crops, the exact timing for sowing can vary. Careful planning and attention to frost dates and soil temperatures can help ensure a successful planting and a bountiful harvest.

PLANTING NEEDS & REQUIREMENTS

Correctly germinating the various Solanaceae vegetable plants from seeds to seedlings is crucial when companion planting for several reasons. Firstly, successful germination ensures that each plant has a healthy start, which is vital for its survival and productivity. Secondly, the timing of germination and transplantation can significantly affect the compatibility and interaction between companion plants.

Each plant in the companion planting system has unique growth rates, maturity times, and seasonal preferences. Therefore, synchronizing the germination and growth of different plants is key to maximizing the benefits of companion planting. For instance, a faster-growing plant can provide necessary shade or ground cover for a slower-growing companion, but only if their growth stages are correctly aligned.

Lastly, healthy seedlings are more resistant to pests and diseases, which can lead to a more resilient and balanced garden ecosystem. Therefore, understanding and applying correct germination practices is a fundamental step in successful vegetable companion planting.

Tomato seeds are typically started indoors about 6-8 weeks before the last expected spring frost. The seeds should be sown in a seed-starting mix, covered lightly with soil, and kept moist but not waterlogged. Tomato seeds germinate best at temperatures between 70°F and 80°F (21°C-27°C).

They usually sprout within 5-10 days under optimal conditions. Once the seedlings have developed their first set of true leaves, they can be transplanted into individual pots. When the danger of frost has passed, and the soil temperature is consistently above 60°F (15°C), the tomato seedlings can be transplanted outdoors.

Potatoes are usually grown from seed potatoes rather than seeds. Seed potatoes are small potatoes or pieces of larger potatoes that include at least one "eye" or sprout. These should be planted directly in the garden once the soil can be worked in early spring and has warmed to at least 45°F (7°C).

Eggplant seeds should be started indoors 8-10 weeks before the last expected spring frost. They should be planted about a quarter-inch deep in a seed-starting mix and kept at a temperature of around 75°F-90°F (24°C-32°C) for optimal germination. Eggplant seeds can take 7-14 days to germinate.

Once the seedlings have two sets of true leaves, they can be transplanted into individual pots. The seedlings should only be moved outdoors once the soil temperature is consistently above 70°F (21°C) and nighttime temperatures remain above 50°F (10°C).

Pepper seeds, both sweet and hot varieties, should be started indoors 8-10 weeks before the last spring frost date. They should be sowed about a quarter-inch deep in a seed-starting mix and kept at a temperature of around 70°F-85°F (21°C-29°C).

Pepper seeds can take anywhere from 7-28 days to germinate, depending on the variety and conditions. Like eggplants, pepper seedlings should have two sets of true leaves before being transplanted into individual pots. The seedlings can be moved outdoors when soil temperatures are consistently above 65°F (18°C) and nighttime temperatures stay above 55°F (13°C).

The process of germinating and transplanting Solanaceae vegetable plants demands precise timing, ideal temperatures, and gentle handling of the fledgling seedlings. By adhering to these steps, you can gift your plants with a robust beginning, setting the stage for a successful growing season.

SPACING & MEASUREMENTS

Proper spacing and measurements when transplanting Solanaceae vegetable seedlings is a critical aspect of successful vegetable companion planting. Every plant requires a certain amount of space to grow and thrive, depending on its size, root structure, and growth habit. In a companion planting setup, adequate spacing ensures that each plant has sufficient room to spread its roots, access nutrients, and receive sunlight without competing with its companions.

Moreover, correct spacing can enhance the beneficial interactions between companion plants. For instance, a taller plant can provide shade for a heat-sensitive companion, but only if they're appropriately spaced. Similarly, ground-covering plants can suppress weeds around taller plants, provided they're not so close as to obstruct the taller plant's growth.

Additionally, proper spacing can help prevent the spread of pests and diseases by ensuring good air circulation. Therefore, careful attention to spacing and measurements during transplantation is vital for creating a balanced and productive companion planting system.

The Solanaceae, or "Nightshade" family, includes several popular vegetables like tomatoes, peppers, eggplants, and potatoes. Each of these has specific spacing requirements to ensure they grow healthily and productively.

Tomatoes are typically large plants that require ample space to grow. Depending on the variety, tomatoes should be planted anywhere from 24 to 48 inches apart in a row, with rows being spaced about 36 to 60 inches apart. This spacing allows for good air circulation, which helps prevent diseases, and also gives the plant enough room to spread out and absorb sunlight.

Peppers, while smaller than most tomato plants, still need a fair amount of space. Plant pepper seedlings 18 to 24 inches apart, with rows set 24 to 36 inches apart. This spacing allows for adequate sunlight and airflow, reducing the risk of disease and encouraging healthy growth.

Eggplants are medium-sized plants that require a bit more room than peppers. Plant eggplant seedlings about 24 to 36 inches apart, with rows spaced 36 to 48 inches apart. This generous spacing allows the plants to spread out and ensures each plant has access to the nutrients it needs from the soil.

Potatoes, despite being grown underground, also need space to thrive. Seed potatoes should be planted about 12 to 15 inches apart in rows that are 30 to 36 inches apart. This spacing allows for the growth of the potato tubers underground and ensures the plants above ground have enough room to spread out and absorb sunlight.

Accurate spacing while planting Solanaceae vegetable seedlings is pivotal to guarantee the vigor and productivity of your garden. By allotting each plant its own personal growth space, you can amplify your yield and keep problems like disease and resource competition at bay.

MAINTAINING SOLANACEAE VEGETABLE PLANTS

Maintaining your Solanaceae vegetable plants is essential in vegetable companion gardening for several reasons. Firstly, regular maintenance ensures that each plant remains healthy and productive, contributing positively to the garden ecosystem. This includes tasks such as watering, fertilizing, pruning, and monitoring for pests and diseases.

Secondly, well-maintained plants are more likely to fulfill their roles in a companion planting setup. For instance, a robust tomato plant can provide the necessary shade for a heat-sensitive companion, but only if it's growing vigorously and healthily. Similarly, a well-tended ground-covering plant can effectively suppress weeds and conserve moisture for its companions.

Moreover, regular maintenance helps prevent any one plant from dominating the garden space or resources, thereby maintaining balance among the companion plants. Lastly, the practice of maintenance keeps you engaged with your garden, allowing you to spot and address any issues early, which is key to a successful and resilient companion garden. Therefore, consistent care and maintenance of your

Solanaceae vegetable plants play a crucial role in optimizing the benefits of vegetable companion gardening.

PRUNING AND THINNING SOLANACEAE VEGETABLE PLANTS

Pruning and thinning vegetables within the Solanaceae family, such as tomatoes, peppers, eggplants, and potatoes, is important in vegetable companion planting for several reasons. Pruning involves removing specific parts of a plant to improve its shape, productivity, or health.

In companion planting, pruning can help manage plant size and shape to ensure that all plants receive adequate sunlight and air circulation, which are critical for disease prevention and optimal growth. For instance, pruning a tomato plant's lower leaves can prevent soil-borne diseases from splashing onto the foliage. Thinning, which involves removing some plants to allow others more space, is equally important. Overcrowded plants compete for light, water, and nutrients, which can lead to stunted growth and increased susceptibility to pests and diseases.

By thinning out seedlings, you can ensure that each plant has the space it needs to thrive while maintaining the balance and harmony in your companion planting setup. Thus, regular pruning and thinning are essential practices for a healthy and productive companion garden.

Tomatoes are usually pruned during their growing stages. Begin pruning when the plant reaches about 1-2 feet tall. Remove the lower branches that touch the ground to prevent soil-borne diseases.

Also, consider removing the suckers - the small shoots that sprout from the junction between two branches. These suckers can take energy away from the main plant. However, be mindful not to over-prune, as leaves are necessary for photosynthesis and fruit production.

Peppers and eggplants can also benefit from some pruning. For these plants, pruning is typically done to shape the plants and encourage them to become bushier. When the plant has 3-4 true leaves, you can pinch off the growing tip. This encourages the plant to branch out, resulting in a bushier plant with more potential for fruit production.

Unlike tomatoes, peppers, and eggplants, potatoes are typically not pruned. However, hilling, which involves piling soil around the base of the plant, is a common practice. This helps protect the developing tubers from sunlight exposure, which can cause them to turn green and become toxic.

Thinning is another crucial practice, particularly for seedlings that were broadcast sown. Once the seedlings have grown their first set of true leaves, you can begin thinning.

Remove the weaker seedlings and leave the stronger ones, ensuring that the remaining plants have enough space to grow. The exact spacing will depend on the specific plant, but generally, aim for at least a couple of inches between each plant.

Understanding the timing and techniques for pruning and thinning the diverse vegetables of the Solanaceae family can profoundly influence their well-being and productivity, particularly in a companion planting arrangement.

By embracing consistent upkeep, you can make certain that each plant has access to the resources it needs to flourish, adding a positive ripple effect to your garden ecosystem.

WATERING SOLANACEAE VEGETABLE PLANTS

Watering your Solanaceae vegetable plants is a fundamental aspect of successful companion planting. These plants have high water demands, especially during their flowering and fruiting stages. Adequate watering ensures that the plants can carry out essential physiological processes like photosynthesis and nutrient uptake.

Moreover, consistent moisture levels in the soil can enhance the symbiotic interactions between companion plants. For instance, some plants help conserve soil moisture for their companions by providing shade or ground cover, but this benefit can only be realized if there's sufficient water to begin with. Furthermore, regular watering can also help mitigate competition for water between companion plants, thereby maintaining a balanced and harmonious garden ecosystem.

However, it's important to avoid overwatering as this can lead to waterlogged soil and root diseases. Therefore, understanding each plant's water needs and providing the right amount of water is crucial for the health and productivity of your Solanaceae vegetable plants in a companion planting setup.

Tomatoes, for instance, require consistent watering, especially during the flowering and fruiting stages. Generally, a tomato plant needs about 1-2 inches of water per week, but this could increase during hot, dry periods. Water deeply and less frequently to encourage deep root growth, which makes the plant more drought-tolerant. Early morning is the best time to water tomatoes to allow any excess water on the leaves to evaporate during the day, reducing the risk of fungal diseases.

Peppers also have high water demands, especially when they are setting fruit. Like tomatoes, they prefer deep, infrequent watering. Aim for about 1-2 inches of water per week, adjusting as needed based on weather conditions. Water early in the day to minimize disease risk.

Eggplants, like their Solanaceae cousins, need consistent moisture, particularly during fruiting. Water them deeply once or twice a week, providing about 1 inch of water each time. Avoid overhead watering to reduce the risk of leaf diseases.

Potatoes require steady watering throughout their growth, but it's particularly crucial during tuber formation. Keep the soil consistently moist but not waterlogged. Overwatering can cause the tubers to rot. As with other Solanaceae vegetables, water early in the day to minimize disease risk.

Understanding the watering needs of each vegetable in the Solanaceae family can help you create a successful companion planting setup. By providing the right amount of water at the right time, you can ensure that each plant thrives and contributes positively to your garden ecosystem.

Organic Fertilisation For Solanaceae Vegetable Plants

Organic fertilization plays a crucial role in the health and productivity of Solanaceae vegetable plants when companion planting. These plants, including tomatoes, peppers, eggplants, and potatoes, have high nutrient demands, and organic fertilizers provide a steady supply of essential nutrients such as nitrogen, phosphorus, and potassium.

Unlike synthetic fertilizers, organic fertilizers release nutrients slowly, providing a long-term nutrient supply that helps maintain soil fertility throughout the growing season. Moreover, organic fertilizers improve soil structure, enhancing its ability to hold water and nutrients, which is particularly beneficial in a companion planting setup where multiple plants share resources.

They also increase the activity of beneficial soil organisms, promoting a healthy soil ecosystem that can suppress pests and diseases. Additionally, organic fertilizers are environmentally friendly, reducing the risk of nutrient runoff that can pollute water bodies.

Therefore, using organic fertilizers in your Solanaceae vegetable garden can ensure that your plants get the nutrients they need for optimal growth while promoting soil health and sustainability.

The various vegetables in the Solanaceae family have unique nutrient needs that can be met with different types of organic fertilizers. Understanding these needs and when to fertilize each plant is crucial for successful companion planting.

CHAPTER 7

Tomatoes, for instance, have high nitrogen and potassium demands, especially during the early stages of growth. An organic fertilizer rich in these nutrients, such as composted poultry manure or a balanced vegetable garden fertilizer, can provide the necessary boost.

Begin fertilizing when you plant the seedlings in the garden, then continue every 2-3 weeks until the plants start setting fruit. At this point, reduce the nitrogen supply to avoid excessive leaf growth at the expense of fruit production.

Peppers also need a good supply of nitrogen and potassium. However, they require more phosphorus than tomatoes, especially during the flowering and fruiting stages, as phosphorus promotes fruit development. Bone meal is an excellent organic source of phosphorus. Start fertilizing when the first true leaves appear, then continue every 2-3 weeks throughout the growing season.

Eggplants, like tomatoes and peppers, benefit from a balanced organic fertilizer. They particularly need consistent nitrogen supply for vigorous growth. Composted manure or a balanced vegetable garden fertilizer can meet these needs. Start fertilizing when you transplant the seedlings, then continue every 2-3 weeks until the plants start flowering.

Potatoes have high potassium demands, which can be met with greensand or kelp meal. Potassium promotes tuber development. Apply a potassium-rich fertilizer when you plant the potatoes, then side-dress with compost or composted manure once the plants start flowering to provide a steady nutrient supply.

Using the right type of organic fertilizer at the right time can significantly enhance the health and productivity of the various vegetables in the Solanaceae family. By understanding each plant's nutrient needs, you can create a successful companion planting setup that promotes optimal growth and yield.

PROTECTING SOLANACEAE VEGETABLE PLANTS

EXTREME TEMPERATURES

Protecting vegetables in the Solanaceae family, from extreme temperatures is crucial when companion planting. These plants are sensitive to both high and low temperatures, and exposure to extreme conditions can affect their growth, health, and productivity.

During periods of high temperatures, these plants may experience heat stress, leading to problems like blossom drop, sunscald, or reduced fruit set. To protect your plants, consider using shade cloths.

These can be placed over the plants during the hottest part of the day to reduce the intensity of the sun. Mulching is another effective strategy. Organic mulch, such as straw or wood chips, can help keep the soil cool and retain moisture, reducing heat stress on the plants.

Regular watering is also crucial, as adequate moisture can help plants cope with high temperatures. However, avoid watering during the hottest part of the day to prevent water loss through evaporation.

In contrast, low temperatures can lead to frost damage, which can be particularly detrimental during the early growing stages. Frost blankets or row covers can provide protection on cold nights. These covers trap heat from the ground, creating a warmer microclimate for the plants.

Also, consider using plastic or fabric cloches for individual plants. These can be especially useful for protecting young seedlings from frost.

Another strategy for dealing with low temperatures is choosing the right companions for your Solanaceae vegetables. Some plants can act as natural windbreaks or help raise the temperature slightly through their respiration process. For instance, tall plants like sunflowers can shield sensitive plants from chilling winds, while dense ground covers can help trap heat near the soil surface.

The importance of protecting Solanaceae vegetables from extreme temperatures cannot be overstated. Temperature stress can significantly impact plant health and yield. Heat stress can cause flower drop, reducing fruit set, while frost damage can kill young plants or damage mature ones, affecting their productivity.

Therefore, implementing strategies to protect your vegetables from extreme temperatures can ensure that they grow and produce optimally, contributing positively to your companion planting setup.

PROTECTING SOLANACEAE VEGETABLES FROM PEST

Protecting the various vegetables in the Solanaceae family from pests is of utmost importance when companion planting. These plants are susceptible to a range of pests that can cause significant damage, affecting their growth, health, and productivity. Pests can defoliate plants, damage fruits, transmit diseases, and even kill plants in some cases.

Therefore, pest management is crucial for maintaining a healthy and productive vegetable garden. Additionally, in a companion planting setup, pests can easily spread from one plant to another due to the close proximity. However, companion planting can also offer pest management benefits, as some plants can deter pests or attract beneficial insects that prey on pests.

Therefore, effective pest protection strategies are key to harnessing the full potential of your Solanaceae vegetable plants in a companion planting setup.

Protecting the different vegetables in the Solanaceae family from pests when companion planting requires a multi-faceted approach. These plants, including tomatoes, peppers, eggplants, and potatoes, are susceptible to various pests, and effective pest management is crucial for their health and productivity.

One of the most effective ways of protecting Solanaceae vegetables from pests is through the strategic use of companion plants. Certain plants can deter pests or attract beneficial insects that prey on pests.

For instance, marigolds are known to repel nematodes, tiny soil-dwelling worms that can damage the roots of Solanaceae plants. Similarly, nasturtiums can deter aphids, a common pest of these vegetables. Planting herbs like basil and dill can attract beneficial insects such as ladybugs and lacewings, which feed on pests.

Regular monitoring is another crucial aspect of pest management. Regularly inspect your plants for signs of pest activity, such as chewed leaves, damaged fruits, or the presence of the pests themselves.

Early detection can allow you to address the problem before it becomes significant. Handpicking can be an effective control measure for larger pests like caterpillars and beetles.

Maintaining good garden hygiene can also help protect your Solanaceae vegetables from pests. Remove plant debris promptly to eliminate potential breeding grounds for pests. Rotate crops each year to disrupt the life cycles of pests and diseases.

In some cases, you might need to resort to organic pesticides. These can provide effective control for persistent or severe pest problems. However, they should be used judiciously to avoid harming beneficial insects. Always follow the manufacturer's instructions when using pesticides.

Safeguarding the assorted vegetables in the Solanaceae family from pests requires a medley of practices, such as companion planting, consistent monitoring, maintaining garden hygiene, and the prudent use of organic pesticides.

By adopting these strategies, you can foster the healthy and productive growth of your plants, paving the way for a fruitful companion planting arrangement.

PROTECTING SOLANACEAE VEGETABLES FROM DISEASES

Protecting the various vegetables in the Solanaceae family from diseases is vitally important when companion planting. These plants can be susceptible to a range of diseases that can significantly impact their health and productivity.

Diseases can cause symptoms ranging from leaf spots and wilts to fruit rots and plant death in severe cases. In a companion planting setup, diseases can spread rapidly due to the close proximity of the plants, making disease management crucial.

Moreover, healthy plants are more likely to produce a good yield and contribute positively to the garden ecosystem. Therefore, implementing effective disease protection strategies is essential for the success of your Solanaceae vegetable garden.

Tomatoes are often affected by diseases like early blight, late blight, and fusarium wilt. Early blight presents as dark spots on older leaves that eventually develop a concentric ring pattern.

Late blight causes water-soaked spots on leaves that turn brown and moldy. Fusarium wilt causes yellowing and wilting of leaves on one side of the plant. Combat these diseases organically by rotating crops, removing infected plants, and using disease-resistant varieties. Copper fungicides can also help control blights.

Peppers can suffer from bacterial spot, a disease that causes small, raised, water-soaked spots on leaves, stems, and fruits. The spots eventually become brown and crusty. Organic control measures include using disease-free seeds, rotating crops, and applying copper-based sprays.

Eggplants are susceptible to verticillium wilt, which causes yellowing, wilting, and browning of leaves, starting from the bottom of the plant. Control this disease by planting resistant varieties, rotating crops, and maintaining a balanced soil pH.

Potatoes can be affected by potato scab, a disease that causes rough, scaly spots on tubers. To prevent this disease, maintain a slightly acidic soil pH and avoid over-fertilizing with manure or compost, as high organic matter content can encourage the disease.

In general, maintaining good garden hygiene can help prevent diseases. Remove plant debris promptly, as it can harbor disease-causing organisms. Water in the morning so the leaves can dry out during the day, reducing the chances of fungal diseases.

Moreover, companion plants can play a role in disease prevention. Some plants have antifungal properties or can improve soil health, thereby helping to protect your Solanaceae vegetables from diseases.

Having a keen understanding of the diseases that can potentially afflict the various vegetables in the Solanaceae family, coupled with applying organic protection measures, can guarantee that your plants remain vibrant and fruitful within a companion planting environment.

HARVESTING SOLANACEAE VEGETABLE PLANTS

The Solanaceae, or "Nightshade" family, includes several popular vegetables such as tomatoes, potatoes, eggplants, and peppers. Each of these plants has a different maturation timeline and harvesting method, which can be influenced by companion planting.

Tomatoes are typically ready to harvest 60-80 days after transplanting, depending on the variety. When companion planted with basil or marigold, it can help in repelling pests and may indirectly speed up growth due to less disease and pest interference.

Harvest tomatoes when they are fully colored and slightly soft to the touch. Use a pair of pruning shears to cut the fruit stem, taking care not to damage the plant or the fruit.

Potatoes are usually ready for harvest 70-120 days after planting, depending on whether you want 'new' potatoes or mature ones. Companion planting with beans can help improve the soil nitrogen level, potentially boosting potato growth.

For new potatoes, carefully dig around the plants, starting a few weeks after the plants have flowered. For mature potatoes, wait until the foliage has died back in late summer or early fall, then dig up the potatoes with a garden fork, being careful not to pierce the tubers.

Eggplants typically take 100-150 days to harvest after transplanting. Companion planting with beans or tarragon can deter pests and enhance growth. Harvest eggplants when the skin is glossy, and the fruit is firm but slightly spongy to the touch. Cut the eggplant off the plant with pruning shears, leaving an inch or so of stem attached.

Peppers, both sweet and hot varieties, usually require 60-90 days to reach maturity after transplanting. Companion plants like basil or onions can deter pests and may indirectly enhance pepper growth. Harvest peppers when they have reached their full size and color, using a sharp knife or pruning shears to cut them off the plant. Be sure to leave a short stub of stem attached to the fruit.

The duration until vegetables from the Solanaceae family are ripe for harvest can differ, and companion planting can be instrumental in boosting robust growth and yield. Nevertheless, it's crucial to keep a vigilant eye on your plants and harvest them at the ideal moment to guarantee you reap the finest quality produce.

CROP ROTATION FOR SOLANACEAE VEGETABLE PLANTS

Crop rotation is a fundamental practice in both conventional and organic farming, including in gardens that implement companion planting. This practice involves changing the type of crop grown in a particular area from season to season or year to year. For Solanaceae vegetables, which include tomatoes, peppers, eggplants, and potatoes, crop rotation can be particularly beneficial.

The primary reason for practicing crop rotation is to prevent the build-up of pests and diseases in the soil. Many pests and diseases are specific to certain plant families. By changing the type of crop grown in an area each season, you can disrupt the life cycle of these pests and diseases, reducing their populations over time. For instance, root-knot nematodes are a common problem for Solanaceae vegetables.

These pests can remain in the soil between growing seasons, ready to attack your next crop. If you plant a non-host crop in the following season, such as a member of the legume family, the nematodes will have nothing to feed on and their numbers will decrease.

Crop rotation can also help improve soil fertility and structure. Different crops have different nutrient requirements and can affect soil structure in different ways.

For example, Solanaceae vegetables are heavy feeders, meaning they take a lot of nutrients, particularly nitrogen, from the soil. Following them with a leguminous crop, which can fix nitrogen from the air into the soil, can help replenish this nutrient.

In a companion planting setup, crop rotation can be implemented by changing the combinations of plants grown together each season. For instance, if you grew tomatoes (a Solanaceae vegetable) with basil (a member of the mint family) one season, you could switch to planting beans (a legume) with corn (a grass) the next season.

This not only helps manage pests and diseases and maintain soil fertility but also allows you to take advantage of different companion planting benefits each season.

Crop rotation is a valuable tool for managing pests and diseases, improving soil health, and maximizing the benefits of companion planting with Solanaceae vegetables. By carefully planning your crop rotation schedule, you can create a healthy and productive garden that thrives year after year.

CHAPTER 8
APIACEAE "CARROT" FAMILY COMPANION PLANTING

The Apiaceae family, also known as the carrot or parsley family, plays a significant role in vegetable companion planting. This diverse family includes many well-known vegetables and herbs, such as carrots, celery, parsley, parsnips, celeriac, fennel, coriander, Dill, anise, and caraway. These plants are not only valued for their unique flavors and nutritional benefits but also for their compatibility with other plants in a garden setting.

When used in companion planting, members of the Apiaceae family can provide numerous benefits, such as improving soil health, attracting beneficial insects, and repelling pests. Understanding the characteristics and needs of these plants is key to successfully integrating them into a companion planting system and maximizing their potential benefits.

Planting companion plants in the Apiaceae family, can provide numerous benefits to your garden. These plants are known for their strong aromatic qualities, which can deter or confuse pests, reducing the need for chemical pesticides. For example, the scent of carrots can mask the smell of nearby onions, helping to deter onion flies.

Additionally, the flowers of many Apiaceae species, such as Dill and coriander, are small and plentiful, making them highly attractive to beneficial insects like bees and predatory insects. These beneficial insects can help with pollination and control harmful pest populations. Furthermore, some members of the Apiaceae family, like fennel, exude compounds from their roots which can repel pests in the soil. Overall, incorporating Apiaceae family plants into your garden can enhance biodiversity, improve pest management, and contribute to a healthier and more productive garden.

APIACEAE FAMILY VEGETABLE PLANTS

The Apiaceae family, often referred to as the carrot or parsley family, features a variety of vegetables that are excellent for companion planting in your garden. This family includes carrots, celery, fennel, parsley, and parsnip. Each of these vegetables brings unique benefits to your garden ecosystem.

CHAPTER 8

Carrots are an essential part of this family and a favorite among gardeners. Carrots grow well with leafy vegetables like lettuce and spinach, which provide shade for the soil, helping to keep carrot roots cool. They also pair well with tomatoes. The tomatoes help to deter carrot flies, and the carrots can loosen the soil around the tomato plants, allowing their roots to penetrate deeper. However, carrots should be avoided near Dill or parsnips as they can attract similar pests.

Celery is another member of the Apiaceae family that works well in a companion planting system. It enjoys the company of plants such as tomatoes, beans, leeks, and onions. These plants can offer celery some protection from the wind and sun. Celery should not be planted near carrots or parsley as they compete for nutrients.

Fennel is unique in that it's known to be allelopathic to many plants, meaning it releases compounds that can inhibit the growth of surrounding plants. Therefore, it's often best to plant fennel separately from other plants. However, it can get along well with Dill, another member of the Apiaceae family.

Parsley is a versatile herb that grows well with asparagus, corn, and tomatoes. The strong scent of parsley can help deter pests from these plants. Conversely, parsley may struggle if planted near lettuce or other herbs in the mint family, as they can compete for resources.

Parsnip, a root vegetable similar to carrots, can benefit from being planted near peas, potatoes, peppers, and beans. These plants can provide shade and ground cover, helping to keep the soil cool for the parsnips. However, parsnips should not be planted near carrots or celery, as they can attract similar pests and diseases.

While the Apiaceae family includes a wide variety of vegetables suitable for companion planting, it's important to remember that each plant has its own specific needs and potential interactions. Understanding these can help you make the most effective use of your garden space and promote a healthy, productive garden.

APIACEAE FAMILY COMPANION VEGETABLES

The Apiaceae family, also known as the carrot or parsley family, includes a variety of vegetables that are well-suited for companion planting. This family comprises plants like carrots, celery, parsnip, fennel, and parsley, each with its unique companion planting partners.

Carrots are a versatile crop that can pair well with several different types of plants. Tomatoes are a great companion for carrots, as the tomatoes repel carrot flies, while the carrots help to aerate the soil around the tomato plants.

Leafy vegetables such as lettuce and spinach can also be beneficial companions for carrots. These plants provide shade for the soil, helping to keep carrot roots cool. However, it's best to avoid planting carrots near Dill or parsnips, as they can attract similar pests.

Celery enjoys the company of plants such as tomatoes, beans, leeks, and onions. These plants can offer celery some protection from wind and excessive sun. Celery should not be planted near carrots or parsley because they compete for nutrients, and proximity can lead to stunted growth.

Parsley is a beneficial herb that grows well with asparagus, corn, and tomatoes. The strong scent of parsley can deter pests from these plants. Conversely, parsley may struggle if planted near lettuce or other herbs in the mint family because they can compete for resources.

Parsnip, a root vegetable similar to carrots, can benefit from being planted near peas, potatoes, peppers, and beans. These plants can provide shade and ground cover, helping to keep the soil cool for the parsnips. However, parsnips should not be planted near carrots or celery, as they can attract similar pests and diseases.

Fennel is a bit of an exception within the Apiaceae family when it comes to companion planting. It's known to be allelopathic to many plants, meaning it releases compounds that can inhibit the growth of surrounding plants. Therefore, it's often best to plant fennel separately from other plants. However, it can get along well with Dill, another member of the Apiaceae family.

When selecting companion plants for your Apiaceae family vegetables, consider the specific needs of each plant. Look at their sun and water requirements, their preferred soil conditions, and their susceptibility to certain pests and diseases.

Good companion plants will have compatible needs and will help each other thrive, either by deterring pests, improving soil health, or providing physical support or shade. It's also important to rotate your crops each year to prevent the buildup of pests and diseases and to maintain soil fertility.

APIACEAE FAMILY NON-COMPANION PLANTS

The Apiaceae family, also known as the carrot or parsley family include a variety of vegetables. While these plants can benefit from many companion planting partnerships, there are also certain plants that they should not be paired with.

Carrots, for instance, should not be planted near Dill. Despite both being members of the Apiaceae family, these two plants can attract similar pests, which can lead to infestations. Additionally, their roots can intertwine and compete for nutrients, leading to stunted growth. Carrots also don't pair well with parsnips for similar reasons.

Celery should be avoided near carrots or parsley. These plants are all heavy feeders, meaning they have high nutrient needs. When planted together, they can deplete the soil and compete with each other for resources. This competition can result in poor growth and reduced yields.

Parsley can struggle if planted near lettuce or other herbs in the mint family. These plants can compete for resources, leading to poor growth. Additionally, parsley and lettuce can attract similar pests, which can lead to increased pest issues when they're grown together.

Parsnip should not be planted near carrots or celery. Like carrots, parsnips can attract carrot flies, and growing these crops together can lead to increased pest problems. Parsnips and celery can also compete for nutrients, leading to poor growth and lower yields.

Lastly, **fennel** is a unique case within the Apiaceae family. It's known to be allelopathic, can inhibit the growth of other plants. Because of this, fennel should generally be planted separately from other plants. Even other members of the Apiaceae family, like carrots and parsley, can be negatively affected by fennel's allelopathic properties.

When planning your garden, it's important to consider these potential negative interactions. By avoiding unfavorable plant pairings, you can help ensure that all of your plants have the resources they need to thrive.

Of course, every garden is unique, and what works best may vary depending on your specific conditions. Therefore, it's always a good idea to keep records and observe how different plant combinations perform in your garden.

THE RIGHT SOIL FOR APIACEAE FAMILY VEGETABLES

The Apiaceae family, also known as the carrot or parsley family, contains a variety of vegetables, each with their own specific soil requirements. By unraveling these specific needs, you can cultivate the most conducive growing environment and hand-select companion plants that harmoniously coexist in your garden.

Carrots, for instance, thrive in deep, loose, well-drained soil. The soil should be free of rocks and heavy clumps to allow the roots to grow straight down and prevent forking. The ideal pH is slightly acidic, between 6.0 and 6.8.

Companion plants like tomatoes, beans, and radishes, which also prefer well-drained soil, can make excellent partners for carrots. The tomatoes and beans can help deter pests, while the radishes can break up the soil, making it easier for carrot roots to penetrate.

Celery prefers rich, fertile soil with plenty of organic matter. It also requires consistent moisture, so well-drained soil is essential to prevent waterlogging. A slightly acidic to neutral pH (6.0 to 7.0) is ideal. Companion plants like tomatoes, leeks, and onions, which have similar soil requirements, can provide celery with some protection from wind and sun while also helping to keep the soil cool and moist.

Parsley thrives in rich, loamy soil with good drainage. It prefers a neutral to slightly acidic pH (6.0 to 7.0). Asparagus, corn, and tomatoes, which can tolerate a similar pH range, make good companions for parsley. These plants can benefit from parsley's strong scent, which deters pests.

Parsnip requires deep, well-drained soil to accommodate its long taproot. It prefers a slightly acidic to neutral pH (6.0 to 7.5). Peas, potatoes, peppers, and beans, which enjoy similar soil conditions, can provide beneficial shade and ground cover for parsnips.

Finally, **fennel** prefers well-drained, slightly acidic to slightly alkaline soil (pH 5.5 to 7.5). However, due to fennel's allelopathic properties, it's often best to plant it separately from other plants. If you choose to plant companions, opt for plants that are not easily affected by allelopathy, such as Dill.

Grasping the unique soil needs of your Apiaceae family vegetables is a key step in nurturing an ideal growth environment and selecting companion plants that align well with them.

Ideal companions will not only share similar soil preferences but also mutually benefit each other by enhancing pest control, promoting soil health, or providing physical support. This understanding can truly transform your garden into a thriving, symbiotic ecosystem.

SOWING APIACEAE FAMILY VEGETABLES

CORRECT SEASON TO SOW APIACEAE VEGETABLE PLANTS

Sowing the different vegetables in the Apiaceae family, in the correct season, is crucial when practicing vegetable companion planting. Each plant in this family, from carrots to

CHAPTER 8

parsley, has its own specific growth cycle and climatic requirements for optimal growth. For instance, carrots prefer cooler weather and should ideally be planted in early spring or late summer, while parsley thrives in cooler fall temperatures.

Sowing these plants in their preferred seasons ensures they get the right temperature, sunlight, and moisture conditions they need to germinate, grow, and produce bountifully. Furthermore, timing your plantings correctly can also help manage pests and diseases which tend to be more prevalent in certain seasons.

Finally, well-timed plantings allow for a harmonious growth pattern among companion plants, ensuring that one does not outgrow or overshadow the other, thus promoting healthier and more productive gardens.

Carrots, known for their preference for cooler weather, are best sown in early spring or late summer. Early spring planting allows carrots to mature with increasing temperatures, while late summer planting leads to a fall harvest when cool weather enhances their sweetness. It's important to note that carrots require a temperature range of 45 to 85 degrees Fahrenheit for optimal germination, ideally around 70 degrees Fahrenheit.

Celery, another member of the Apiaceae family, is more sensitive to temperature changes. This vegetable requires a long growing season under cool conditions, but it doesn't tolerate frost. It's recommended to start celery seeds indoors about 10-12 weeks before the last expected frost date and then transplant them outdoors when temperatures consistently range between 60 and 70 degrees Fahrenheit.

Fennel, a perennial herb, prefers milder climates and well-drained soils. Similar to carrots, fennel is best sown in early spring or late summer. An early spring planting ensures a summer harvest, while a late summer planting yields a fall crop.

Parsley, a biennial plant often treated as an annual, also thrives in cooler weather. It can be planted in the early spring or fall. A spring planting provides leaves throughout the summer and a crop of seeds in the fall, while a fall planting will yield a bountiful harvest the following spring.

Parsnip, a root vegetable in the carrot family, also prefers cool weather for optimal growth. It's typically sown in early spring, right after the last frost, as it requires a long growing season. Parsnip seeds can take up to three weeks to germinate, and the roots are usually ready for harvest in late fall or early winter, after the first frost, which helps sweeten the roots.

Gaining insight into the special seasonal needs of each vegetable in the Apiaceae family is a vital step towards triumphant planting and harvesting. Right-on-cue timing not only fosters vigorous plant growth but also supercharges yield, making every bit of your gardening labor truly pay off. This understanding can morph your gardening pursuit into a rewarding harvest adventure.

PLANTING NEEDS & REQUIREMENTS

The correct germination of the different vegetables in the Apiaceae family, from seeds to seedlings, is vital when implementing vegetable companion planting. Each vegetable species has its unique germination requirements, including temperature, moisture, and light conditions.

Ensuring these needs are met helps the seeds sprout healthily and grow into strong seedlings. When these seedlings are robust, they can better coexist with other plants in a companion planting setup. Healthy seedlings are more resistant to pests, diseases, and adverse weather conditions, reducing the risk of these factors affecting their companion plants.

Furthermore, successful germination also ensures that the plants mature at the right time, maintaining the balance in a companion planting system where each plant species plays a specific role. For instance, some plants provide shade, others deter pests, and some enrich the soil. Hence, proper seed germination is a stepping stone to an efficient and productive vegetable companion planting system.

Carrots are relatively easy to germinate. They prefer a soil temperature of around 50-85 degrees Fahrenheit, with optimal germination occurring at about 80 degrees Fahrenheit. To start, prepare your soil by removing any rocks or debris, then sow the seeds directly into the ground about a quarter-inch deep.

Carrot seeds should be spaced about 2 inches apart to allow room for growth. The seeds typically germinate in one to three weeks, depending on the soil temperature. Once the seedlings reach 2 inches tall, they can be thinned out to ensure proper growth.

Celery has a longer germination period and prefers cooler temperatures between 60 and 70 degrees Fahrenheit. Start celery seeds indoors 10-12 weeks before the last expected frost date. Sow the seeds on top of the soil and lightly press them in, but don't cover them as they need light to germinate.

Keep the soil consistently moist. Celery seeds will typically germinate in 7-14 days. Transplant the seedlings outdoors when they have 5-6 leaves and the outdoor temperatures are consistently in the preferred range.

Fennel prefers warmer temperatures for germination, ideally between 60 and 70 degrees Fahrenheit. Start fennel seeds indoors about 4-6 weeks before the last frost date, or sow them directly outdoors once the danger of frost has passed.

Fennel seeds should be sown about a quarter-inch deep and will typically germinate in 7-14 days. Transplant or thin seedlings to about 12 inches apart once they reach 4-6 inches tall.

Parsley seeds can be a bit tricky to germinate as they have a thick seed coat. Soaking the seeds overnight can help speed up germination. Sow the seeds about a quarter-inch deep in soil that's between 50 and 85 degrees Fahrenheit. Parsley seeds will usually germinate in 14-30 days. Transplant seedlings when they are about 2 inches tall, spacing them 6-8 inches apart.

Parsnips prefer cooler soil temperatures for germination, between 50 and 70 degrees Fahrenheit. They have a long germination period and can take up to 28 days to sprout. Sow the seeds directly into the garden about half an inch deep and 3 inches apart. Once the seedlings are 1 inch tall, thin them to about 6 inches apart.

Successfully kick-starting the germination process for the diverse vegetables in the Apiaceae family is your gateway to a bountiful harvest. Grasping the unique temperature and spacing requisites of each plant is crucial to nurturing healthy, robust seedlings that are primed and ready for transplanting.

This understanding is the first brushstroke in your masterpiece of a thriving vegetable garden.

SPACING & MEASUREMENTS

Proper spacing and measurements when transplanting Apiaceae vegetable seedlings are crucial in vegetable companion planting for several reasons. First, each plant requires sufficient space to grow and expand, not just above the ground but also below the surface, where roots spread out in search of water and nutrients.

Overcrowding can lead to competition for these resources, hindering the growth and development of the plants. Second, appropriate spacing reduces the risk of disease transmission by ensuring better air circulation, which can prevent the buildup of moisture that often leads to fungal diseases.

Third, proper spacing allows each plant to receive adequate sunlight, essential for photosynthesis. Finally, in a companion planting setup, certain plants benefit others by improving soil quality, deterring pests, or providing shade. Proper spacing ensures these beneficial relationships can occur without one plant overshadowing or outcompeting another. Thus, correct spacing and measurements contribute significantly to a healthy, productive vegetable garden.

Carrots are typically planted directly from seeds, but if you're transplanting seedlings, they should be spaced about 2-3 inches apart. This spacing allows each carrot ample room to develop its root, which is the edible part of the plant. Be careful not to plant the seedlings too deeply, as this can hinder their growth.

Celery plants require more space due to their larger size and leaf spread. When transplanting celery seedlings, it's recommended to space them about 10-12 inches apart in rows that are 18-24 inches apart. This ensures each plant has enough room to grow without competing for resources.

Fennel, similar to celery, requires a bit more space. When transplanting fennel seedlings, space them about 12-18 inches apart in rows that are 24-36 inches apart. This allows enough room for the large bulbous base of the fennel to develop properly.

Parsley plants are smaller and can be spaced a bit closer together. When transplanting parsley seedlings, they should be spaced about 6-8 inches apart. This allows enough space for each plant to spread out and ensures that they won't compete for sunlight and nutrients.

Parsnip, like carrots, develops a large root underground, so it needs room to grow. When transplanting parsnip seedlings, space them about 3-6 inches apart in rows that are 12-18 inches apart. This ensures that the roots have ample room to develop.

Getting the spacing and measurements right when planting Apiaceae vegetable seedlings is a secret ingredient in their growth and yield recipe. It's like ensuring each plant has its own room to stretch, grow, and access the essential resources.

This careful consideration not only promotes healthier plants but also paves the way for a bountiful harvest, making your gardening efforts a success.

MAINTAINING APIACEAE VEGETABLE PLANTS

Maintaining your Apiaceae vegetable plants is essential in vegetable companion gardening for a multitude of reasons. These plants play several roles in the garden, including attracting beneficial insects, repelling pests, and improving soil health. For instance, parsley attracts predatory insects that help control pests, while carrots and parsnips have deep roots that can break up compacted soil, enhancing its structure.

However, these benefits can only be realized if the plants are healthy and thriving. Regular maintenance, such as watering, weeding, fertilizing, and monitoring for pests and diseases, ensures that your Apiaceae plants can perform their companion roles effectively. Furthermore, maintaining your plants helps to maximize their productivity, leading to a more plentiful harvest. Thus, regular care and maintenance of your Apiaceae vegetable plants is a cornerstone of successful vegetable companion gardening.

PRUNING AND THINNING APIACEAE VEGETABLE PLANTS

Pruning and thinning vegetable plants within the Apiaceae family is a critical practice in vegetable companion planting. These processes contribute to plant health, productivity, and the overall success of the garden. Pruning involves removing specific parts of a plant, such as dead or overgrown branches, to improve its shape and growth.

For instance, pruning parsley can stimulate bushier growth, leading to higher yields. On the other hand, thinning refers to the removal of some plants to reduce crowding and competition for resources. Carrots and parsnips, for example, often need thinning after germination to provide adequate space for root development. In a companion planting setup, proper spacing achieved through thinning can prevent one type of plant from overshadowing or outcompeting another.

Moreover, both pruning and thinning can enhance air circulation among plants, reducing the risk of fungal diseases. Therefore, these practices are essential for maintaining a healthy and productive companion vegetable garden.

When it comes to **Carrots**, thinning rather than pruning is crucial. Carrots are typically sown directly into the soil and can often germinate very closely together. Once they've grown to about 2 inches in height, usually a few weeks after sowing, they should be thinned. This involves removing some seedlings to ensure that the remaining ones are spaced about 2-3 inches apart. Thinning allows each carrot ample room to develop its root, which is the edible part of the plant.

Celery, unlike carrots, benefits from both pruning and thinning. Seedlings should be thinned once they reach about 3-4 inches tall, leaving about 10-12 inches between each plant. As for pruning, remove any yellow or brown leaves throughout the growing season to keep the plant healthy and encourage more growth.

Fennel also benefits from thinning and pruning. Thin the seedlings when they are about 4-6 inches tall, leaving about 12-18 inches between each plant. Prune fennel by cutting back the oldest and largest stalks at the base where they meet the bulb, promoting bushier growth.

Parsley plants should be pruned regularly throughout the growing season to encourage bushy growth. You can do this by snipping off the tops of the stems just above a leaf node. If the plants are too close together, thin them out so that there's about 6-8 inches of space between each plant.

Parsnip, similar to carrots, requires thinning rather than pruning. Once the seedlings are about 2 inches tall, thin them out so that there's about 3-6 inches of space between each plant. This gives the large parsnip roots enough room to develop.

Unlocking the secrets of when and how to prune and thin your Apiaceae vegetable plants can significantly boost their health and productivity. It's like providing your plants with a tailored fitness regime that strengthens them, ultimately leading to a more fruitful harvest in your companion planting garden.

This knowledge could be the ace up your sleeve in your gardening journey, propelling your harvest from satisfactory to spectacular.

WATERING APIACEAE VEGETABLE PLANTS

Watering your Apiaceae vegetable plants is a critical aspect of companion planting. These plants, including carrots, celery, fennel, parsley, and parsnip, have varying water needs that must be met to ensure their healthy growth and development.

Proper watering encourages deep root growth, which is particularly important for root vegetables like carrots and parsnips. Moreover, adequate hydration helps the plants withstand pest attacks and diseases better. In a companion planting setup, ensuring each plant's water needs are met is crucial because different plants can have different requirements.

Overwatering or underwatering one plant could negatively impact its companions. Hence, understanding and providing the appropriate amount of water for each plant in the Apiaceae family is key to successful vegetable companion planting.

Carrots, for instance, require consistent moisture, particularly during their early growth stages. Water them thoroughly after planting, then aim to provide about 1 inch of water per week. However, avoid overwatering as this can lead to root rot. As the carrots mature, they can tolerate slightly drier conditions, but it's still important to maintain regular watering.

Celery plants are heavy drinkers and require consistent, deep watering. Aim to provide about 1-1.5 inches of water per week, divided into two or three watering sessions. This helps to keep the soil consistently moist but not waterlogged. During hot, dry periods, celery may need additional water.

Fennel prefers a moderately moist soil, so aim to water it deeply once a week. However, be mindful not to overwater, as this can lead to root rot. In hot and dry conditions, check the soil regularly and water if the top 2 inches are dry.

Parsley likes evenly moist soil, so try to water it deeply once or twice per week, providing about 1 inch of water each time. During hot weather or in well-drained soil, parsley may need more frequent watering.

Parsnip, like its carrot cousin, needs consistent moisture for best growth. Aim to provide about 1 inch of water per week, watering deeply to encourage the roots to grow down into the soil. Once established, parsnips can handle some dry conditions, but regular watering will yield the best results.

Remember, these are general guidelines, and actual watering needs can vary based on factors such as soil type, weather conditions, and the specific needs of companion plants. Always check the soil moisture levels before watering and adjust your watering schedule as needed. By doing so, you'll ensure that your Apiaceae vegetable plants remain healthy and productive in your companion planting garden.

CHAPTER 8

ORGANIC FERTILISATION FOR APIACEAE VEGETABLE PLANTS

Organic fertilization is crucial for Apiaceae vegetable plants when companion planting for several reasons. First, these plants have specific nutrient needs that must be met to ensure their healthy growth and development.

Organic fertilizers can provide a balanced supply of essential nutrients, such as nitrogen, phosphorus, and potassium, in a form that's easily accessible to the plants. Second, organic fertilizers improve the soil structure, enhancing its ability to hold water and nutrients, which is particularly beneficial for deep-rooted plants like carrots and parsnips.

Moreover, organic fertilizers are rich in organic matter, which can support a diverse array of beneficial soil microorganisms. These microbes play a key role in nutrient cycling, helping to make nutrients more available to the plants.

Lastly, in a companion planting setup, using organic fertilizers can help create a balanced ecosystem where different plants can benefit from the nutrients added to the soil, promoting overall garden health and productivity. Therefore, organic fertilization is an integral part of successful vegetable companion planting with Apiaceae plants.

Carrots, for instance, benefit from a balanced organic fertilizer, such as compost or well-rotted manure, which provides a good mix of nitrogen, phosphorus, and potassium.

These root vegetables don't require a lot of nitrogen, as too much can lead to excessive top growth at the expense of root development. Apply the fertilizer a few weeks before planting to allow it time to break down in the soil.

Celery is a heavy feeder and requires plenty of nitrogen to develop its lush, green stalks. An organic fertilizer rich in nitrogen, like composted poultry manure or a plant-based meal like alfalfa meal, would be beneficial.

Apply the fertilizer at planting time and again midway through the growing season to support its rapid growth.

Fennel also appreciates a balanced organic fertilizer. Compost or well-rotted manure can be added to the planting hole and mixed with the existing soil. Fennel doesn't require a lot of feeding, so one application at planting time should suffice for the growing season.

Parsley, being a leafy green, requires ample nitrogen for its foliage growth. A nitrogen-rich organic fertilizer, such as composted poultry manure or worm castings, can be applied at planting time and then again midway through the growing season to replenish nutrients.

Parsnip, similar to carrots, benefits from a balanced organic fertilizer but doesn't require excessive nitrogen. Compost or well-rotted manure can be incorporated into the soil a few weeks before planting.

Keep in mind, these are guiding principles, and the true fertilizer necessities can shift based on variables like soil fertility, climate conditions, and the distinctive needs of companion plants.

Think of regular soil testing as a health check-up for your garden, helping you decode your soil's nutrient profile and fine-tune your fertilization plan accordingly. By providing the right type and amount of organic fertilizers, you can ensure that your Apiaceae vegetable plants thrive in your companion planting garden.

CHAPTER 8

PROTECTING APIACEAE VEGETABLE PLANTS

EXTREME TEMPERATURES

Protecting vegetables in the Apiaceae family from extreme temperatures is a crucial aspect of companion planting. This is because extreme temperatures can cause stress to these plants, hindering their growth and productivity. Both excessively high and low temperatures can lead to a variety of issues, from bolting and wilting to frost damage.

During periods of extreme heat, it's important to provide adequate water to Apiaceae vegetables. Plants such as celery and parsley, which require a consistently moist soil, can quickly wilt under hot conditions. Regular, deep watering in the early morning or late evening can help keep the soil cool and prevent moisture loss through evaporation.

Mulching is another effective way to protect against high temperatures. Organic mulches like straw or compost can help maintain soil moisture, regulate soil temperature, and prevent weed growth. Mulch can be particularly beneficial for root vegetables like carrots and parsnips, keeping their roots cool and moist.

Shade cloth can also be used to protect the plants from intense midday sun. It can be particularly beneficial for leafy greens like parsley, which can wilt or develop scorched leaves under high heat.

In contrast, during periods of extreme cold, protective measures are needed to prevent frost damage. Floating row covers, cloches, or cold frames can provide a protective barrier against cold winds and frost. They can be particularly useful for extending the growing season for cool-weather crops like celery or fennel.

Furthermore, choosing the right companions can also aid in temperature regulation. Taller plants can provide shade for shorter ones, protecting them from intense sun. Similarly, ground-covering plants can help keep the soil cool and moist, benefiting the root development of carrots and parsnips.

Protecting Apiaceae vegetables from extreme temperatures is essential for their survival and productivity. By implementing these strategies, you can create a more resilient garden that can withstand temperature fluctuations, ensuring a successful harvest from your companion planting efforts.

PROTECTING APIACEAE VEGETABLES FROM PEST

Protecting the various vegetables in the Apiaceae family from pests is vitally important when companion planting. These plants, including carrots, celery, fennel, parsley, and parsnip, can be susceptible to a range of pests that can cause significant damage if left unchecked.

Pests not only cause physical harm to the plants but can also transmit diseases, further affecting plant health and productivity. In a companion planting setup, an infestation on one plant can quickly spread to its neighbors, potentially impacting the entire garden.

Moreover, certain pests can multiply rapidly under favorable conditions, making them harder to control if not promptly addressed. Therefore, implementing effective pest management strategies is crucial to safeguard the health of your Apiaceae vegetable plants and ensure a successful harvest in your companion planting garden.

Carrots, for instance, can be prone to carrot fly attacks. These pests are attracted to the smell of bruised carrot foliage, so it's important to handle your plants carefully. Companion planting with aromatic herbs like rosemary or sage can help mask the scent and deter carrot flies. Additionally, using floating row covers can physically prevent these flies from laying eggs on the carrot plants.

Celery can be attacked by pests such as celery leaf miners and aphids. Introducing beneficial insects, like ladybugs and lacewings, can help control aphid populations. Leaf miners can be harder to manage, but regular inspection of the leaves and removal of any infested ones can help keep their numbers down. Companion planting celery with leek can also help deter leaf miners.

Fennel is known to attract aphids, but these can be controlled by encouraging beneficial insects or by spraying the plants with a mild soap solution. However, fennel should be isolated from most other plants in a companion planting setup, as it can inhibit the growth of many other plants.

Parsley can suffer from parsley worm, which later turns into a beautiful black swallowtail butterfly. If the infestation is not severe, you might choose to share your parsley with these creatures.

However, if you need to control them, handpicking is an effective method. Companion planting parsley with tomatoes can help repel tomato hornworms.

Parsnips can be affected by parsnip webworms. Regular monitoring and handpicking can help keep their population under control. Floating row covers can also be used to prevent these pests from laying eggs on the plants.

Remember, maintaining a healthy garden is the best defense against pests. This includes proper watering, fertilization, and crop rotation practices.

Also, attracting beneficial insects and birds to your garden can provide natural pest control. By understanding the specific pest threats to your Apiaceae vegetables and taking proactive measures, you can help ensure the success of your companion planting garden.

PROTECTING APIACEAE VEGETABLES FROM DISEASES

Protecting the various vegetables in the Apiaceae family from diseases is a critical aspect when companion planting. Diseases can significantly impact plant health, affecting their growth and yield. Many plant diseases are infectious and can quickly spread from one plant to another, especially in a companion planting setup where plants are grown close together.

If not promptly addressed, these diseases can potentially wipe out an entire crop. Furthermore, certain diseases can persist in the soil or plant debris for several years, posing ongoing challenges to future plantings. For these reasons, implementing effective disease management strategies is crucial to maintain the health of your Apiaceae vegetable plants, ensuring a successful and productive companion planting garden.

Various diseases can affect vegetable plants in the Apiaceae family, impacting their health and productivity. Identifying these diseases early and implementing organic control measures is crucial in a companion planting setup.

CHAPTER 8

Carrots, for instance, can be affected by carrot leaf blight, which manifests as yellow spots on the leaves that eventually turn brown. To manage this disease, use resistant varieties whenever possible and practice crop rotation to break the disease cycle.

Regularly remove plant debris from the garden to eliminate potential sources of infection. For severe infections, organic fungicides based on copper or sulfur can be used.

Celery is susceptible to diseases like celery mosaic virus and fusarium wilt. Celery mosaic virus causes mottling and curling of leaves. Unfortunately, there's no cure for viral diseases, so infected plants should be removed and destroyed.

Fusarium wilt causes yellowing of leaves and wilting of the plant. Using disease-resistant varieties and ensuring good soil drainage can help prevent this disease.

Fennel can suffer from rust, which appears as orange pustules on the underside of leaves. Rust can be managed by removing and destroying infected leaves. Ensure good air circulation around the plants to reduce humidity levels, which can discourage the development of rust. Organic fungicides containing sulfur or copper can also help control this disease.

Parsley can be affected by leaf spot, causing circular brown spots on the leaves. This disease can be managed by removing infected leaves, practicing crop rotation, and maintaining good sanitation in the garden. An organic fungicide can be applied if the disease is widespread.

Parsnips can suffer from parsnip canker, a fungal disease that causes sunken, dark lesions on the root. To prevent this disease, ensure good soil drainage, avoid damaging the roots, and rotate crops regularly. There are no effective organic treatments for parsnip canker once it has taken hold, so prevention is key.

Remember, the best defense against diseases is a healthy garden. Providing your plants with the right growing conditions, including adequate light, water, and nutrients, can strengthen their natural defenses against diseases.

By understanding the specific disease threats to your Apiaceae vegetables and taking proactive measures, you can help ensure the success of your companion planting garden.

HARVESTING APIACEAE VEGETABLE PLANTS

The vegetables within the Apiaceae family each have their unique growth cycles and harvesting methods, which can be influenced by factors such as the specific variety, growing conditions, and companion plants.

Carrots are typically ready for harvest anywhere between 50 to 80 days after planting, depending on the variety. You can start checking for readiness when the tops of the carrots are about 3/4 inch in diameter. To harvest, gently loosen the soil around the carrot with a garden fork and pull the carrot out by its greens. Be careful not to damage the root during this process.

Celery generally takes about 100 to 120 days to reach maturity. It's ready to harvest when the stalks are about 6 to 8 inches tall. To harvest celery, cut the entire plant at the soil line using a sharp knife. Alternatively, you can harvest individual stalks as needed, starting from the outermost ones.

Fennel is usually ready for harvest 90 to 115 days after planting. The bulb should be harvested when it is about the size of a tennis ball. Cut the bulb at the soil level with a sharp knife, leaving some of the root in the ground if you want the plant to produce a second, smaller bulb.

Parsley can be harvested throughout the growing season, starting about 70 to 90 days after planting. Harvest the outer leaves first, cutting them off at the base. This encourages the plant to produce new growth from the center.

Parsnips are typically ready for harvest 100 to 130 days after planting, but they often taste sweeter if allowed to experience a frost before harvesting. To harvest parsnips, loosen the soil around the root with a garden fork, then pull the root out by its greens.

Remember, regular harvesting can often encourage further growth, so don't be shy about picking your vegetables. However, avoid over-harvesting, as this can weaken the plant and reduce its productivity.

By understanding the specific harvesting needs of your Apiaceae vegetables, you can ensure a steady and healthy yield from your companion planting garden.

CROP ROTATION FOR APIACEAE VEGETABLE PLANTS

Crop rotation is a critical practice in gardening and farming, including when growing Apiaceae vegetables in a companion planting setup. It involves changing the type of plant grown in each area of the garden in a planned sequence over several seasons. This practice helps to maintain soil fertility, reduce pest and disease problems, and promote healthy, productive plants.

Apiaceae vegetables, such as carrots, celery, fennel, parsley, and parsnips, each have different nutrient requirements and pest and disease profiles. By rotating these crops, you can ensure that the soil nutrients are used more evenly over time, reducing the need for heavy fertilization.

For instance, after growing a nitrogen-consuming crop like celery, you might follow it with a legume that can fix nitrogen back into the soil.

Crop rotation also helps break the life cycles of pests and diseases that are specific to certain plant families. Many pests and diseases survive in the soil or plant debris between growing seasons and can build up if the same crop is grown in the same location year after year.

By planting a different family of crops in the subsequent season, you can disrupt these cycles and reduce the pest and disease pressure on your Apiaceae vegetables.

When planning a crop rotation scheme for Apiaceae vegetables, consider their role in the rotation sequence. These crops are generally considered "root and leaf" crops because they use a lot of potassium and some nitrogen but not much phosphorus. Therefore, they are often followed by "fruiting" crops (like tomatoes or peppers) that need high levels of phosphorus.

A simple crop rotation plan for a companion planting garden could be as follows: In the first year, plant Apiaceae vegetables along with some beneficial companions. In the second year, plant legumes in the same place where the Apiaceae vegetables were grown and move the Apiaceae vegetables to where the legumes were. In the third year, plant fruiting crops in the spot where the Apiaceae vegetables were in the first year, and so on.

In conclusion, crop rotation is an effective, organic way to manage soil fertility and control pests and diseases in your companion planting garden. By understanding the needs and characteristics of your Apiaceae vegetables and planning your rotations carefully, you can create a healthier, more productive garden.

CHAPTER 9
CROP ROTATION GUIDE

Constructing a crop rotation plan while factoring in companion planting can be an astute strategy that serves multiple beneficial purposes for your garden. It's a proactive approach to preserve the integrity of your soil, act as a natural deterrent against pests, and elevate your garden's overall yield. It's not just about planting; it's about planning for success. Here are the essential steps you should follow.

Identify the Plant Families: Start by categorizing your plants according to their families. This is important because plants from the same family often have similar nutrient needs and are susceptible to the same diseases and pests.

Understand the Crop Needs: Each type of crop has its own specific requirements in terms of sunlight, water, and nutrients. Also, some crops, like beans and peas, enrich the soil with nitrogen, while others, like corn and tomatoes, are heavy feeders that deplete soil nutrients.

Plan Your Rotation: The basic rule of thumb in crop rotation is not to plant the same family of crops in the same place for at least three years. This helps to prevent the build-up of diseases and pests and gives the soil a chance to recover. An example of a four-year rotation might be: Year 1 – legumes, Year 2 – leafy vegetables, Year 3 – fruiting vegetables, Year 4 – root vegetables.

Incorporate Companion Planting: Companion planting involves placing crops near each other for mutual benefit. For example, planting marigolds near tomatoes can help repel harmful nematodes, and planting carrots near tomatoes can help each other grow. Think about these relationships when planning your garden layout.

Document Your Plan: Keep a detailed record of where and when you plant each crop. This will make it easier to plan your crop rotation in the future and help you identify any recurring pest or disease issues.

Revise and Adapt: Based on your observations and experiences, don't hesitate to revise your plan. If certain combinations of plants work well together, remember to repeat them in the future. If some areas of your garden have persistent problems, consider changing what you plant there.

Remember, the goal of crop rotation and companion planting is to create a balanced and sustainable ecosystem that enhances soil fertility and plant health. It may take some trial and error, but with careful planning and observation, you'll create a thriving garden.

SIX-YEAR ROTATION PLAN

Crafting a crop rotation timetable that incorporates the vegetable families of Brassica, Alliums, Cucurbitaceae, Leguminosae, Solanaceae, and Apiaceae is a smart approach to regulating soil fertility while keeping pests and diseases in check. By diversifying the plant families in your garden each year, you can break the life cycles of specific pests and diseases and prevent them from establishing. It's like setting up a natural defense mechanism for your garden while optimizing its productivity. Here's an example of a six-year crop rotation plan.

Year 1 - Leguminosae (Fabaceae) Family: This family includes peas, beans, lentils, soybeans and chickpeas. They are known for their ability to fix nitrogen in the soil, thus improving soil fertility.

Year 2 - Solanaceae Family: This group includes tomatoes, peppers, potatoes, and eggplants. These plants are heavy feeders, benefiting from the nitrogen left by the legumes.

Year 3 - Cucurbitaceae Family: This family includes crops like cucumbers, squash, pumpkins, and melons. They also enjoy rich soil but are less demanding than Solanaceae.

Year 4 - Apiaceae Family: This includes carrots, celery, and parsley. They can cope with poorer soil conditions after the heavy feeders.

Year 5 - Allium Family: This family includes onions, garlic, and leeks. These crops are generally less demanding on soil nutrients.

Year 6 - Brassicaceae Family: This includes broccoli, cabbage, kale, and radishes. Brassicas can handle the cooler temperatures and can be planted in the fall or early spring.

Remember, these schedules are just a guide. Your garden's specific conditions, your local climate, and the specific crops you want to grow can all influence your crop rotation plan. Keeping records of what you plant each year and how well it grows can help you adjust your plan as needed.

CHAPTER 10
ACKNOWLEDGEMENTS

We would like to express our deepest gratitude to the incredible team at Green Roots for their knowledge, experience, and commitment that made this book possible. Special thanks to Charles Craig, Annie Hayford, Jessica Reid, Adam Spencer, and Nicole Robinson for their invaluable contributions.

Your dedication to making a positive impact in people's lives and developing the community through gardening is truly unmatched. This book is the culmination of over 20 years of collective expertise, experience, insight, and passion in the gardening field. We are extremely proud to have created this comprehensive resource meant to assist gardeners worldwide at all levels of experience.

AFTERWORD

The art of vegetable companion planting is far more than a mere gardening technique; it is a testament to the interconnectedness of life. Each plant, with its unique traits and requirements, has the potential to support, protect, and enhance the growth of others. This mirrors the fundamental truth of our own existence in this world - we thrive best when we respect, value, and foster each other's strengths.

Gardening, particularly companion planting, teaches us patience, resilience, and the value of nurturing relationships. As we nurture our plants, we cultivate our patience, waiting for seeds to sprout and grow according to their own rhythms and timelines.

We learn resilience as we adapt to changing weather conditions, fight off pests, and bounce back from failed crops. We understand the importance of relationships as we observe the symbiotic interactions between our companion plants.

Moreover, gardening is a powerful tool for wellness. It provides a sanctuary, a place to disconnect from the stresses of daily life and reconnect with nature. The physical activity involved in gardening promotes physical health, while the satisfaction of watching your garden flourish fosters mental well-being.

The simple act of tending to your plants, observing their growth, and ultimately harvesting the fruits of your labor can bring immense joy and peace.

Beyond personal development, gardening, especially companion planting, offers profound lessons about sustainability and ecological balance. It teaches us to work with nature rather than against it, promoting biodiversity and healthy ecosystems. It reminds us of our responsibility to care for the Earth, fostering a deeper connection to our environment and encouraging more sustainable living practices.

In essence, through the practice of vegetable companion planting, we can find a path to personal enlightenment. It encourages mindfulness as we tune into the needs of our plants and respond to them.

It fosters gratitude as we appreciate the bounty that nature provides, and it cultivates a sense of wonder as we witness the incredible intricacies and harmonies of life. In the garden, we are all students, continually learning about plants, about life, and about ourselves.

In the end, a garden is not just a collection of plants but a reflection of the gardener's heart and soul. By embracing the practice of companion planting, we not only grow vegetables but also sow the seeds of personal growth, wellness, and enlightenment.

As we draw to the close of this enriching journey through the world of vegetable companion planting, it's important to reflect on the knowledge and practices you've gained from this book. You've discovered the unique characteristics and

AFTERWORD

needs of various vegetable families - Brassica, Alliums, Cucurbitaceae, Leguminosae, Solanaceae, and Apiaceae - and how they can be paired for mutual benefit.

We started our exploration with the Brassica family, learning about their preference for cool weather and their compatible companions such as beets, celery, onions, and potatoes. We delved into the Alliums, understanding that their strong scent can deter pests, benefiting many other vegetables, particularly carrots and tomatoes.

The Cucurbitaceae family, encompassing melons, cucumbers, and squash, taught us about the benefits of the "Three Sisters" method, a time-honored tradition of companion planting corn, beans, and squash together.

The Leguminosae family, including peas and beans, highlighted the importance of nitrogen-fixing plants and their role in enriching the soil for other crops.

With the Solanaceae family, which includes tomatoes, peppers, and eggplants, we learned about the importance of crop rotation and choosing companions that deter common pests. And finally, the Apiaceae or carrot family showed us that even root vegetables have preferred companions and how proper timing and positioning can lead to more successful growth.

Throughout this book, you've not only learned about the theory of companion planting, but also the practical aspects of implementing these strategies in your own garden. We've discussed everything from proper plant spacing and temperature requirements to pest control and soil health. You've gained an understanding of how to select the best companion plants based on their growth habits, pest interactions, and growing season requirements.

As you venture out into your garden, armed with this wealth of information, remember that gardening is as much an art as it is a science. It requires patience, observation, and willingness to learn from experience. Not every companionship will work perfectly every time, and that's okay. The goal is to continually experiment, observe, and adjust until you find what works best for your unique garden.

Companion planting is a powerful tool that can greatly improve the health and yield of your garden. As you apply what you've learned about the Brassica, Alliums, Cucurbitaceae, Leguminosae, Solanaceae, and Apiaceae families, we truly hope you'll discover the joy and satisfaction that comes from cultivating a thriving, harmonious vegetable garden and would love to share this experience with you via our Facebook gardening community - **facebook.com/groups/greenroots/**

Now that you're well-equipped to start your companion planting journey, we would appreciate if you could give an honest review of this guide. Your feedback and thoughts help us determine whether we did an excellent job of assisting you in improving your gardening skills. Feel free to post them in the comments and reviews section of your purchased retailer, and we'll keep an eye out for them.

"Garden is not just a hobby, but a way of life" - Green Roots

ALSO BY GREEN ROOTS

Fruit and Veggies 101 - Salad Vegetables : Gardening Guide on How to Grow the Freshest & Ripest Salad Vegetables (Perfect for Beginners)

Fruit and Veggies 101 Summer Fruits - Gardening Guide on How to Grow the Freshest & Ripest Summer Fruits (Perfect For Beginners) Includes - Fruit Salad, Smoothies & Fruit Juices Recipes

Fruit And Veggies 101 - The Winter Harvest: Gardening Guide on How To Grow the Freshest & Ripest Winter Vegetables (Perfect for Beginners)

Fruit and Veggies 101

THE WINTER HARVEST

Gardening Guide On How To Grow The Freshest & Ripest Winter Vegetables

(Perfect For Beginners)

GREEN ROOTS

CHAPTER 11
GLOSSARY

Acidic

Something that forms or becomes acid and has a pH of less than 7.

Allelopathic

Refers to the biological phenomenon where one plant inhibits the growth of another by releasing certain biochemicals into the environment.

Aeration

The act of circulating air through a garden, soil, and plants.

Aged manure

Old manure that has matured through a long period by letting it sit in a container.

Alkaline

Something that contains alkali and has a pH above 7.

Aphids

Tiny insects which consume the liquid plants produce, such as sap.

Aerate

The process of introducing air into the soil to improve its structure and promote root growth.

Alliums

A family of plants that includes onions, garlic, leeks, and chives. They are known for their strong scent, which can deter many pests.

Apiaceae

Also known as the carrot or parsley family, this group includes vegetables like carrots, celery, parsley, and fennel. They are often used in companion planting for their ability to attract beneficial insects.

Bacteria

A microorganism that causes disease and, at other times, improves the well-being of an organism.

Buttoning

A condition affecting certain vegetables, especially those in the cabbage family, like broccoli and cauliflower. Buttoning occurs when these plants form small, button-like heads prematurely instead of developing a single large one

Biodegradable

Something that can decompose into the soil and not harm the soil or other living organisms in it.

Bolting

When vegetable crops prematurely run to seed, usually making them unusable

Blunt

Something that is not sharp but softer around its edges and unable to penetrate through something.

Blanch

A method for growing vegetables. A condition in which a plant's young shoots are covered to block light, preventing photosynthesis and the production of chlorophyll, leaving them pale in color.

Bulb

A plant's fruit or organ grows in soil right above its roots and is typically edible when it's a vegetable plant.

Bushy

Something that is overgrown or grows to be dense, big, and has lots of leaves.

Beneficial Insects

Insects that help control pest populations by preying on them or acting as pollinators. Examples include ladybugs, lacewings, and bees.

Brassica

A plant family that includes cabbage, broccoli, kale, and Brussels sprouts. These plants are often companion planted with aromatic herbs or Alliums to deter pests.

CHAPTER 11

Cabbage loopers

An insect or moth tends to be found crawling and laying eggs on cabbages. This insect is a cabbage pest that destroys crops.

Calcium carbonate

Insoluble chalk is natural and white. This is also called ground limestone.

Collar

A round object is used to cuff the base of a plant to protect it from pests such as worms and maggots.

Compaction

The compression of soil particles removes air pockets and hardens the soil. It is considered harmful when gardening and if you want to achieve successful results.

Companion planting

Planting two or more plants next to each other and is protective of each other to avoid disease and pests. It can improve harvest results and improve growth.

Compost

A combination of biodegradable plants, objects, or waste that has been mixed to rot and build up nutrients necessary to soil health and fertility.

Container garden

A garden of plants grown in a pot that holds soil.

Crop rotation

Planting various crops in succession on the same piece of land helps to improve soil health, maximize nutrients, and reduce pest and weed pressure. This practice is known as crop rotation.

Cutworms

A damaging and destructive moth larva is a vegetable pest found in soil and on plants.

Companion Planting

A gardening method that involves growing different types of plants together for mutual benefit, often in terms of pest control, pollination, or nutrient uptake.

Crop Rotation

The practice of growing different types of crops in the same area in sequential seasons to improve soil health and reduce pest and disease problems.

Cucurbitaceae

A plant family that includes squash, cucumber, and melon. These plants often benefit from being planted with corn and beans, a combination known as "Three Sisters."

Debris

Remains or objects in the soil, such as rocks and previously dead crops, need to be removed to maintain the health of your garden.

Drainage

The process by which liquids or water is expelled from something, such as soil.

Drilling Tractor

A gardening sowing machine that drills holes into the ground and helps a gardener avoid manual soil drilling to plant his plants.

Ecosystem

Different biological organisms interact with each other to maintain an environment.

Evaporation

Water that turns into vapor.

Fertile soil

Soil that is healthy enough to give plants all nutrients they need to grow successfully until harvest.

Fertilization

Making soil fertile through the use of fertilizers.

Frost

Ice crystals can form on plants when temperatures are freezing or too cold.

Frost Cloth

A covering made of insulation that is positioned over plants, shrubs, trees, and crops to shield them from frost, wind, and chilly weather.

Fungus

Living organisms feed on other living organisms and create mold or discolored plants when present. They can destroy plants and cause disease.

Germinate

When a plant starts to grow out of a shell and form shoots or leaves.

Harvest

A collection of mature and ripe plants and their fruit. It's when your plants have matured, and you collect them from their stems.

Heart rate

How fast or slow are your heartbeats? It's a number or calculation which determines the heart's speed.

Humus

Decomposed organic matter consists of soil and compost.

Hybrid seed

Seeds have been altered and are offspring of two different types of seed varieties of the same plant.

Interplanting

Growing two or more types of plants together in the same space to maximize the use of garden space and enhance productivity.

Leguminosae

Also known as Fabaceae or the legume family, this group includes peas, beans, and lentils. These plants can fix nitrogen from the air into the soil, benefiting other plants grown with them.

Mesh

A material you lace over your garden plants that protects them from insects and pests.

Minerals

Substances are naturally occurring and are needed to produce fertile soil and healthy plants.

Moisture

Dampness is caused by diffused water or liquid.

Mulch

Decayed matter, such as compost, is placed on the soil's surface to lock moisture in or protect the soil from harsh weather conditions.

Nitrogen

A nutrient is needed to give plants their green color and healthy leaves.

Nutrients

Elements that feed plants the necessary food they need to grow.

Organic matter

Decomposed humus is in the soil and is essential in growing healthy vegetables.

Organic produce

Food that has been made or grown without the use of chemical alterations.

Pathogens

Organisms that cause disease in plants. These can include fungi, bacteria, viruses, nematodes (tiny worm-like creatures), and even certain types of insects.

Pesticides

Organic or chemical substances kill or repel insects and other pests from a garden.

Pests

Living organisms are destructive to a garden and need to be repelled or prevented from reaching plants.

pH

A chemistry figure which communicates a scale of alkalinity or acidity. It helps you know how alkaline or acidic soil is.

Phosphate

Phosphoric acid is a salt needed for the soil's health.

Potassium

It is a nutrient that helps plants grow and is essential in their life cycle.

Pruning

Maintain a garden by cutting or trimming dead or potentially unwanted parts of a plant.

Pest Control

Methods used to manage and reduce damage from pests, which can include cultural practices, biological control, and organic or synthetic pesticides.

Roots

The bottom stingy and firm bits of a plant grow and stretch into the soil. They absorb the nutrients and water for a plant's needs.

Seedling

A small and recently germinated plant that is ready to be planted.

Soggy

A mushy, soft, and overly damp area such as soil.

Soilless

Matter which seeds can be grown in and is an alternative to soil.

Sowing

The act of planting, drilling, or scattering a seed onto or into the soil to grow.

Sprout

When a plant produces its first shoots or leaves.

Stem

The structure of a plant that supports all its branches, leaves, and fruit.

Suckers

Plant suckers are vigorous vertical growth originating from a plant's root system or lower main stem.

Solanaceae

A plant family that includes tomatoes, peppers, and eggplants. These plants often benefit from being planted with basil or marigold, which can deter certain pests.

Succession Planting

The practice of planting crops in a staggered manner so that as one crop is harvested, another one is ready to take its place.

Thinning

Separating seedlings clumped together or removing some overcrowded plants from the soil to space out your garden to give others the chance of growing properly.

Transplanting

When you take a plant from one soil, area, or tray into another area or garden, this is also known as replanting it into another space.

Trap Crop

A plant that is used to attract pests away from the main crop. The pests are then easier to control on the trap crop.

Weed Control

Methods used to manage and reduce the growth of weeds, which can compete with crops for light, water, and nutrients. This can include mulching, hand weeding, and using weed-suppressing plants.

BIBLIOGRAPHY

Admin. (2022a, July 31). *A Complete Guide To Growing Lettuce From Seed - Grower Today*. *Grower Today*. https://www.growertoday.com/growing-lettuce-from-seed/

Admin. (2022b, December 23). *Looking To Supercharge Your Tomato Plants? Try Companion Planting! – Handyman tips*. DIY News Hubb. https://diynewshubb.com/2022/12/23/looking-to-supercharge-your-tomato-plants-try-companion-planting-handyman-tips/

Admin. (2022c, December 23). *The benefits and techniques of crop rotation in agricultural production*. Gardenmaz. https://gardenmaz.com/the-benefits-and-techniques-of-crop-rotation-in-agricultural-production/

Admwp. (2022, October 20). How to Water Seedlings from the Bottom Water Purifier. *Water Purifier*. https://ewaterpurifier.com/how-to-water-seedlings-from-the-bottom/

Agri, L. A. (2023). Planting green beans - Planting, growing and harvesting. *Life and Agri*. https://lifeandagri.com/planting-green-beans/

Allie. (2022). How To Grow Brussel Sprouts In Containers - A Complete Guide. *Gardening With Allie*. https://gardeningwithallie.com/how-to-grow-brussel-sprouts-in-containers/

Anna. (2022a, October 29). Popular herbs with shallow roots - Grower today. *Grower Today*. https://www.growertoday.com/herbs-with-shallow-roots/

Anna. (2022b, October 29). Popular herbs with shallow roots - Grower today. *Grower Today*. https://www.growertoday.com/herbs-with-shallow-roots/

AspiringYouths. (2023, June 24). *Advantages and disadvantages of crop rotation*. https://aspiringyouths.com/advantages-disadvantages/crop-rotation/

Barnett, E. (2023). Identifying and preventing common pest infestations on poinsettias. *ShunCy*. https://shuncy.com/article/what-pests-are-most-likely-to-attack-poinsettias

Bill. (2022, December 18). *Maximizing Yield In Your Vegetable Garden: Some Tips And Tricks - Virtual Seeds*. Virtual Seeds. http://virtualseeds.com/maximizing-yield-in-your-vegetable-garden-some-tips-and-tricks/

Boucher, E. (2023, January 12). Amend Soil For Vegetable Garden | Vegetable Gardening News. *Vegetable Gardening News*. https://www.vegetablegardeningnews.com/amend-soil-for-vegetable-garden/

ClubRoot of Canola | Disease | Government of Saskatchewan. (n.d.). Government of Saskatchewan. https://www.saskatchewan.ca/business/agriculture-natural-resources-and-industry/agribusiness-farmers-and-ranchers/crops-and-irrigation/disease/clubroot-of-canola

Common Diseases – Alive tree care. (n.d.). https://alivetreecare.com/common-diseases/

Cooper, J. (2023a). Determining the optimal growing space for skullcap herbs. *ShunCy*. https://shuncy.com/article/how-much-space-does-skullcap-need

Cooper, J. (2023b). Identifying different varieties of clematis: an easy guide. *ShunCy*. https://shuncy.com/article/how-do-you-identify-different-types-of-clematis

Cyr, A. (2022). Enjoy the last fruits — or alliums — of summer. *The Charlotte News*. https://www.charlottenewsvt.org/2022/11/17/enjoy-the-last-fruits-or-alliums-of-summer/

Dhruv, A. (2022, October 28). *The Best Vegetable Garden Soil Recipe For Healthy Plants – Best metal landscape edging and fertilizer for vegetables.* https://deebrownmusic.com/2022/10/28/the-best-vegetable-garden-soil-recipe-for-healthy-plants/

Dwank. (2022, September 26). *Nitrogen deficiency in plants - causes, symptoms, and treatment - Dwank.com*. Dwank.com. https://dwank.com/nitrogen-deficiency-in-plants/

Eggplant or aubergine – Firefly farm and Mercantile. (n.d.). https://fireflyfarmandmercantile.com/collections/eggplant-or-aubergine

Ethans, L. (2022). How To Improve Garden Soil in Winter. *BackyardBoss*. https://www.backyardboss.net/improve-garden-soil-in-winter/

Farm4Trade Suite. (n.d.). https://www.farm4tradesuite.com/blog/regenerative-agriculture-3-c-s-for-a-better-use-of-carbon-in-farming

Flower Tent. (2021, October 22). *IMPATIENS DOWNY MILDEW - Flower Tent*. Flower Tent - Quality Flowers at a Fair Price in Convenient Locations. https://www.flowertent.com/tips/impatiens-downy-mildew-2/

Gardener, C. (2022). What is manure organic fertilizer? *Growing Life Organic*. https://gardenguide4all.com/what-is-manure-organic-fertilizer/

Gardener, C. (2023a). How To Grow Organic Vegetables in Raised Beds. *Growing Life Organic*. https://gardenguide4all.com/how-to-grow-organic-vegetables-in-raised-beds/

Gardener, C. (2023b). What is crop rotation in farming? *Growing Life Organic*. https://gardenguide4all.com/what-is-crop-rotation-in-farming/

Gardener, M. (2021, March 5). 9 Best Turnip Companion Plants of 2023 {With PHOTOS}. *GardeningBank*. https://gardeningbank.com/turnip-companion-plants/

Gardener's Guide Serie – Mossy Feet Books. (n.d.). Mossy Feet Books. https://mossyfeetbooks.com/category/gardeners-guide-serie/

BIBLIOGRAPHY

Gordon, A. (2022). The best companion plants for potatoes. *luv2garden.com*. https://luv2garden.com/best-companion-plants-for-potatoes/

Grant, A., & Grant, A. (2023, March 15). Southern Pea powdery mildew control – Treating southern peas with powdery mildew. *Gardening Know How*. https://www.gardeningknowhow.com/edible/vegetables/black-eyed-peas/southern-pea-powdery-mildew.htm

Green english peas. (n.d.). https://skatteridad.web.app/34444/16357.html

Green, K. (2023, April 4). Growing Potatoes - Determinate vs. Indeterminate Varieties. *zone3vegetablegarden*. https://www.zone3vegetablegardening.com/post/growing-potatoes-determinate-and-indeterminate

Growing Cabbages from Sowing to Harvest. (2018, July 13). GrowVeg. https://gardenplanner.almanac.com/guides/growing-cabbages-from-sowing-to-harvest/

Help your garden survive a summer drought. (2018, August 9). GrowVeg. https://gardenplanner.almanac.com/guides/help-your-garden-survive-a-summer-drought/

Herk, R. (2022, December 29). Pea Plants: How To Grow Peas - Allo Farms. *Allo Farms*. https://www.allofarms.com/how-to-grow-pea-plant/

How to trim a zucchini plant. (2020, September 3). Garden Guides. https://www.gardenguides.com/12412286-how-to-trim-a-zucchini-plant.html

Howe, C. W. (2021). How (and why) to prune tomato plants. *Homestead How-To*. https://homesteadhow-to.com/how-and-why-to-prune-tomato-plants/

Japanese beetles. (n.d.). Almanac.com. https://www.almanac.com/pest/japanese-beetles

Jensen, A. (2023a). How many onions will one onion grow. *ShunCy*. https://shuncy.com/article/how-many-onions-will-one-onion-grow

Jensen, A. (2023b). Protecting Frankincense Trees from Pest Infestations: Preventative Tips and Techniques. *ShunCy*. https://shuncy.com/article/how-can-you-prevent-pests-from-attacking-frankincense-trees

Jensen, J. (2023a). The amazing benefits of companion planting in your herb garden. *Joanne Jensen*. https://joannejensen.com/benefits-of-companion-planting-herb-garden/

Jensen, J. (2023b). The amazing benefits of companion planting in your herb garden. *Joanne Jensen*. https://joannejensen.com/benefits-of-companion-planting-herb-garden/

Jensen, J. (2023c). The amazing benefits of companion planting in your herb garden. *Joanne Jensen*. https://joannejensen.com/benefits-of-companion-planting-herb-garden/

Joan Clark. (2021, June 22). 11+ awesome tips for growing your own tomatoes. Tips Bulletin. https://www.tipsbulletin.com/how-to-grow-tomatoes/

Kennedy, L. (2023). Growing Cucumbers: How and When To Pick Cucum-

BIBLIOGRAPHY

bers (2023). *Little Yellow Wheelbarrow.* https://www.littleyellowwheelbarrow.com/how-to-harvest-cucumbers/

Kim. (2020). How To Get Rid Of Flea Beetles. *Homestead Acres.* https://www.homestead-acres.com/how-to-get-rid-of-flea-beetles/

Leeth, F. (2017). Growing facts for Beans and Peas. *Backyard Gardener.* https://www.backyardgardener.com/garden-tip-articles/garden-guide/growing-facts-for-beans-and-peas/

Luckyhomeofanupama. (2022). Best Borage Companion Plants Uses & benefits. *Homeluxuryz.* https://homeluxurys.com/best-borage-companion-plants-uses-benefits/

Lynne, K. (2022). How To Start Seeds Indoors – The Easiest Way. *New Life on a Homestead.* https://www.newlifeonahomestead.com/start-seeds-indoors/

MadMadViking. (2023). How To Grow Basil In A Pot On Your Patio. *My Urban Garden.* https://www.my-city-garden.com/how-to-grow-basil-in-a-pot-on-your-patio/

Marie, B. K. (2019, March 21). *A Beginners' Guide To Growing Organic Food This Spring - Gluten-Free Living.* Gluten-Free Living. https://www.glutenfreeliving.com/gluten-free-foods/diet/a-beginners-guide-to-growing-organic-food-this-spring/

Market Gardener Institute. (2023, July 13). *The most detailed course on organic farming | Market Gardener Masterclass.* https://themarketgardener.com/the-market-gardener-masterclass/

Matagouri/tūmatakuru. (n.d.). https://www.doc.govt.nz/nature/native-plants/matagouri-wild-irishman/

Mathew, E. (2021). Cucumber leaves turning white. *Autenica Portaland.* https://autenicaportland.com/cucumber-leaves-turning-white/

Mcdonald, C. (2020, November 12). *How do I germinate buddleia seeds? – spudd64.com.* https://www.spudd64.com/how-do-i-germinate-buddleia-seeds/

Mildew Diseases of plants: Powdery or downy? (2011, August 5). Uconnladybug's Blog. https://uconnladybug.wordpress.com/2011/08/05/mildew-diseases-of-plants-powdery-or-downy/

Mohammad, A., & Mohammad, A. (2023). How to use worm castings in vegetable garden? | Vegetable GardenerX. *Vegetable GardenerX | Grow What You Eat.* https://vegetablegardenerx.com/how-to-use-worm-castings-in-vegetable-garden/

Natural Bone Meal - Earth Science. (2022, September 13). Earth Science. https://www.earthsciencegrowing.com/products/natural-bone-meal/

News. (2017, July 10). Wildseed Farms. https://shop.wildseedfarms.com/blogs/news

Organic farming enhances soil microbial abundance and activity—A meta-analysis

BIBLIOGRAPHY

and meta-Regression. (n.d.). WUR. https://www.wur.nl/en/Publication-details.htm?publicationId=publication-way-353234333838

Organic SHALLOT GROWING GUIDE | Filaree Organic Garlic Farm. (n.d.). https://filareefarm.com/organic-shallot-potato-onion-growing-guide/

Patterson, S. (2022). 13 Common Tomato Problems & How To Fix Them. *Rural Sprout.* https://www.ruralsprout.com/common-tomato-problems/

PKFarmer. (2022). How to plant Brussels sprouts. *Pk Farmer | Agriculture - Farming - Livestock.* https://pkfarmer.com/plant-brussels-sprouts/

Prairie Road Organic Seed. (n.d.). *NEW! Tomatillo: Mexican strain.* https://www.prairieroadorganic.co/products/tomatillo-mexican-strain

Ryan. (2022, December 8). How To Harden Off Seedlings? The Best Way To Make Your Plants Grow Strong! » Beagreens. *Beagreens.* https://beagreens.com/how-to-harden-off-seedlings/

Saha, P. (2023). Growing Beans At Home Everything From Planting To Harvesting [In A Nutshell]. *Gardening ABC.* https://gardening-abc.com/how-to-grow-beans-at-home/

Saleem, M. I. (2021, March 12). How to grow broccoli in your raised beds? *Bed Gardening.* https://www.bedgardening.com/how-to-grow-broccoli-in-your-raised-beds/

Seeds, I. (2023). Grow Your Own Organic Vegetables in a Sustainable way. *Inherited Seeds.* https://inheritedseeds.com/blogs/news/growing-your-own-organic-vegetables-in-a-sustainable-way

Simmons, C. (2022, July 22). *Growing Shallots In Containers.* Garden Planters. https://gardenplanters.net/growing-shallots-in-containers/

Sophia. (2022, December 9). How to use neem oil on houseplants? - HousePlantsInfo.com. *HousePlantsInfo.com.* https://houseplantsinfo.com/how-to-use-neem-oil-on-houseplants/

sowtrueseed.com. (n.d.). *Eggplant Seeds - Listada de Gandia, ORGANIC.* Sow True Seed. https://sowtrueseed.com/products/eggplant-seeds-listada-de-gandia-organic

Squash (Summer) Grow Guide. (n.d.). GrowVeg. https://gardenplanner.agriscaping.com/plants/us-and-canada/how-to-grow-summer-squash/

Support, Support, & Support. (2022). What is companion planting? and how will it benefit my Maine garden? *Stone Solutions Maine - for All Your Stonework and Masonry Projects - Portland and Southern Maine.* https://stonesolutionsmaine.com/what-is-companion-planting-and-how-will-it-benefit-my-maine-garden/

Tamara. (2023). The secret to easy gardening, Use mulch for no weeding! *The Reid Homestead.* https://thereidhomestead.com/the-secret-to-easy-gardening-no-weeding/

The Garden Club of Bermuda. (2021, February 10). *Companion planting guide*

BIBLIOGRAPHY

- *The Garden Club of Bermuda*. https://gardenclubbermuda.org/education/planting-guides/companion-planting-guide/
- Today, E. (2022). New guide highlights IPM for boxwood pests. *Entomology Today*. https://entomologytoday.org/2022/06/16/guide-boxwood-integrated-pest-management/
- Veroutsos, E. (2022). 13 of The Best and Worst Companion Plants for Cabbage. *BackyardBoss*. https://www.backyardboss.net/best-and-worst-companion-plants-for-cabbage/
- *Want more from your veggie garden? Here's how to properly lay out your field.* (2017, November 27). DIYEVERYWHERE.COM. https://diyeverywhere.com/2017/11/27/want-more-from-your-veggie-garden-heres-how-to-properly-lay-out-your-field/?src=sidexpromo&eid=62761&pid=62761
- Wendy. (2021, December 10). *Organic gardening benefits and basics*. https://gardeningcode.com/organic-gardening-benefits-and-basics/
- Wolthoorn, B. (2022, December 30). *Fusarium wilt - Plant Pests*. Plant En Plagen. https://www.plantenplagen.nl/en/plantenplagen/ffusarium-wilt/#more-12269

Made in United States
Cleveland, OH
17 January 2025

13580756R00182